JINNAH

MOHAMMED ALI JINNAH AND HIS SISTER, MISS FATIMA JINNAH

[*Frontispiece*

JINNAH
Creator of Pakistan

*

By HECTOR BOLITHO

Failure is a word unknown to me.
MOHAMMED ALI JINNAH

LONDON
JOHN MURRAY ALBEMARLE STREET W

First published November 1954
Reprinted May 1956
Reprinted March 1957
Reprinted October 1960
Reprinted September 1964

Printed in Great Britain by Cox & Wyman, Ltd., London, Fakenham and Reading

CONTENTS

Part 1. BOYHOOD IN KARACHI 3
A STUDENT IN LONDON 8
THE YOUNG ADVOCATE 14
THE YOUNG POLITICIAN 22

Part 2. TALK OF ALEXANDER 31
BACKGROUND FOR PAKISTAN 36
1906–1910 44
1910–1913 49
AN ESSAY IN FRIENDSHIP 54
A GENTLEMAN 'OF RECOGNIZED POSITION' . 59
THE LUCKNOW PACT 61
GANDHI, ANNIE BESANT, AND EDWIN SAMUEL MONTAGU 67

Part 3. JINNAH'S SECOND MARRIAGE: 1918 . . . 73
THE YEARS OF DISILLUSIONMENT . . . 78
1921–1928 86
THE 'PARTING OF THE WAYS' 92
EXILE: 1930–1934 96

Part 4. RETURN TO INDIA: 1935–1937 109
1937–1939 115
1940: 'PAKISTAN' 125

Part 5. A BIRTHDAY PRESENT 133
1940–1942 136
1942–1944: AN ASSASSIN, AND THE DOCTORS . 141
1944: JINNAH, GANDHI, AND LIAQUAT ALI KHAN 148

CONTENTS

Part 6.	1945–1946	157
	1946–1947	167
Part 7.	1947: PARTITION	177
Part 8.	FLIGHT INTO KARACHI	193
	THE BRITONS WHO STAYED	199
	IN THE GARDEN	210
	ZIARAT, AND THE LAST TASK	214
	THE LAST DAYS	219
Bibliography		228
Index		229

ILLUSTRATIONS

MOHAMMED ALI JINNAH AND HIS SISTER, MISS FATIMA JINNAH
Frontispiece

THE HOUSE IN NEWNHAM ROAD—JINNAH'S BIRTHPLACE	4
THE SIND MADRASAH SCHOOL, KARACHI	6
M. A. JINNAH, ABOUT THE TIME OF HIS SECOND MARRIAGE	73
PANDIT JAWAHARLAL NEHRU AND M. A. JINNAH, AT SIMLA, IN 1946	114
M. A. JINNAH AND MAHATMA GANDHI, IN 1944	151
M. A. JINNAH AND LIAQUAT ALI KHAN, IN 1947	151
MISS FATIMA JINNAH, M. A. JINNAH, LIAQUAT ALI KHAN AND BEGUM LIAQUAT ALI KHAN	166
M. A. JINNAH ADDRESSING MUSLIM LEAGUE MEETING, KINGSWAY HALL, DECEMBER 1946	166
LORD MOUNTBATTEN LISTENING TO MR JINNAH'S INAUGURAL SPEECH AS THE FIRST GOVERNOR-GENERAL OF PAKISTAN AUGUST 14, 1947	198
KARACHI: THE DAY OF MOHAMMED ALI JINNAH'S BURIAL	226

ACKNOWLEDGEMENTS

DURING the two years I have spent in writing this book, I have visited both Pakistan and India, and have spoken to some two hundred people who knew Mohammed Ali Jinnah. My record of his life and achievement will, I hope, prove my gratitude to them. A full list of their names would serve no purpose, but I wish to mention some who have helped me with particular problems in my work.

Jinnah's early years, as a lawyer in Bombay, were described to me by Sir Cowasjee Jehangir, Mr Motilal Setalvad, former Advocate-General of Bombay, Mr G. N. Joshi, Mr Kanji Dwarkadas, and Rajah Sir Maharaj Singh, former Governor of Bombay.

Those who helped me with the years of Jinnah's political struggle include Begum Liaquat Ali Khan, who has been especially generous in giving me reminiscences and in reading my manuscript; also Diwan Chaman Lall, and Mr M. H. Saiyid, author of *Mohammed Ali Jinnah (A Political Study)*, who allowed me the use of his own researches, when I was in Karachi. Other Pakistani writers who provided me with valuable material include Mr Mohammed Noman, Mr Altaf Husain, editor of *Dawn*, Mr S. M. Ikram, Mr Fareed S. Jafri, former editor of *The Civil and Military Gazette* (Karachi), Mr Rafiq M. Khan, and Mr Nasim Ahmed.

I am grateful to the doctors, especially Surgeon-Commander Jal R. Patel, and Lieut.-Colonel Ilahi Bakhsh, who attended Mr Jinnah; also to Sister Phyllis Dunham, who nursed him when he was dying. Their accounts of his growing malady, and the circumstances of his death, have greatly strengthened my narrative.

The younger men who served Jinnah in his later years include Mr K. H. Khurshid, his secretary, Captain S. M. Ahsan and Lieutenant Mazhar Ahmed, his naval As.D.C., and Wing-Commander Ata Rabbani, his air A.D.C., who were helpful with stories about their master and in teaching me to appreciate the lively hopes of Pakistan.

Some fifty Britons who served in the sub-continent, before and since the transfer of power in 1947, have talked to me, and some of

ACKNOWLEDGEMENTS

them have loaned me letters and diaries. Of these, I am especially obliged to Vice-Admiral J. W. Jefford, General Sir Frank Messervy, Colonel E. St J. Birnie, Colonel Geoffrey Knowles, and Sir Francis Mudie.

My chapter on 'Partition' presented many problems. The facts have been checked by General Lord Ismay, Sir Eric Miéville, and Mr Alan Campbell-Johnson, who were with Admiral Earl Mountbatten during his term as Viceroy; and by Mr Ian Stephens, former editor of *The Statesman*. They have made corrections and suggestions, but any shade of opinion that may have crept into the narrative is my own.

The entire manuscript has been read by Sir Hawthorne Lewis, former Reforms Commissioner to the Government of India, and afterwards Governor of Orissa, by Sir Francis Low, for many years editor of *The Times of India*, Mr Edwin Haward, former editor of *The Pioneer* and Mr Majeed Malik, Principal Information Officer to the Government of Pakistan. Their vigilance has, I hope, brought my errors down to a minimum.

I wish also to thank Mr Derek Peel, who has helped me with research from the beginning to the end of my task.

H. B.

SALISBURY, WILTS,
1954

PART ONE

BOYHOOD IN KARACHI

THE map of the west coast of India shows Kathiawar Peninsula, between the gulfs of Cutch and Cambay, thrust into the Arabian Sea, like a great challenging fist. This was the native land of the parents of Mohammed Ali Jinnah, who fought for, and created, the Muslim state of Pakistan.

Long before Jinnah was born, his parents migrated to the fishing port of Karachi, on the edge of the Sind desert. It was then a small town of some 50,000 people. The dust from the desert came down on them in hot clouds : it invaded their food, their clothes and their lungs. On one side was the parched earth, pleading for water : to the west was the sea, from which they made their living.

Today, Karachi is the throbbing capital of the biggest Muslim country in the world : refugees, officials, and business men have swelled the population to a million and a quarter. Thousands of masons toil, from dawn to dark, turning more and more acres of the desert into blocks of offices, and dwellings, so that, from the air, the edge of the city seems to increase, overnight, like grey lava flowing into the sand.

Ancient bunder boats still come into the harbour from coastal ports, their huge sails bowing amiably over the smooth blue water ; but there are also the big ships of international commerce, from Liverpool, Tokyo and the Baltic. And there are destroyers, tossing the foam from their bows as they steam in from torpedo practice : busy, proud ships, of the youngest navy in the world.

In the heart of the bustling new city is old Karachi ; the town of mellow houses that Jinnah knew, as a boy. Some of the streets are so narrow, and the houses so low, that the camels ambling past can look in the first-floor windows. In one of these narrow streets, Newnham Road, is the house—since restored and ornamented with balconies—where Mohammed Ali Jinnah was born. The date is uncertain : in the register of his first school, in Karachi, the day is recorded as October 20, 1875 ; but Jinnah always said that he had been born on Christmas Day—in 1876. If the 1876 date is correct, he was seven days old when Queen Victoria was proclaimed Kaisar-i-Hind, on the Plain of Delhi. He was born in the year that Imperial India was created, and he lived to negotiate, with Queen Victoria's great-grandson, for its partition and deliverance from British rule.

In one of the tenement houses in old Karachi there lives Fatima Bai, a handsome old woman, aged eighty-six ; one of the few persons alive who can remember Mohammed Ali Jinnah when he was a boy. She was a bride of sixteen, married to one of Jinnah's cousins, when she arrived in the family home in Karachi. The year was 1884 : Jinnah was then seven years old.

Fatima Bai lives with her son, Mohammed Ali Ganji, in rooms at the top of a flight of bare stone stairs. I went there one evening and she received me in her own room, in which there were her bed, an immense rocking-chair, and a wardrobe where, among the bundles of clothes, the few existing documents—the family archives —were kept.

Mohammed Ali Ganji spread the papers on the bed, beside his mother, and then gave me the bones of the early story.

Although Jinnah's immediate ancestors were Muslims—followers of the Khoja sect of the Aga Khan—they came, like so many Muslim families in India, of old Hindu stock. Mohammed Ali Ganji said that the family migrated to the Kathiawar Peninsula from the Multan area, north of the Sind desert, long ago. From Kathiawar, they moved to Karachi, where they settled, and prospered in a modest way.

When Jinnah was six years old, he was sent to school in Karachi. When he was ten, he went on a ship to Bombay, where he attended the Gokul Das Tej Primary School, for one year. He was eleven when he returned to Karachi, to the Sind Madrasah High School ; and he was fifteen when he went to the Christian Missionary Society High School, also in Karachi.

Mohammed Ali Ganji said, "In the same year that he was at the Mission School, he was married by his parents, as was the custom of the country, to Amai Bai, a Khoja girl from Kathiawar. In 1892 he went to England to study law and, while he was there, his young wife died. Soon afterwards, his mother died, and his father became very poor. . . ."

THE HOUSE IN NEWNHAM ROAD—JINNAH'S BIRTHPLACE

Fatima Bai raised her hand and interrupted her son: she said, "He was a good boy; a clever boy. We lived, eight of us, in two rooms on the first floor of the house in Newnham Road. At night, when the children were sleeping, he would stand a sheet of cardboard against the oil lamp, to shield the eyes of the children from the light. Then he would read, and read. One night I went to him and said, 'You will make yourself ill from so much study,' and he answered, 'Bai, you know I cannot achieve anything in life unless I work hard.'"

As Fatima Bai finished her story, an old man appeared at the door; a smiling old Muslim with tousled, snow-white hair. His name was Nanji Jafar. He came in, sat in the rocking-chair and said that, as far as he knew, he was in his 'eighties'. Though he had been at school with Jinnah, all he could recall was, "I played marbles with him in the street."

When I asked, "Can you remember anything that he said to you?" he looked from beneath his thick white brows and repeated, "I played marbles with him in the street."

I asked him to close his eyes and to see, once more, the coloured glass marbles in the dust. Nanji Jafar closed his eyes and dug deeper into his memory: then he told his only anecdote of Jinnah's boyhood. One morning, when Nanji Jafar was playing in the street, Jinnah, then aged about fourteen, came up to him and said, "Don't play marbles in the dust; it spoils your clothes and dirties your hands. We must stand up and play cricket."

The boys in Newnham Road were obedient: they gave up playing marbles and allowed Jinnah to lead them from the dusty street to a bright field where he brought his bat and stumps for them to use. When he sailed for England at the age of sixteen, he gave Nanji Jafar his bat and said, "You will go on teaching the boys to play cricket while I am away."

All Jinnah's story is in the boyhood dictum—'Stand up from the dust so that your clothes are unspoiled and your hands clean for the tasks that fall to them.'

* * *

The chief peril in writing about Mohammed Ali Jinnah lies in the spurious anecdotes that are already confusing the facts of his story.

BOYHOOD IN KARACHI

Sorting these facts from the legends is not easy. In her appreciation [1] of Jinnah, written in 1917, Mrs Naidu described him as 'the eldest son of a rich merchant . . . reared in careless affluence.' This picture is false : as Fatima Bai said, the family lived in two rooms of a house, set among the bedlam of rickshaws and camel-carts.

Jinnah's father was a hide merchant—a lean man named Jinnah Poonja : his wife, who bore him seven children, is never more than a vague shadow in the story. Her eldest child was Mohammed Ali, the boy who grew up and made a forlorn, scattered multitude into a nation. Then came Rahmat, Maryam, Ahmed Ali, Shireen, Fatima, and Bande Ali, all of whom remained obscure, except Fatima, who qualified as a dentist, and who, in later years, became her brother's close and devoted companion.

Pakistanis sometimes enjoy the delights of gossip more than the science of history, and they are already weaving legends about Jinnah's name. There is a tale, repeated in the Pakistani magazines, of an astrologer who stopped Jinnah one day in the street, when he was still a schoolboy. The astrologer practised a little abracadabra and told him that there were 'signs' that he would grow up to be a 'king'.

Another story is told of Jinnah being so poor that he sat under the light of a lamp-post to study his books ; and that he spent all his leisure from school in the police courts, listening to the wrangling of the advocates. There is no proof of this : in later life, he referred to only one boyhood visit to a law court, with his father. When he saw his first advocate, in gown and bands, he said, "I want to be a barrister." [2]

Little is known of these early years. Jinnah was neither a letter-writer nor a diarist ; nor did he care to reminisce about the past. But it is certain that he was neither Mrs Naidu's 'eldest son of a rich

---

[1] *Mohomed Ali Jinnah, An Ambassador of Unity, His Speeches and Writings. 1912–1917*, with a biographical appreciation by Sarojini Naidu. (Ganesh & Co., Madras.)

Mrs Naidu became one of Mohammed Ali Jinnah's few devoted friends. She was a remarkable and talented woman. She had been a student at Girton College, Cambridge, during 1896–97, but she found the English climate 'too trying' and returned to India. After Partition, she became the first woman Governor of an Indian Province—Uttar Pradesh—where she died in March, 1949.

[2] *Immortal Years*, Sir Evelyn Wrench (Hutchinson, 1945), pp. 132–3.

THE SIND MADRASAH SCHOOL, KARACHI

merchant . . . reared in careless affluence,' nor a poor boy reading beneath a street lamp : the truth lies in between.

★ ★ ★

Over the gateway of the Sind Madrasah School in Karachi are the words, ENTER TO LEARN—GO FORTH TO SERVE, carved in the stone. The time came when Mohammed Ali Jinnah had to 'go forth' into the world—armed only with his matriculation from the Bombay University, gained at the Mission School, and his determination to stand up from the dust. In his earliest photograph he appears as a lean boy, with high cheekbones, and heavy lips that suggest a sensuousness his character belied ; eyes with more power than warmth, and beautiful, slim hands, which he used with an actor's skill, even when they were bony and old.

There are no letters, and only one remembered phrase, to make the boy of almost sixteen more real. The one, curious phrase persists in almost every piece of writing that recalls Jinnah's early years : he is described as 'that tall, thin boy, in a funny long yellow coat.'

At the time when Jinnah finished his schooling, there was an Englishman, Frederick Leigh Croft, working as an exchange broker in Bombay and Karachi. He was heir to a baronetcy—a thirty-two-year-old bachelor, described by a kinswoman who remembers him as 'something of a dandy, with a freshly picked carnation in his buttonhole each morning ; a recluse and a wit, uncomfortable in the presence of children, whom he did not like.' But he liked Mohammed Ali Jinnah, and was impressed by his talents. Frederick Leigh Croft ultimately persuaded Jinnah Poonja to send his son to London, to learn the practice of the law.

Mohammed Ali Jinnah was not yet sixteen when he sailed across the Arabian Sea, towards the western world which was to influence his mind, his ambition, and his tastes ; which was to imbue him with an Englishness of manner and behaviour that endured to his death.

★ ★ ★

A STUDENT IN LONDON

THE ledgers kept at Lincoln's Inn in the 1890's were given for salvage during the 1939-45 war; the contemporary shipping lists no longer exist, and Jinnah's English bankers lost their records during a bombing raid. There seems to be no way of finding out when or how he came to England, except that the year was 1892. Only his reader's ticket for the British Museum has been saved, and it gives his London address as 35 Russell Road, Kensington. The house, which still stands, is one of a modest row that face the immense glass arch of Olympia : the view from the windows is over a busy suburban railway line. Jinnah once said, of his arrival in England, 'I found a strange country and unfamiliar surroundings. I did not know a soul, and the fogs and winter in London upset me a great deal, but I soon settled down and was quite happy.'[1]

Jinnah's achievement as a student was remarkable : he passed his examinations in two years. If the 1876 birth-date is to be believed—the date also given in the records of the Law Society—he was not yet eighteen : but he had to remain in England two more years, to complete the formalities required by Lincoln's Inn. Dr Ashraf[2] recalls Jinnah telling him that he was ' the youngest Indian student ever to be called to the Bar.' But there are no details of the hours of diligent study that brought about this feat of scholarship ; of the habits, formed beside an oil-lamp in the house in Newnham Road, and projected to the reading-rooms of the law libraries, and the British Museum.

Mrs Naidu wrote of Jinnah some years later, ' It seems a pity that so fine an intelligence should have denied itself the hall-mark of a University education.' Jinnah apparently withstood the temptations of literature, and art, and even of history. His mind seldom doted on the past, and it would seem that his habits in London were narrowed down—that his way was from lectures in Lincoln's Inn, to debates in the House of Commons, without any pausing in the National Gallery on the way. He was to do two things brilliantly in his life : he was to become a great advocate, and he was to create a nation. From the beginning, he did not dissipate his energies with hobbies,

[1] *Immortal Years*, Sir Evelyn Wrench, p. 132.
[2] Dr Mohammed Ashraf was Vice-President of the Union of the University of Aligarh in 1921.

nor his strength in dalliance. His chief passions were in his mind.

In an address to the Karachi Bar Association, in 1947, Jinnah recalled, " I joined Lincoln's Inn because there, on the main entrance, the name of the Prophet was included in the list of the great law-givers of the world." [1] He spoke of Muhammad as " a great statesman, and a great sovereign." His appreciation of the Prophet was realistic : perhaps his political conscience, as a Muslim, had already begun to stir, while he was in England.

Jinnah told Dr Ashraf that, during the last two years in London, his time was " utilized for further independent studies for the political career " he already " had in mind ". Jinnah also said, " Fortune smiled on me, and I happened to meet several important English Liberals with whose help I came to understand the doctrine of Liberalism. The Liberalism of Lord Morley was then in full sway. I grasped that Liberalism, which became part of my life and thrilled me very much."

This awakening in politics coincided with significant personal changes. Up to April 1894, Mohammed Ali Jinnah had used his boyhood name, Jinnahbhai—*bhai* being a suffix used in the Gujrati language, which was his mother tongue. On April 14, 1894, he adopted the English fashion in names and became *Mr* Jinnah, the form he used for the rest of his life. He had also abandoned his ' funny long yellow coat' and adopted English clothes ; and—perhaps encouraged by the sight of Mr Joseph Chamberlain in the House— he had bought his first monocle.

It must have been an important moment in the development of his courage, and his personality, when he went to an optician's shop in London and bought the first of the many monocles, which he wore during the next fifty years—even at the end, when he was being carried into his capital on a stretcher ; a dying warrior, holding the circle of glass between his almost transparent fingers.

* * *

Jinnah had said that ' the Liberalism of Lord Morley ' thrilled him very much. The thrill must have been intensified on June 21, 1892, when he read of the Royal Assent to the Amendment to the Indian Councils Act, empowering the Viceroy to increase the numbers in the Legislative and Provincial Councils—an amendment that gave

[1] He must have had in mind G. F. Watts' fresco 'The Law Givers' in the New Hall.

the people of India, for the first time, 'a potential voice' in the government of their country.

The beginning of Jinnah's partiality for Liberalism was well-timed. At the end of May 1892, Mr Gladstone spoke 'with a vigour and animation most remarkable in a man of eighty-two.'[1] He was rewarded in the following August, when the Liberals came into power after six years of Tory rule under Lord Salisbury.

The early 1890's offered refreshing opportunities for any young novice in politics, newly arrived from India, anxious to learn, and naturally in love with agitation and reform. In 1893, when Jinnah must have recovered from his loneliness and 'settled down', he was able to listen to some of the lively debates over Mr Gladstone's Irish Home Rule Bill: he was able also to study English reactions to affairs in India, and Egypt; to watch the growing power of Labour, and to develop his sympathy with the political emancipation of women—a reform that became a fixed part of his political creed when he returned to India.

There was another stirring innovation, nearer his own heart. Jinnah arrived in London in time to watch—perhaps to help—the election of the first Indian, Dadabhai Naoroji, to the British Parliament, as member for Central Finsbury.

Dadabhai Naoroji was a Parsee, aged sixty-seven at the time of his return : for many years he had been a business man in London. Photographs of him, in later life, reveal some of the reasons why he came to be known as the 'Grand Old Man of India'. His humorous old eyes, long white beard, and relaxed hands, proclaim the teacher, about whom young Indians gathered, to learn—rather than the furious agitator in love with change for its own sake.

When Dadabhai Naoroji announced his intention to stand as Liberal candidate for Central Finsbury, Lord Salisbury committed the clumsy folly, in a speech at Edinburgh, of saying, " I doubt if we have yet got to the point of view where a British constituency would elect a black man." The Scottish electors shouted " Shame ! " and the indignation spread south—as far as Windsor, where Queen Victoria, attended by Indian servants and engrossed in her study of Hindustani, was much displeased.

The unhappy insult—addedly unfortunate because Dadabhai Naoroji

[1] Mr Balfour to the Queen, May 28, 1892.

had a paler skin than Lord Salisbury—soon made the Parsee Liberal into a hero. The chapters in his biography,[1] describing the controversy awakened by the election in Finsbury, make an exciting story. Women's Suffrage was one of his aims, and he was therefore overwhelmed by women helpers. Among the letters sent to him was one from Florence Nightingale : ' I rejoice beyond measure,' she wrote, ' that you are now the only Liberal candidate for Central Finsbury.'

Dadabhai Naoroji was elected, with a majority of three, and the quick-tongued Cockneys who had voted for him turned his difficult name into ' Mr Narrow-Majority.'

Mohammed Ali Jinnah was caught up in the excitement of the Finsbury election, and he prospered under the influence of Dadabhai Naoroji, whom he was to serve, as secretary, fourteen years later. It is reasonable to suppose that Jinnah learned much from Naoroji's speeches ; that he absorbed some ideas from the Grand Old Man. The nature and quality of these ideas are revealed in the first speech which Dadabhai Naoroji made in the House of Commons on August 9, 1892, during the No Confidence debate following the Speech from the Throne. He said :

> My election for an English constituency is a unique event. For the first time, during more than a century of settled British rule, an Indian is admitted into this House as a Member for an English constituency. . . .
>
> I desire to say a few words in analysis of this great and wonderful phenomenon. The spirit of British rule, the instinct of British justice and generosity, from the very commencement, when Parliament seriously took the matter of Indian policy into its hands, about the beginning of this century, decided that India was to be governed on the lines of British freedom and justice. Steps were taken—without any hesitation—to introduce Western education, civilization, and political institutions in that country ; and the result was that, aided by a noble and grand language, in which the youth of that country began to be educated, a great movement of political life—I may say *new* life—was infused into a land which had been decaying for centuries.

[1] *Dadabhai Naoroji: The Grand Old Man of India*, R. P. Masani (George Allen & Unwin Ltd., 1939).

The British rulers of the country endowed it with all their own most important privileges. A few days ago, Sir, you demanded from the Throne the privileges which belong to the people, including freedom of speech, for which they have fought and shed their blood. That freedom of speech you have given to us, and it enables Indians to stand before you and represent in clear and open language any desire they have felt.

By conferring those privileges, you have prepared for this final result—of an Indian standing before you in this House, becoming a Member of the great Imperial Parliament of the British Empire, and being able to express his views openly and fearlessly before you.

Mr Gladstone, Mr Balfour, Mr T. P. O'Connor, and the other speakers during the debate, might have wondered where Dadabhai Naoroji's passions would lead him next. He was expected, as 'an ardent Gladstonian', to support his leader in the debate: but, as *The Times* reporter wrote, he 'dilated with radiant *naïveté* on the splendour of his victory in Central Finsbury', and concluded 'without saying one word' on the matter in hand.

Dadabhai Naoroji continued:

The glory and credit of this great event—by which India is thrilled from one end to the other—of the new life, the joy, the ecstasy of India at the present moment, is all your own: it is the spirit of British institutions and the love of justice and freedom in British instincts which has produced this extraordinary result, and I stand here in the name of India to thank the British people that they have made it at all possible for an Indian to occupy this position, and to speak freely in the English language of any grievance which India may be suffering under, with the conviction that, though he stand alone, with only one vote, whenever he is able to bring forward any aspiration, and is supported by just and proper reasons, he will find a large number of other Members from both sides of the House ready to support him and give him the justice he asks. This is the conviction which permeates the whole thinking and educated classes of India. . . .

Mohammed Ali Jinnah heard this speech, from the Visitors' Gallery of the House of Commons, and he no doubt absorbed its lessons.

★ ★ ★

EXPERIENCE AS AN ACTOR

These fragments of fact about Jinnah do not yet make him real: he is only half-clear, as in a first pencil sketch for a portrait, without colour, depth, or humour. There are but two stories of these student days, that show him as a human being, away from his reading-lamp and the Gallery of the House of Commons. Many years later, when Mahatma Gandhi and Pandit Jawaharlal Nehru were in prison in India, a friend said to Jinnah, " All the leaders have been arrested at some time or other, except you." Jinnah answered, " Oh, I also have had my friction with the police. It was on Oxford and Cambridge Boat Race night, when I was a student in London. I was with two friends and we were caught up with a crowd of undergraduates. We found a hand cart in a side street, so we pushed each other up and down the roadway, until we were arrested and taken off to the police station. But I am afraid we were not imprisoned: we were let off with a caution."

Also, there was a spell away from his studies, when he toured England with a Shakespearean company. In 1946, Jinnah recalled this incongruous adventure to Mr Nasim Ahmed [1]—he described his experiences as a prompter, and the occasion when he played Romeo. No more is known, although there is a legend, unproven, that for a time he was with Miss Horniman's famous repertory company.

There is little trace of influence on his vocabulary, or in his speeches, from this nodding acquaintance with Shakespeare. There was but one episode, in the far future, when Gandhi asked Jinnah how he wished to be addressed. Jinnah answered, " I thank you for your anxiety to respect my wishes in the matter of the prefix you should use with my name. What is a prefix after all? ' A rose by any other name would smell as sweet.' "

Jinnah was never to become excited by the charm of words: his prose, written or spoken, was bald and factual. Many years later, when he was drafting a statement, with the help of Liaquat Ali Khan and one of his secretaries, he became impatient with their search after fine sentences, and said, " I don't care for beautiful language: I only wish to see my idea come through."

*   *   *

[1] London correspondent of *Dawn* newspaper.

THE YOUNG ADVOCATE

MOHAMMED ALI JINNAH returned to India in the autumn of 1896. He was then a qualified barrister, aged almost twenty, and devoted to the Liberalism he had absorbed from Gladstone, Morley, and Dadabhai Naoroji. English had become his chief language, and it remained so, for he never mastered Urdu : even when he was leading the Muslims into freedom, he had to define the terms of their emancipation in an alien tongue. His clothes also remained English, until the last years of his life, when he adopted the *sherwani* and *shalwar* of the Muslim gentleman. And his manner of address was English : he had already assumed the habit, which he never gave up, of shaking his finger at his listener and saying, " My dear fellow, you do not understand."

When he arrived back in Karachi, Jinnah must have felt like a stranger among his own people. His mother was dead ; also his child wife, who could not have contributed much to his experience of human relationships. And his father had lost whatever little fortune he had saved. Jinnah was perhaps ill at ease within the confines of the two rooms in Newnham Road : nor was there much help or encouragement for him as a young barrister seeking clients.

During four years, Jinnah had been absorbed into the life of London : he had talked with scholars and he had heard the great voices in Westminster, busy with the riddles of government. He had listened also to the young reformers, lively with new ideas. He might have been alarmed as he tried to resume his old habits in Karachi ; a town devoted to trade and shipping, and small talk. His hands—spread so eagerly towards life in London—were now tied for lack of opportunity. There is one story, often told but never verified, that he was offered work in a law office, on the understanding that he married the lawyer's daughter. He was aloof from such shabby bargaining : he left the depressing sands of Karachi for Bombay, with its High Court, its tradition in the law, and all the sweets of opportunity to attract an ambitious young man.

Mohammed Ali Jinnah sailed for Bombay in 1897, but he was to endure three more years of penury, and disappointment, before he began to climb. Mr M. H. Saiyid, who was Jinnah's secretary in later years, has written [1] of this lean time. 'The first three years were of great hardship and although he attended his office regularly every day, he wandered without a single brief. The long and crowded foot-paths of Bombay may, if they could only speak, bear testimony to a young pedestrian pacing them every morning from his new abode . . . a humble locality in the city, to his office in the Fort . . . and every evening back again to his apartments after a weary, toilsome day spent in anxious expectation.'

At the turn of the century, Jinnah's fortunes changed, through the kindness of the acting Advocate-General of Bombay, John Molesworth MacPherson,[2] who invited the young lawyer to work in his chambers. Mrs Naidu wrote [3] of this as 'a courteous concession—the first of its kind ever extended to an Indian,' which Jinnah remembered as 'a beacon of hope in the dark distress of his early struggles.'

Early in 1900, there was a vacancy for a Presidency Magistrate in Bombay—an office that required generous recommendation. Jinnah was hopeful; and he was also enterprising. He sat, ' gazing through a window . . . smoking a cigarette,' wondering what he could do: a cab passed by and 'an idea struck him': he jumped into the cab and drove 'straight to the office of Sir Charles Ollivant, the then Member in charge of the Judicial Department'. Jinnah went in and asked for the appointment. He obtained the necessary recommendation from Mr MacPherson, and, within a few weeks, he became a temporary Presidency Magistrate. The material struggle was over : now he earned enough money to buy a carriage, to move to a better apartment, and to bring his sister, Fatima, from Karachi, and send her to the Bandra Convent school.

Bombay was a maze of caste and religious distinctions, and it was therefore a brave innovation to send a young Muslim girl to a Catholic convent. An anonymous author recalled the circumstances of this early gesture, of Jinnah to his sister, in a magazine article,[4] written fifty years later. 'In those days the people of her community

---

[1] *Mohammed Ali Jinnah (A Political Study)*, M. H. Saiyid (Sh. Muhammad Ashraf, Lahore, 1945), p. 7.
[2] Created Sir John Molesworth MacPherson, 1911.
[3] *An Ambassador of Unity*, p. 4.
[4] *Illustrated Weekly of Pakistan*, September 10, 1950.

THE YOUNG ADVOCATE

could not be reconciled to the idea of her joining the Convent as a boarder. Many efforts were made to dissuade her from doing so. There was a regular hue and cry. The dovecots of orthodoxy went up in flutters. The innocent young Fatima became the target for wagging tongues.'

We are told, in this flourish of words, that Miss Jinnah's brother was at her side, ' to give all the courage that she needed to stand up to the opposition that had come from the torch bearers of orthodoxy.' Jinnah drove to the convent to arrange for his sister to be admitted ; he went with her ' on an inspection round of the school premises ', and, when she had settled down to her studies, ' he used to visit her every Sunday, travelling all the way from Bombay to Bandra on horse-back.'

The relationship between brother and sister endured through the vicissitudes of half a century ; to the day of Jinnah's public tribute to her, after the creation of Pakistan, when he said, ". . . my sister was like a bright ray of light and hope, whenever I came back home and met her. Anxieties would have been much greater and my health much worse, but for the restraint imposed by her." She alone kept a place in his cautious affections, from the childhood days in Newnham Road, to the years of his triumph.

* * *

Although Pakistan and India were irrevocably divided, largely through Mohammed Ali Jinnah's imagination and persistence, he is still remembered with respect among the older Hindu lawyers of Bombay. In the heart of the city is the lofty Victorian-Gothic building where Jinnah began to practise, soon after his term as temporary Presidency Magistrate ended, in November 1900. Two splendid policemen, in gold and blue turbans, stand before an iron cage in which the prisoners are kept. Beyond them is a big dark office, in which some twenty lawyer's clerks tap out the wisdom of their masters on twenty typewriters. It was in this room that Jinnah began his career as an advocate, fifty-four years ago. In another room along the passage sits an old man who can remember Jinnah's first arrival at his chambers, which he filled with furniture "more splendid than anyone else would afford."

The old advocate was very willing to talk of these early days. He said, "I expect you know the story of Jinnah, at the beginning of his career; of his answer when Sir Charles Ollivant offered him a permanent appointment, at 1,500 rupees a month. Jinnah refused and said he expected to make that sum *every day*. Oh yes, he had a lot of brass and dash. But he was right. Once he was established, he probably earned more than any other lawyer in Bombay."

The advocate then summoned two friends from a neighbouring office, and all three, in turn, told their stories of Jinnah. The second of them had known him when he was " still rather poor." " But," he said, " his clothes were always his great distinction. He was even more independent in those lean years than he was later on. But he was so scrupulously honest. Difficult! Oh, yes. Although I have never heard of his doing an injustice, or a shady act. It was not in his nature."

The third advocate then said, " Of course, you know the story of how the *real* turn came in Jinnah's fortunes? In 1903, the President of the Municipal Corporation was a Scotsman—James MacDonald. He was a very important man—manager of all the affairs of the Bombay Corporation. There was a big case being tried in the High Court and the place was so full that the doors had to be closed. Inside the Court was an enclosure reserved for the lawyers. When Jinnah arrived—he was quite unknown then—there was nowhere for him to sit. He saw that James MacDonald was occupying one of the chairs reserved for the lawyers and he asked him to move. Naturally, he refused, so Jinnah went to the Clerk of the Court and demanded that MacDonald be removed. The Clerk was reluctant, until Jinnah threatened to appeal to the judge. Then the wretched Clerk simply had to go and ask MacDonald to yield up his place to Jinnah. MacDonald must have been an unusual sort of man. Instead of being furious, he gave up his chair, asked Jinnah's name, and, soon after, appointed him to act for the Corporation for a fee of 1,000 rupees a month."

The second advocate interrupted, " Jinnah's faith in himself was incredible. You must have read the story of his reply to the judge who said to him, ' Mr Jinnah, remember that you are not addressing a third-class magistrate.' Jinnah answered, ' My Lord, allow me to warn you that you are not addressing a third-class pleader.' . . . And that reminds me of the nice story of a rich Hindu landowner who protested at the amount of Jinnah's fee. He replied, 'You can't travel in a Pullman on a third-class ticket.'"

The third old gentleman spoke again: "Oh, I remember him once when I was collecting for a relief fund. I went up to him in the Bar Library and handed him the subscription list. He took it, placed his monocle in his eye, read the list, handed it back to me and said, 'I'm not interested.'"

The second advocate resumed his story: he said, "You must realize that Jinnah was a great pleader, although not equally gifted as a lawyer. He had to be briefed with care, but, once he had grasped the facts of a case, there was no one to touch him in legal argument. He was what God made him, not what he made himself. God made him a *great* pleader. He had a sixth sense: he could see around corners. That is where his talents lay. When you examine what he said, you realize that he was a very clear thinker, though he lacked the polish that a university education would have given him. But he drove his points home—points chosen with exquisite selection—slow delivery, word by word. It was all pure, cold logic."

The first advocate then told another story. "One of the younger men practising at that time—younger than Jinnah—was M. A. Somjee, who became a High Court Judge. They were appearing, as opposed counsel in a case which was suddenly called on for hearing. Mr Somjee was in another court at the time and the solicitor instructing him asked Jinnah to agree to a short adjournment. Jinnah refused. The solicitor then appealed to the judge, who saw no objection, provided Jinnah would agree. But Jinnah would *not* agree: he stood up and said, 'My learned friend should have anticipated this and he should have asked me personally for an adjournment.'

"Jinnah's arrogance would have destroyed a man of less will and talent. Some of us used to resent his insolent manner—his overbearing ways—and what seemed to be lack of kindness. But no one could deny his power of argument. When he stood up in Court, slowly looking towards the judge, placing his monocle in his eye—with the sense of timing you would expect from an actor—he became omnipotent. Yes, that is the word—*omnipotent*."

"Maybe," said the third advocate, "but, always, with Jinnah, one comes back to his honesty. Once when a client was referred to him, the solicitor mentioned that the man had limited money with which to fight the suit. Nevertheless, Jinnah took it up. He lost—but he still had faith in the case and he said that it should be taken to the Appeal Court. The solicitor again mentioned that his client had no money. Jinnah pressed him to defray certain of the appeal expenses out of his own pocket, and promised to fight the case without any fee for himself. This time, he won ; but when the solicitor offered him a fee, Jinnah refused—arguing that he had accepted the case on the condition that there was no fee."

" I'll tell you another story along that line," said the second advocate. " There was a client who was so pleased with Jinnah's services in a case, that he sent him an additional fee. Jinnah returned it, with a note, ' This is the amount you paid me——. This was the fee——. Here is the balance——.' "

When the three lawyers were asked, " Did you merely admire Jinnah, or did any of you become fond of him ? " one of them answered, " Yes, I was genuinely fond of him, because of his sense of justice. And because, with all the differences and bitterness of political life, I believe he was a man without malice : hard, maybe, but without malice."

★ ★ ★

Two of the advocates who spoke of Jinnah were Hindus : one was a Parsee. Some time later, a veteran Muslim barrister gave his different, perhaps more penetrating, impression of Jinnah's work at the Bar. " One must realize," he said, " that when he began to practise, he was the solitary Muslim barrister of the time : there may have been one or two others, but they did not amount to a row of pins. This was in a profession made up mostly of Hindus and Parsees. Perhaps they were over-critical of a Muslim—who came from business stock—setting up such a standard of industry. There was no pleasure in Jinnah's life : there were no interests beyond his work. He laboured at his briefs, day and night. I can see him now ; slim as a reed, always frowning, always in a hurry. There was never a whisper of gossip about his private habits. He was a hard-working, celibate, and not very gracious young man. Much too serious to attract friends. A figure like that invites criticism, especially in the lazy East, where we find it easier to forgive a man for his faults than for his virtues.

THE YOUNG ADVOCATE

"I can just remember Jinnah's first big chance, in 1907, in what came to be known as The Caucus Case. This arose out of a petition, filed by certain citizens in Bombay, alleging that the Municipal Corporation elections had been 'rigged' by a 'caucus' of Europeans, with the object of defeating Sir Pherozeshah Mehta—of keeping him out of the Council. Sir Pherozeshah Mehta was a Parsee, an elder statesman of the Congress, much respected and with great influence in the local administration. At that time, Jinnah was working in Sir Pherozeshah Mehta's chambers. He was appointed by the petitioners to act for them in securing annulment of the elections. The case was lost, but Jinnah gained great prestige for the way he handled it: as the Americans say, he 'made the headlines' for the first time. And also, it was a great compliment to his talents that he had been chosen to state the case of Sir Pherozeshah, himself a distinguished barrister. This was the first of many instances when Jinnah was trusted by an older man; a man who was wise enough to see past the defence of arrogance—for I am sure it was only a defence—into the source of Jinnah's very real talents.

"As to the accusation that he was a brilliant advocate, but a poor lawyer! It is easy for lawyers who lack the talent to plead, to accuse the men they are obliged to brief, of having scant knowledge of the law. I would put that down to human nature: Jinnah knew his law all right.

"I admit that Jinnah's methods were sometimes extraordinary. A judge once asked him to 'speak up'. 'We cannot hear you, Mr Jinnah,' he said. Jinnah replied, 'I am a barrister, not an actor.' The judge was patient, but he had to interrupt again—'Mr Jinnah, I must ask you to speak louder.' Jinnah answered, 'If you will remove that pile of books in front of you, you might be able to hear what I have to say.'

"I can tell you other such stories, but there is an explanation for them, in Jinnah's strange character. I think his apparent rudeness was linked with his deep honesty. This may be difficult to believe, but you must relate Jinnah's integrity to the wholly different ethics of the life surrounding him—in a land where private ethics are rather shaky.

"There was a well-known businessman, Haji Abdul Karim, who had to appear in Court on a serious charge. He went to Jinnah and asked him how much it would cost to take up the case. Jinnah answered bluntly, 'Five hundred rupees a day.'

"The businessman was cautious and he asked, 'How long will the case go on? I have five thousand rupees with me. Will you accept this to cover the whole of your fees?'

"Jinnah answered, 'I am not prepared to accept this amount. Five hundred rupees a day is my fee, and you must engage me on these terms or find another lawyer.'

"Abdul Karim accepted the terms, and Jinnah won the case, in three days. He accepted his fee of fifteen hundred rupees with good grace.

"There is another story," concluded the barrister, "concerning myself. Although I once or twice acted as magistrate in cases where Jinnah appeared before me, I was actually his junior in years. My father was related to Jinnah's family and, at the beginning of my career—when I returned to Bombay from Gray's Inn—my father took me to Jinnah, at his chambers. He said, 'Here is my son—make him as brilliant as you are.' Jinnah's answer was typical: he said to my father, 'Your son can come and work in my chambers, but he must make his own brilliance, by himself.'"

* * *

During these years of Jinnah's early success as a lawyer, he met Mrs Sarojini Naidu, the first sophisticated, intelligent woman to observe his talents; to see beyond the arrogance of the young advocate. She wrote of him:

> Never was there a nature whose outer qualities provided so complete an antithesis of its inner worth. Tall and stately, but thin to the point of emaciation, languid and luxurious of habit, Mohomed Ali Jinnah's attenuated form is the deceptive sheath of a spirit of exceptional vitality and endurance. Somewhat formal and fastidious, and a little aloof and imperious of manner, the calm hauteur of his accustomed reserve but masks—for those who know him—a naive and eager humanity, an intuition quick and tender as a woman's, a humour gay and winning as a child's. Pre-eminently rational and practical, discreet and dispassionate in his estimate and acceptance of life, the obvious sanity and serenity

of his worldly wisdom effectually disguise a shy and splendid idealism which is the very essence of the man.

Mrs Naidu's warm regard for Jinnah was shared by many other young women who saw, as *pride*, what his lawyer friends called *arrogance*. Among them was an old Parsee lady, still living on Malabar Hill, who remembers Jinnah at the age of twenty-eight. She has said of him, " Oh, yes, he had charm. And he was *so* good-looking. Mind you, I am sure he was aware of his charm : he knew his own strength. But when he came into a room, he would bother to pay a compliment—to say, ' What a beautiful *sari* ! ' Women will forgive pride, or even arrogance, in a man like that."

* * *

THE YOUNG POLITICIAN

WHEN Mohammed Ali Jinnah was old and full of authority, he liked to relax in the company of young people, with whom he would chuckle and joke, with patience that he seldom offered his contemporaries. After he had listened to boy students who came to him with their eager plans for improving the world, he would usually shake his finger at them and say, " Don't enter politics until you have made your pile."

Jinnah had obeyed this dictum himself : he waited until 1906, when he was thirty years old and safe in his career and his fortune, before he began any active work in the political affairs of India. His first aim was the Indian National Congress.

Mahatma Gandhi once said that it was ' a matter of the greatest pleasure ' to him that the Congress was ' first conceived in an English brain.' The brain was that of Allan Octavian Hume, a Secretary of the Indian Government, who realized the need for a national forum in which ' the picked men, the most highly educated of the nation,' could meet each year to ' secure greater freedom . . . a more impartial administration,' and a ' larger share in the management ' of their ' own country.'

On March 1, 1883—when Mohammed Ali Jinnah was still at school in Karachi—Hume had written a letter in which he said that if fifty men ' good and true can be found to join as founders ', an Indian Congress could be established. He was no sentimentalist : he challenged the people of India to produce the fifty wise men who would ' renounce personal ease and pleasure ' for India's cause. ' Let there be no more complaining of Englishmen being preferred to you,' he wrote. '. . . if you lack that public spirit, that highest form of altruistic devotion that leads men to subordinate private ease to the public weal, that patriotism that has made Englishmen what they are, then rightly are these preferred to you, rightly and inevitably have they become your rulers. And rulers and task-masters they must continue, let the yoke gall your shoulders ever so sorely, until you realize and stand prepared to act upon the eternal truth that self-sacrifice and unselfishness are the only unfailing guides to freedom and happiness.'

The Indian National Congress was formed, with this lofty purpose, and the first session was opened in Bombay, in 1885. The character of Congress did not continue in Hume's terms of ' altruistic devotion,' and it soon yielded to the vagaries of human nature : the members sometimes allowed their egos to come first, and the ' public weal ' second. It was nevertheless true that this noble hope for India's ' freedom and happiness ' was the image, not of the Indians themselves, but of one of the English ' rulers and task-masters.'

The founder members of Congress were mostly men who had been taught in English universities, or by English teachers in India. During the early sessions, they showed no impatience with the slow, safe tempo of British reforms. Gopal Krishna Gokhale—afterwards a patron and friend of Jinnah—admitted that the " present contract between India and England " was " a providential arrangement." W. C. Bonnerjee, the first President of Congress, said, ". . . much has been done by Great Britain for the benefit of India." He was grateful for the " order," the " railways," and the " inestimable blessings of Western education." Dadabhai Naoroji, returned from his political enterprises in Westminster, spoke of the " benefits of English rule," of the " darkness of Asiatic despotism," and the " light of free English civilization."

These compliments were printed in English newspapers, and they salved the British conscience : there seemed no reason to suppose that more could be done for India. Doctors, nurses, missionaries, social workers and teachers, travelled out and spent the best years of their lives in the Indian hospitals and schools : there was much benevolence, to cancel any selfish wish among the few who sought the rewards of profit, or power.

But the English had repeated, in India, the errors of their own educational reforms at home. The intellectual emancipation had begun at the top : rural and primary schools, technical and industrial teaching, were neglected. An Indian scholar wrote that ' a British pattern of character and education had been imposed on the upper classes, but nothing had been done to develop the indigenous ego of the Indian people.'

This higher education had bred a number of young political malcontents, who spoke against their " white overlords " and of freedom from the " shackles of British rule." In May 1905, they were encouraged by the victory of the Japanese over the Russians. The Viceroy reported that the news of this major conquest of a ' white ' people by ' coloured ' Asiatics, ' reverberated through the whispering galleries of the East.' The whispers became loud, and defiant, five months later, when Bengal was partitioned [1]—a measure that gave the bolder agitators the signal they needed. There were terrible outrages in East India, and an organized boycott of goods imported from Britain. The rulers were forced into stern punishments and reprisals.

One of the alarming effects of the Bengal episode was on the character of Congress, so mild in its policy up to then. The dramatic appeal of the extremists, against the British, startled all India, and, to hold their own as a political force, liberal-minded men like G. K. Gokhale and Dadabhai Naoroji had to assume a more belligerent look.

[1] There were two main reasons for dividing the over-populated province of Bengal : first, it was hoped that *two* provinces, with two governors, could be administered more efficiently ; and secondly, that the depressed Muslims —living mostly in East Bengal—would no longer suffer under the inquisitions of the wealthy Hindu landlords and moneylenders of Calcutta and West Bengal. For the Muslims, partition brought the promise of social and economic emancipation : for the Hindus, a threat to both their prosperity, and independence. The division of the province led to riots, and antagonism that was never subdued, even when the Act of Partition was annulled. See p. 50.

PARTITION OF BENGAL

At the next meeting of Congress—the first attended by Jinnah—Gokhale denounced the Government of India for its "determination to dismember Bengal at all costs." He said that the measure arose from "a decision to suit everything to the interests and convenience of the Civil Service." Gokhale first recalled the inauguration of Congress, in 1885, under the influence of "a remarkable outburst of enthusiasm for British rule." At the end of his speech, he announced a lively change of policy : he said, "Above all, there is a general perception now of the goal towards which we have to strive. . . . The goal of the Congress is that India should be governed in the interests of the Indians themselves, and that in course of time a form of government should be attained in this country similar to what exists in the self-governing colonies of the British Empire."

The story of the political currents that flowed in this time is told in a hundred books of reference : it is necessary only to describe those immediate events that must have influenced Jinnah at this important period of his life, when, having made his ' pile '—or the foundations of it—he decided to ' enter politics.'

It might seem that the old astrologer in Karachi was still busy with his prophetic scratchings in the dust ; busy arranging the pattern of coincidences in Jinnah's life. He had been born only a few days before Queen Victoria was proclaimed ' Kaisar-i-Hind ' ; he arrived as a student in London in the year of Mr Gladstone's last great Liberal victory—the year of Dadabhai Naoroji's election to Parliament. In 1906, when Jinnah decided to ' enter politics ', the Liberals were again in power in England, with Sir Henry Campbell-Bannerman as Prime Minister, Mr John Morley as Secretary for India, and six members of Parliament who were ' Anglo-Indians ', pledged to the cause of freedom in the country they knew so well.

On February 26, 1906, John Morley said in the Commons, " This Parliament presents a considerable number already of new features ; and it is a new feature, and one, I think, on which we ought to congratulate ourselves, that this afternoon we have had six maiden speeches in succession from Gentlemen who have shown themselves possessors of a competent knowledge of Indian subjects. . . . I think a debate of this kind can do nothing but good to this country and also to our interests in India."

The debate, on the partition of Bengal and the unrest in India, had inspired each of these six new members to make a long speech, explaining India's misfortunes and needs, as they had never been presented to the Commons before. The text of the speeches must have been heartening to readers of *The Times of India* next morning, and Mohammed Ali Jinnah must have noted all this with satisfaction. He may have read Sir Henry Cotton's statement, that " Sympathy is the keynote of successful administration in India " ; and Sir John Jardine's plea, that " the natives of the country should be employed in the administration of the country as much as possible and as far as was consistent with good government."

This disturbing debate in the British Parliament coincided with Jinnah's first active move in the politics of his own country : during the important 1906 session of the Indian Congress, held in Calcutta, he was private secretary to Dadabhai Naoroji. He had heard his old master, in Westminster, fourteen years before, speaking of " British justice and generosity " : now he listened to him declaring, " All our sufferings of the past centuries demand before God and men reparation. . . . The British people would not allow themselves to be subjected for a single day to such an unnatural system of government as the one which has been imposed upon India for nearly a century and a half. . . . We do not ask favours. We only want justice. Instead of going into any further divisions or details of our right as British citizens, the whole matter can be comprised in one word—' Self-government,' or ' Swaraj '. . . ."

So the Grand Old Man—the once-gentle mediator of the Finsbury electorate—now in his eighty-first year, became a warrior. His slogan, ' Swaraj '—*Our Raj*—was writ on the new banner of Congress. Behind the banner marched Jinnah, at the age of thirty, with most of the attributes of great reformers. Those attributes have been described as ' immense enthusiasm, a desire for adventure, a powerful persuasiveness, a keen sense of the spirit and the requirements of the day, and a certain mysticism.' Jinnah had all these, except mysticism. His advent into public life—with this small rôle at Dadabhai Naoroji's heels—was welcomed by all except his admirer, Mrs Naidu, who wrote, ' *Hai-hai*, what has happened to this beautiful boy ? Why has he meddled in politics ? '

★ ★ ★

"THE NIGHTINGALE OF BOMBAY"

The old Parsee lady, still living in Bombay, recalls both Jinnah and Mrs Naidu during this year, when the advocate became the young politician. "Yes," she has said, "I remember Sarojini Naidu: she was in love with Jinnah, but he was never in love with her. He was cold and aloof; his career was all that mattered to him. She wrote love poems to him, but he was not the man to be enticed by romantic verses: he was fastidious and virtuous, and he spent his evenings with his law court briefs. They used to call Mrs Naidu, 'The Nightingale of Bombay'. I am afraid that, as far as Jinnah was concerned, she sang in vain."

The extravagance of Mrs Naidu's devotion must have been embarrassing to a man of Jinnah's nature: she wrote,

> In the noon-tide hours, O Love, secure and strong,
> I need thee not. . . .
> But in the desolate hour of midnight, when
> An ecstasy of starry silence sleeps
> On the still mountains and the soundless deeps,
> And my soul hungers for thy voice. . . .

Mrs Naidu's conception of Mohammed Ali Jinnah was over-coloured: the true portrait of him at this time has an El Greco look, with grey, cold depths—lean, pale hands, which he washed almost every hour, and eyes that searched into a man's conscience. Except for the heavy lips, his face was that of a zealot—a puritan, but one who made no laws for others that he did not already keep himself.

There is a vague story that Jinnah made a speech in Congress on the opening day of the 1906 session. But there is no proof of this; no words are recorded to let us know what was in the mind of the calm, relaxed figure, who was so curiously free from those extremes of emotion usually found in his race.

When another old friend of this time was asked, "But was Jinnah absolutely without passion?" he answered, "It may sound ridiculous, but I believe his only passion was for newspapers. He had them sent from all over the world: he cut pieces out of them, annotated them, and stuck them into books. He would do this for hours—all through his life, he loved newspapers."

The habit endured forty years later, even when he was dying—the eager interest in what was happening, everywhere. Always, he was to peer ahead : the past had no allure for him. When he went to see one of the great Parsee aristocrats of Bombay, in his fabulous palace by the sea, Jinnah would hurry through the galleries thronged with treasures; ancient bronzes brought from southern India, and exciting, delicate Moghul paintings. All he sought was a sofa, in a corner, where he could ensnare his host and talk politics—at him, rather than with him—late into the night.

PART TWO

TALK OF ALEXANDER

IT is refreshing to leave Karachi and, after a long journey, come to the trees, the gardens and the stately tombs of Lahore. Karachi, the once arid fishing village, seems bewildered by its own size and prosperity. The city grows: immense, expressionless office buildings buzz with the extravagant fuss of government; white villas multiply in the gleaming sun, and there are new hotels, brash as the saxophones that split the silence of their courtyards. There is also another world, hiding behind this façade of 'progress'. On the edges of the city are the hovels of the poor—the survivors of the biggest migration of human beings in all the history of the world; the herds of refugees, clutching the bright star of an ideal in one hand and the poor man's ration of rice in the other. The thousands of rush huts seem to float in the mud and slime: one overturned oil-stove could transform them into a terrible forest of flame.

In the city are the stacks of cotton bales, piled high, like gigantic slabs of stone trying to form pyramids. They are watched night and day by stalwart Pathans, who sometimes dance when their vigil is over, waving their big swords as they stamp on the earth. (The cotton must be guarded against fire, for this is most of the fortune, and the security, of West Pakistan.)

The most delightful sounds in Karachi are the camel and donkey bells, enlivening the tatterdemalion of the streets. Among the shining motor-cars, the men in Western clothes and the women in saris, walk the dwindling number of wives in purdah, covered from head to toes in their tawdry white *burkas*. They look like bell-tents on the march: peering at this new world that Mohammed Ali Jinnah made, through the eyeholes of their curious shrouds, they do not seem to belong to lively, emancipated Pakistan.

The colours of the earth in Karachi are dun and feeble, but the ever-changing light that comes over the sea is splendid. In the morning it is watery turquoise, and clean, like English light. Later in the day it becomes fierce gold. At sunset, for a brief moment, the sea is a flood of burgundy. Then comes the night, covering all the harshness with stars, hanging so low that they look like trembling tassels of silver, rather than fixed points of light.

The train from Karachi arrives in Lahore in the evening. The contrast, after the barren desert—the stingy dryness of the sand—is surprising. The trees of Lahore have deep, fat roots, for the earth is also deep, and well watered. They seem to be immense as oaks in an English park: in the half-darkness they are like herds of elephants, moving against the sky.

With the sense of depth, in the earth of the Punjab, comes a sense of the depth of its history. Alexander the Great passed near Lahore, after he defeated Porus, ruler of the land between the Chenab and the Jhelum rivers, in 326 B.C. One hundred miles north of Lahore, the strong, solemn Jhelum still flows by: it is possible to stand on the river-bank and think of Alexander's flotilla making its way down, to the wild meeting with the waters of the Chenab, and then on to the Indus, and the sea. There are great stretches of quiet, dead land on the river-bank, unchanged in this new Muslim state, where a lonely man might listen for the chanting of Alexander's oarsmen, making their slow, perilous journey home.

Mohammed Ali Jinnah remained unaware of these voices of history: otherwise he might have been inspired by the figure of Porus, who rode into battle on an elephant, and Alexander, astride the valiant Bucephalus. Jinnah might have comprehended, and enjoyed the words they exchanged. "How shall I treat you?" Alexander asked the vanquished warrior. Porus answered, "As one king treats another."

Within a few miles of where Alexander rode, at the head of his army, the monumental Pakistan Resolution was to be passed, in 1940. At the vast meeting of Muslims, in Lahore, within a bowl of earth called the Wrestling Ring, the decision was to be made—that the Muslim people of India would sever themselves from the Hindus and form their own nation. Today, in the rainy season, the Wrestling Ring is flooded, and children play there, laughing and splashing in the water—some of them riding on the backs of buffaloes. There are no signs, of Alexander upon his charger, or of Jinnah, hypnotizing a multitude with the promise that they would be free, and strong. Yet, an alert listener might hear their similar voices; the one, from more than two thousand years ago, saying, "It is sweet to live with courage," and Jinnah's voice, saying, "Failure is a word unknown to me."

* * *

The history of Lahore is recorded in the names of its monuments and streets—from the age of the Moghul Emperors, to the advent of Mohammed Ali Jinnah. The gardens, and bazaars, the fortresses and the tombs, reveal the four ages of Punjab history; from the heyday of the Moghul kings, to the present regime of the free Muslims; from *Akbari Mandi*—the market named after Akbar the Great, who began to rule in 1556—to *Jinnah Gardens*, named in our time. In between are the Sikh and British names, to account for the intervening centuries.

There is one object, set up as a monument, in Lahore—Zam-Zamma, or Kim's Gun—which has watched all these changes of power. The gun is beautifully engraved: it was cast in 1757, and known first by its Afghan name, *Malik-i-Maidan*—The King of the Battlefield. The name Zam-Zamma was the soldiers' onomatopoeic description of the splendid booming sound, when the gun was fired. During the Sikh conquest of the Punjab, Zam-Zamma was captured, and preserved as a trophy. When the British came, they decided that its fighting days were over: to celebrate the visit of the Duke of Edinburgh, in 1870, the gun was placed on a platform and 'declared open', as a monument to peace. Today, it presents a benign look to the passing traffic: idlers lean against it, and boys climb over its barrel. 'Kim' was perhaps the first of these:

> He sat, in defiance of municipal order, astride the gun Zam-Zamma on her brick platform opposite the old Ajaib-Gher—the Wonder House, as the natives call the Lahore Museum. Who holds Zam-Zamma, that 'fire-breathing dragon', holds the Punjab; for the great green-bronze piece is always first of the conqueror's loot.

Beyond Kim's Gun, which is set within a merry-go-round of traffic, are the great names, painted on walls and street-ends, such as *Aurangzeb Street*, *Shish Mahal Park*, and *Kochai Chabuk Sawaran* (the street of the horse-trainers); names that survive from Moghul times, during which the first English voices were heard in the Punjab. William

Hawkins came, as emissary from the Court of James I, and, following him, in 1615, Sir Thomas Roe, to encourage the sale of English goods in the Moghul Empire.

The wars and terrors of three hundred years have not banished all the ghosts of these splendid times, before the Sikhs ravaged the Punjab. Within the old, walled city of Lahore, in a fine big house opposite *Barood Khana*—another Moghul name, meaning ' the arsenal '—there lives Mian Amiruddin, who served Mohammed Ali Jinnah, when the time came, and who fought hard for Pakistan. Guests at his table may hear, through the wall, what seems like the muffled beat of a drum : Mian Amiruddin will explain that the noise comes from the silver beaters at work, and, a few minutes later, his servant will bring in a dish of rich almond paste and other delicacies, wrapped in little sheets of pure silver, beaten until it is gossamer thin. While his guests are eating the fragments of silver, he will tell them that it is " good for the heart " ; and that when the Queen of Sheba went to Solomon, she took him sweets wrapped in sheets of pure gold and silver, so fine that he was able to eat them. Mian Amiruddin will then say, " The Moghul rulers of India also ate their sweetmeats wrapped in silver."

* * *

The next group of street-names records the terrible history of the Punjab in the early eighteenth century, when the Sikhs ' laid their ruthless hands ' on the land. Latif writes, in his history of Lahore, of the evils that followed the last of the Moghul rulers. ' During the commotions that followed the death of Bahadur Shah, the Sikhs emerged from their mountain retreats and laid waste the Punjab from Ambala to Lahore.' Then, ' The mosques were defiled, the houses burnt, the women outraged and the Muslims slaughtered . . . the whole country was ravaged. Mosques and tombs were razed to the ground . . . they slaughtered the inhabitants indiscriminately, without regard to age or sex. They butchered, bayoneted, strangled, shot down, hacked to pieces, and burnt alive, every Mahomedan in the place. . . . '

Britons, shocked by such tales of devilry in India, might recall that, about the same time, there was a generation alive in England who could remember the excesses of the Civil War ; that little more than fifty years had passed since Cromwell's body was dragged through London on a sledge, followed by the 'universal outcry and curses of the people.'

Of Sikh names that survive in Lahore, there are *Guru Nanak Street*, named after the originator of the Sikh sect ; *Guru Arjun Nagar, Chawk Phula Singh*, and *Chawk Jhanda Singh*—a ' chawk ' being a square or market place. There is also *Maharaj Ranjit Singh Road*, in memory of the famous one-eyed Sikh ruler who made a treaty with the British, and kept it.

Set among these native street-names are memorials to British India —the names planted there after the Punjab was annexed, in 1849. There is *The Mall*, the main shopping street—and other good English names like *Egerton Road, Cooper Road*, and *Nicholson Road*. The pattern of British rule in the last half of the nineteenth century comes alive in these streets : there is *Mayo Road*, named after the great Viceroy who was assassinated in the Andaman Islands, in 1872 : there are *Aitchison Park*, and *Lawrence Road*, in memory of Sir John (later Lord) Lawrence, the ' Saviour of India ' in his time, who was Lieutenant-Governor of the Punjab from 1846 to 1859, and then Viceroy, after Lord Elgin, in 1864.

But there are signs, already, that this is part of a new state, eager to plant its own memorials on the land. The *Lawrence Gardens* have been changed to *Jinnah Gardens*, and the sunken rose-garden within the park is named after Miss Fatima Jinnah.

The memories in the gardens are of neither Moghul, Sikh, nor Briton. Between the artificial hills, aflame with poppies, cinerarias, and carnations, is a sweep of grass : here, early in the morning, the robust young Punjabis wrestle and lift weights, pausing now and then to enjoy the sight of their own muscles, in big, incongruous looking-glasses erected for this purpose on the lawn. They are the generation in which Mohammed Ali Jinnah had every hope—young men, excited by tomorrow rather than yesterday, who are to be the **real** makers of Pakistan.

* * *

BACKGROUND FOR PAKISTAN

THERE is a span of history to be comprehended before Mohammed Ali Jinnah is brought back into the story : from the wane of the Moghul rulers, to the re-awakening of the Muslims, under Jinnah's will, almost two and a half centuries later. In between were the years of increasing humiliation for the Muslims, from causes within, and without, themselves.

The first part of the story is told, concisely, in one paragraph of the *Encyclopædia Britannica* [1] :

> On the death of Aurangzeb in 1707, the decline of the Mogul empire set in with extraordinary rapidity. Ten emperors after Aurangzeb are enumerated in the chronicles, but none of them has left any mark on history. His son and successor was Bahadur Shah, who reigned only five years. Then followed in order three sons of Bahadur Shah, whose united reigns occupy only five years more. In 1739 Nadir Shah of Persia, the sixth and last of the great Mahommedan conquerors of India, swept like a whirlwind over Hindustan, and sacked the imperial city of Delhi. Thenceforth the Great Mogul became a mere name, though the hereditary succession continued unbroken down to the time of the Mutiny. Real power had passed into the hands of Mahommedan courtiers and Mahratta generals, both of whom were then carving for themselves kingdoms out of the dismembered empire, until at last British authority placed itself supreme over all.

This 'authority' of the British began with the valiant exploits of Clive, and became 'supreme over all' a century later, with Napier's conquest of Sind in 1843, the destruction of Sikh authority over the Punjab in 1849, and the annexation of Oudh in 1856. In 1856 also, Lord Canning arrived in India as Governor-General, having declared, before he sailed :

> I wish for a peaceful term of office. But I cannot forget that in the sky of India, serene as it is, a small cloud may arise, no larger than a man's hand, but which, growing larger and larger, may at last threaten to burst and overwhelm us with ruin.

[1] *India* (History), Sir William Wilson Hunter and James Sutherland Cotton, 11th edition, Vol. 14, p. 404.

The 'small cloud' arose in the following year, when the sepoys of the Bengal army mutinied 'and all the valley of the Ganges from Patna to Delhi rose in open rebellion.' In one month, 30,000 native troops deserted from the army in northern India.

Three statements, from the many made before the transfer of the government of India to the Crown, reveal the British reaction to the horrors that spread, and endured, for a year and a half. At Balmoral, Queen Victoria and Prince Albert opened a map of India, and studied the reports of the massacre at Cawnpore; 'the hideous, unheard-of murders . . . unspeakable cruelties done to poor ladies and children.' The Queen wrote to the Empress Augusta of the 'one thousand Europeans, besieged, hungry and in terror,' within the walls of Lucknow; and of the terrible dangers of the twenty-four thousand Britons, at the mercy of a million rebel Indians. She added, '. . . there is hardly a family who has not lost a relation or is not in anxiety about them.' The Queen thought 'no punishment . . . severe enough' for the 'perpetrators of these awful horrors', but she agreed that the 'innocent ones,' whatever their race or religion, 'should not be made to suffer.'

Prince Albert wrote, with informed detachment, to the Prince of Prussia:

> The Indians are not a people capable of conquering independence for themselves, to say nothing of maintaining it. Since the days of Bacchus and Nimrod, India has constantly been overrun and conquered by new races—the Assyrians and Persians, the Greeks under Alexander, the Hiungnu, Tartars, Arabians, and others, down to the most recent times. The conquerors have brought under the yoke and oppressed the races whom they found in possession, but have neither rooted them out nor absorbed them; thus they remain intermingled, but without national coherence.

The third statement was part of a letter written from India, by Lord Canning to Lord Granville, President of the Council,

> As long as I have breath in my body, I will pursue no other policy than that I have been following: I will not govern in anger. Justice, and that as stern and inflexible as law and might can make it, I will deal out. But I will never allow an angry and

indiscriminating act or word to proceed from the Government of India, as long as I am responsible for it.

Among the races described by Prince Albert as 'intermingled, but without national coherence,' were the fifty-odd million Muslims who, with the decline of the Moghul Empire, had lost pride, property, and power, especially in the Hindu-dominated areas, where they lived in degradation and misery, excluded from all but humble posts in the British administration.[1]

The tragic circumstances of the Muslims at last bred the leader they needed. His name was Syed Ahmed Khan—the first Muslim in India who dared to speak of 'partition'; the first to realize that, mutual absorption being impossible, the Hindus and Muslims must part. He was the father of all that was to happen, ultimately, in Mohammed Ali Jinnah's mind.

There is a photograph of Syed Ahmed Khan, taken when he was a very old man. He had the splendid eyes, the noble brow and the strong, yet benevolent, look associated with wise leadership. In the photograph, these features are given a patriarchal air because of his immense white beard. Beneath are printed his name and ultimate titles : The Hon'ble Dr. Sir Syed Ahmed Khan Bahadur, K.C.S.I., LL.D.

Syed Ahmed Khan was born in 1817, of a family that claimed spiritual sanctity because of their descent from the Prophet. His father was a religious recluse ; his mother, a daughter of the Prime Minister at the Moghul Court. Syed Ahmed Khan might therefore have embraced the traditions and conventions of his forbears, without question. But he was marked for lonely and independent flight : when he was a baby, his aristocratic grandfather noted his 'unusually large hands and feet,' and said, " A burly rustic has been born in our family."

---

[1] ' Sir William Hunter, in a remarkable book [*The Indian Mussalmans*] publshed shortly after the Mutiny, gives a striking picture of the decaying Muslim middle class in Bengal. They had lost their traditional positions in the police, courts of law, magistracy, army, and revenue offices. Of 240 Indian pleaders admitted to the Calcutta bar between 1852 and 1868 only one was a Muslim. There were no Muslim covenanted officers or High Court judges. In all the government-gazetted appointments of the province, they filled only 92 places out of 1,338.' *The Making of Pakistan*, Richard Symonds (Faber, 1950), p. 26.

Like Mohammed Ali Jinnah, born almost sixty years later, Syed Ahmed Khan was plunged from security to poverty when he was still in his 'teens : like Jinnah, he studied the law. He began work as a clerk ; but such were his scholarly habits and energies that at the age of twenty-four he was a *Munsif*, or sub-judge. From 1846 to 1854 he worked in the law courts in Delhi, growing in experience, mind and character. The once-important Moghul city had lost much of its princely glamour, but, out of the shabbiness and rubble, new Muslim thought was springing. Syed Ahmed Khan found himself surrounded by young voices chanting the virtues of Reform, and he soon became their leader. He had been bred on the basic theology of Islam, but he was too lively in mind to be obsessed with the past, or to be sentimental about the maladies of his people. Some years later he wrote of the Muslims :

> They are under the influence of false and meaningless prejudices, and do not understand their own welfare. In addition, they are more jealous of each other and more vindictive than the Hindus and suffer more from a sense of false pride. They are also poorer, and for these reasons I fear that they may not be able to do much for themselves.

Syed Ahmed Khan was something of a changeling in the Muslim brood—a realist, and too cautious to be trapped into frenzy. During these early years, when he watched the Muslims wilting in their fight for survival, against the astute Hindus, he believed that the only hope for his people was in co-operation with the British.

In 1857, at the time of the Mutiny, Syed Ahmed Khan was forty years old and he had been in the judicial service for almost twenty years—still a young man, but mellow with experience. During the Mutiny, he proved his partiality for the British by shielding some of them in his bungalow : when a mob of fanatics came to his door, he went out, unarmed, and turned them away.

When the Mutiny ended, Syed Ahmed Khan wrote an honest and startling book, *The Causes of the Indian Revolt*, which was to influence and help to change the fortunes of India. The book was distributed only to British officials : some of them thought it ' highly seditious ', but they heeded its warnings. His language was mild, compared with the fiery charges made by Burke, in the British Parliament, seventy-five years before. Syed Ahmed Khan's plea, for government 'of the people, by the people, for the people,' makes sound and polite reading now. He wrote: 'Most men agree . . . that it is highly conducive to the welfare and prosperity of Government—indeed, it is essential to its stability—that the people should have a voice in its councils.' Other sentences confirmed the reasonableness of his argument: 'The people have no means of protesting against what they might feel to be a foolish measure, or of giving public expression to their own wishes.' Then this bitter comment on the cause of so much mischief in the British conduct of India: 'There is no real communication between the governors and the governed, no living together or near one another, as has always been the custom of the Mohammadans, in countries which they have subjected to their rule.' Syed Ahmed Khan stated that 'it was for the Government to try and win the friendship of its subjects, not for the subjects to try and win that of the Government'. He added, 'Now the English Government has been in existence upwards of a century, and up to the present hour it has not secured the affections of the people.'

Among the many British officials whose consciences were stirred by these criticisms was Allan Octavian Hume: he wrote, 'It was after reading Syed Ahmed Khan's book on the causes of the Indian Mutiny that I first felt the need for having a forum of public opinion of India and eventually the Indian National Congress came into existence.'

Before describing the arrival in Congress of Mohammed Ali Jinnah, as secretary to Dadabhai Naoroji, in 1906, other events and thoughts in the story of Syed Ahmed Khan must be observed; events and thoughts that influenced the formation of Jinnah's mind and ambitions.

As early as 1867, Hindu leaders in Benares began a movement to replace Urdu—the chief language of the Muslims—by Hindi. This episode convinced Syed Ahmed Khan that the two communities—Muslim and Hindu—would never "join wholeheartedly in anything." He made this statement to the British Divisional Commissioner [1] at Benares, and added, "At present there is no open hostility between the two communities, but on account of the so-called 'educated' people, it will increase immensely in future. He who lives will see."

Thus was born the thought, of the parting of the peoples, to which Mohammed Ali Jinnah became the heir, although many years were

[1] Mr Alexander Shakespear.

to pass before he acknowledged that it was his destiny to fulfil Syed Ahmed Khan's disturbing prophecy.

The next great achievement which was to influence Jinnah, was the founding of Aligarh University—first called the Mohammedan Anglo-Oriental College—at Aligarh, in the United Provinces.

The foundation-stone of the College was laid in 1877 by the Viceroy, Lord Lytton; but the vision, and the will that made a reality of the vision, was Syed Ahmed Khan's. He aimed to produce—through the College—an educated ' upper ' class of Muslims who might lead their people out of despair and ignorance, towards humanism and intelligent government. English professors and lecturers, including Sir Walter Raleigh, and Sir Thomas Arnold, the great orientalist, served on the staff of the College; and during the next fifty years, an entirely new class of Muslims was bred in India—scholars, reformers, teachers and politicians who, for the first time, were able to wave a lamp of hope before their co-religionists; hope of dignity, and emancipation.

Among the many evils corrected by Aligarh was the sad state into which the Muslim language had deteriorated. When the Muslims had been degraded and excluded from public office, their language had been reduced to a minority tongue. They were no longer aware of the trends of contemporary thought, for they produced little literature of their own, nor could they read what other men were writing. Aligarh helped to disperse this cloud of ignorance. Their own language, Urdu, regained its self-respect, as a language of scholarship and not merely an untidy means of speech. Also, English and European literature was made available to the students, and they became alive to the spread of Liberalism in England. Aligarh taught its Muslim students to think for themselves, in both English and Urdu, and they were encouraged to revive their own literature.

Syed Ahmed Khan also founded the Mohammedan Educational Conference, ' to engender enthusiasm for social reforms, modern education, and general economic and intellectual progress.' Until the Muslim League was founded, in 1906, the Mohammedan Educational Conference was the first and only parliament for the Muslims in India.

During the birth of these lofty intentions, the enmity between the Hindus and Muslims increased: it became all the more savage because of the ' so-called educated ' people, who had learned to organize and direct their rancour. In 1893 there were vicious anti-Muslim riots in Bombay. (Sir Syed Ahmed Khan was then seventy-seven years old : he had been knighted in 1877 and he was the undisputed leader of his people.) In *Makers of Pakistan and Modern Muslim India*,[1] the effect of these riots is described : ' This state of affairs intensified Syed Ahmed's fears. He began to wonder that, if under the British rule, Hindus wished to exercise so much pressure against normal civic rights of Muslims, what would be the state of affairs if the British left India and the reins of government passed into the hands of the majority community.'

Sir Syed Ahmed Khan was ' full of grave apprehensions ' about the fate of the Muslims. In a speech in 1883, ten years before the Bombay riots, he had said, " Now suppose that all the English . . . were to leave India . . . then who would be the rulers of India ? Is it possible that under these circumstances, two nations—the Mohammedan and Hindu—could sit on the same throne and remain equal in power ? Most certainly not. It is necessary that one of them should conquer the other and thrust it down. To hope that both could remain equal is to desire the impossible and the inconceivable."

There was another Muslim leader, the Aga Khan, who was also aware of the importance of British rule to the safety of his people. In his book, *India in Transition*, he wrote of the state of the Muslims during the last decade of the nineteenth century :

> The average Indian Moslem looked upon himself as a member of a universal religious brotherhood, sojourning in a land in which a neutral Government, with a neutral outlook, kept law and order and justice. . . . While his allegiance was to Queen Victoria, his political self-respect was satisfied by the existence of the Sultans at Constantinople and Fez, and of the Shah and Khedive at Teheran and Cairo. The fact that the British Government was the mainstay and support in the diplomatic arena of the independent Mahommedan States was naturally a source of continued gratification to him.

* * *

During most of this time, Mohammed Ali Jinnah was still in England, unaware that Sir Syed Ahmed Khan was creating, for him,

[1] A. H. Albiruni (Ashraf, 1950), p. 46.

the two beliefs that were to dominate the latter half of his life : that separation of the two chief races in India was inevitable, and that only through education might the Muslims find the way to freedom, peace and reason.

When the first generation of Aligarh students was already helping the Muslims towards a larger life and freedom of heart, Jinnah was still tramping between Lincoln's Inn, the British Museum, and his lodgings in Russell Road. Later, when he was a middle-aged man, he spent many days at Aligarh, talking to the students—usually in the rôle of stern disciplinarian, concerned with their responsibilities rather than their ambitions or grievances. One evening, some students of another college called on him, to seek his guidance. When some of them were critical of their elders, Jinnah interrupted them with the question, "How many of you have lamps on your bicycles?" Only one could say "Yes." Jinnah quickly answered, "Do not criticize others when you yourselves have not yet learned to respect the sanctity of the law."

This was his outward method with the young. But, behind the brusque words, was tenderness. Aligarh was largely the focus for this emotion when he was older : there he could find the young thinkers who would listen to the phrases of wisdom he liked to scatter when he was in a mood for moralizing.

Proof of this devotion to Aligarh lies in the two or three short pages of his will, written on some sheets of Legislative Assembly paper, on May 30, 1939, eight years before the Partition of India. Subject to family bequests and gifts to certain institutions, Jinnah ordered the rest of his fortune to be shared between Aligarh University, Islamia College at Peshawar, and the Sind Madrasah in Karachi, where he had been a schoolboy.

Jinnah never revised his will, even after Partition. Although Aligarh was then in alien territory, he did not withdraw his gesture. Through the long months, in 1948, when he knew that he was dying, he did not change his mind. Over small things—the rationing of tea to his staff, the price of a tie, the amount of petrol used in his car— he could be exasperatingly penny-wise : over any immense issue, such as this endowment of Aligarh, there was no rancour or pettiness in his heart.

★ ★ ★

1906-1910

IF Mohammed Ali Jinnah had gone to Aligarh, in 1892, instead of venturing across the seas to England, and Lincoln's Inn, his belief in the parting of the Muslims and Hindus might have developed much earlier. As it was, his political awakening had come in the British House of Commons, when he was 'thrilled' by the revival of Liberalism under Gladstone. It was with the same conception, and aims, that he joined the Indian Congress, on the side of such Moderates as Dadabhai Naoroji and G. K. Gokhale. At Aligarh, he might have joined the early Muslim intellectuals; he might have believed, while still in his 'teens, in the prophecies of Sir Syed Ahmed Khan. But Jinnah did not admit this enlightenment until he was a much older man.

By 1906, Aligarh College was twenty-eight years old, and many of the ex-students had become an effective force in politics. They had learned an important lesson, following the partition of Bengal. The outside world—including even the new Liberal Government in England, with its pro-Indian sympathies—had interpreted the outcry of Congress against the partition as the voice of all India. The six new members, who spoke in the Commons on February 26, 1906, referred to " the Indians " and " the natives of the country "—not to the diverging interests of Hindus and Muslims. (At that time, of the 756 members of the Indian Congress, the Muslims numbered only seventeen.)

The speeches made in Westminster, and articles published in English newspapers, about this time, reveal the unwillingness of the British to realize that ' the natives of the country ' were not all of one mind; that, in many parts, Hindus and Muslims were opposed and living in discord. There was talk of appeasing the ' Indians ' by cancelling the partition of Bengal, *immediately*—an act that would have robbed the Muslims of the only encouraging piece of legislation in their favour since the Mutiny. The vehemence of the Hindu protest in Congress, against the partition, convinced educated Muslims that they could be redeemed only if they created their own political force and their own leadership. Out of these circumstances the Muslim League was formed.

On October 1, 1906, the Viceroy, Lord Minto, received a deputation of thirty-five leading Indian Muslims at Viceregal Lodge, in Simla.

FORMATION OF MUSLIM LEAGUE

The Aga Khan, then twenty-nine years old, described the plight of his co-religionists: he pressed "upon the Government of India the Muslim view of the political situation created by the partition of Bengal," and asked that his people should be guarded against any "political concessions" that might be "hastily made to the Hindus," and which would "pave the way for the ascendancy of a Hindu majority."

At the close of a long reply, the Viceroy said:

> I am entirely in accord with you. . . . I can only say to you that the Mohammedan community may rest assured that their political rights and interests as a community will be safeguarded in any administrative reorganization with which I am concerned, and that you and the people of India may rely upon the British *Raj* to respect, as it has been its pride to do, the religious beliefs and the national traditions of the myriads composing the population of His Majesty's Indian Empire.

The Muslims nevertheless relied on their own strength: on December 30, 1906, the All-India Muslim League was formed, at Dacca, with three main objectives:

> (*a*) To promote, amongst the Mussalmans of India, feelings of loyalty to the British Government and to remove any misconception that may arise as to the intentions of Government with regard to Indian measures.
>
> (*b*) To protect and advance the political rights of the Mussalmans of India and respectfully represent their needs and aspirations to the Government.
>
> (*c*) To prevent the rise among the Mussalmans of India of any feeling of hostility towards other communities without prejudice to the other aforesaid objects of the League.

Sir Percival Griffiths states in *The British Impact on India*, 'Whatever may have been the other effects of the foundation of the Muslim League, it set the seal upon the Muslim belief that their interests must be regarded as completely separate from those of the Hindus, and that no fusion of the two communities was possible.' He added, 'The philosopher might deplore the fact that Hindus and Muslims thought of themselves as separate peoples, but the statesman had to accept it.'

The Muslims of India had at last begun to re-create their own political history.

This brief outline leads to the next chapter in the story of Mohammed Ali Jinnah : but it is history in which he had no active part. He went his way, increasing his reputation and fortune as an advocate, and ignoring both the extremists in Congress and the sectarian aims of the League. When any cause affecting the Muslims came up, he gave it just and due sympathy ; but the impression of him, during these first years in politics, is of a dispassionate lawyer, observing the prejudices of his fellow-countrymen with a quizzical eye, and waiting for the right moment in which to raise his own voice.

He was at the Congress meeting in Surat in December 1907, when the extremists became so violent in their anti-British opinions, and in their criticism of the moderate Congress leaders, that one of them took off a shoe and flung it at Sir Pherozeshah Mehta, the distinguished Parsee veteran statesman. After this untoward incident, the session broke up in disorder. Jinnah was also present, in April 1908, when these extreme Nationalists were expelled and Congress declared its aim to be independence and self-government for India, within the secure pattern of the British Empire.

On November 2, 1908—the fiftieth anniversary of the assumption by the Crown of the Government of India—Jinnah was able to read the promise of the King-Emperor, that the time had come when ' the principle of representative institutions ' might be ' prudently extended.' The Address continued, ' Important classes among you, representing ideas that have been fostered and encouraged by British rule, claim equality of citizenship, and a greater share in legislation and government. The politic satisfaction of such a claim will strengthen, not impair, existing authority and power.'

There was one sentence that gave heart to the cold and formal Address, suggesting that King Edward VII might have worked on the phrasing himself. When he visited India, as Prince of Wales, in 1875–6, he had been shocked by the ' rude and rough manner ' of some of the officials : in a letter to his mother he had written, ' Natives of all classes in this country will, I am sure, be more attached to us if they are treated with kindness and with firmness at the same time, but not with brutality or contempt.'

The memory of this young experience, from thirty-three years before, may have urged him to add, at the close of his Address— ' Administration will be all the more efficient if the officers who conduct it have greater opportunities of regular contact with those whom it affects. . . .'

Before coming to the reforms that followed the King-Emperor's Address—and which gave Mohammed Ali Jinnah his first lively opportunity in the direct government of his country—it would be helpful to consider what is meant by the 'Government of India', as it was composed in 1908. In England, the Secretary of State for India was assisted by the Council of India, which was made up of ten to fifteen members, at least nine of whom must have lived or served in India for ten years or more. (At that time they included a Muslim, and a Hindu, appointed in 1907.) The 'Government of India', *in* India, was led by the Viceroy, assisted by an executive council, or cabinet, of six members, with the Commander-in-Chief as an extraordinary member; and this body enjoyed almost arbitrary rule over some three hundred million Indian subjects.

In November 1909—a year after the King-Emperor's Address—the Indian Councils Act enlarged the Viceroy's executive council into the Imperial Legislative Council, by the addition of 35 nominated members and 25 elected members, 'with special representation for Mohammedans and landowners.' The new Imperial Legislative Council thus became a debating body, in which, for the first time, the elected representatives of the people had the right to criticize, and promote, the government of their country.

Mohammed Ali Jinnah's ascent to power began with this reform: at the age of thirty-three he became one of the 'elected' members of the Council, by choice of the Muslims of Bombay.

The first meeting of the Imperial Legislative Council was held at Calcutta, on January 25, 1910. The new members belonged to a variety of religions and they took their oaths in a variety of ways and languages. Mr Macpherson, the Legislative Secretary, made his pledge on the Bible; the Hon. Maharajadiraj of Burdwan kissed a 'Gita'—the holy book of Krishna—which he produced from his pocket; the Raja Partab Bahadur Singh of Partabgarh, another Hindu, took his oath in Urdu; Sir David Sassoon, a Jew, placed a handkerchief on his head and kissed the Old Testament. The description of the ceremony [1] does not mention how Mohammed Ali Jinnah

---

[1] *Speeches of the Earl of Minto, 1905-1910*, p. 372.

took his oath, but one presumes that he observed this duty in the Muslim way, on the Koran—and in English.

Jinnah was not an intimidated novice: almost immediately he crossed swords with the Viceroy, Lord Minto, during a debate regarding the plight of Indians in South Africa. This was his first essay in political duelling: he treated the incident with the aggressive self-confidence he had always displayed in the Law Courts of Bombay. In both rôles, of advocate and councillor, his manner was similar. Jinnah said:

> My Lord, I beg to support the Resolution that has been placed before the Council. The Honourable the mover put the question before the Council so clearly and concisely that there is very little left for anyone else to say. But the importance of this question requires that at least some of us should say a few words and express our feelings on this Resolution. If I may say at the outset, it is a most painful question—a question which has roused the feelings of all classes in this country to the highest pitch of indignation and horror at the harsh and cruel treatment that is meted out to Indians in South Africa.

The Viceroy interrupted:

> I must call the Honourable gentleman to order. I think that is rather too strong a word, 'cruelty'. The Honourable Member must remember that he is talking of a friendly part of the Empire, and he really must adapt his language to the circumstances.

Jinnah replied:

> Well, my Lord, I should feel inclined to use much stronger language, but I am fully aware of the constitution of this Council, and I do not wish to trespass for one single moment; but I do say this, that the treatment that is meted out to Indians is the harshest which can possibly be imagined, and, as I said before, the feeling in this country is unanimous.

Next morning, the Indian newspapers made much of the story, and, from then on, Jinnah was treated as 'news', although his manner with reporters was as brusque as with other men. To the end of his life, he made no effort to court popularity or to appease the press.

The fact that Jinnah's first speech in the Council concerned the Indians in South Africa, draws attention to the other men who were to be his opponents in the ultimate conflict between the Muslims and Hindus. In February 1910, Mohandas Karamchand Gandhi, Barrister-at-Law (Inner Temple, 1889)—almost forty-one years old—was leader of the many thousands of Indians settled in South Africa : he had already evolved the theory of 'Passive Resistance', which became the root of his policy after he returned to India. Pandit Jawaharlal Nehru, the more scholarly of the three reformers—who later became Gandhi's most devoted disciple and successor—had by that time come down from Cambridge and was studying law at the Inner Temple. All three men, who were to become the great protagonists in India's deliverance, were graduates of English Inns of Court.

In the same month, when Jinnah had already learned how to argue with a Viceroy ; when Gandhi was fighting the cause of the Indians in the Transvaal, and Nehru was completing the saga of Harrow, Trinity, and the Inner Temple, Prince Louis of Battenberg, the future Earl Mountbatten of Burma—who was to be the mediator and judge in the final conflict—was a boy of nine and a half years, not yet at his preparatory school.

* * *

1910-1913

KING EDWARD VII died on May 6, 1910, and six months later Lord Hardinge was appointed Viceroy. At the close of 1911, he welcomed King George V and Queen Mary to India, and to the fabulous Durbar at Delhi.

The King had already visited India, as Prince of Wales, in 1905, and he had talked with many of the leaders, among them Gopal Krishna Gokhale. Sir Walter Lawrence, a veteran in Indian affairs, wrote of their meeting : ' At one of the large receptions . . . the Prince had retired to an alcove for five minutes' rest. . . . I saw in the throng an old friend of mine, a great Indian, Mr Gokhale. . . . I took him into the alcove and introduced him to the Prince of Wales. . . . After a few words the Prince said, "I have been reading your speech at Benares, in which you said that it would be better for India if the Indians had a much larger part in the administration. I have now been travelling for some months in India . . . and I have never seen a happier-looking people. . . . Would the peoples of India be happier if you ran the country?"

'Mr Gokhale replied, "No, Sir, I do not say they would be happier, but they would have more self-respect."

'"That may be," said the Prince; "but I cannot see how there can be real self-respect while the Indians treat their women as they do now."

'"Yes," said Mr Gokhale, "that is a great blot." . . .'

The Prince had continued his journey, enjoying the sight of an ornate temple here—there a lovely mosque. That the temple was Hindu and the mosque Mohammedan did not seem to disturb him, and thus he missed the chief cause of friction in India. But he echoed his father's humanism: in some notes that he wrote when the journey was over, he admitted that he could not help 'being struck by the way in which all salutations by the Natives were disregarded by the persons to whom they were given'; and that he 'could not help noticing that the general bearing of the European towards the Native was to say the least unsympathetic.'

This impression must have endured in his incredible memory: in 1910, when plans were being made for his second visit and for the Durbar, he 'laid it down that "all classes should have a chance of seeing him close at hand."' [1]

At the end of the Durbar, when the Viceroy had finished his speech, 'the King, to the surprise of all, himself rose, and in a clear voice proclaimed . . . the revision of the partition of Bengal and the transference of the capital to Delhi.' [2]

There is no record of Mohammed Ali Jinnah's feelings over the 'revision', which was a victory for the Hindu-controlled Congress, and a sorrow for the Muslim League. The Muslims could no longer hope that the British would protect them against the superior forces of the Hindus; and the Muslim League could no longer be justified in a policy described by Mrs Naidu as 'too narrow and too nebulous.' At their next session, in December 1912, which Jinnah attended, the

[1] *King George V. His Life and Reign*, Harold Nicolson (Constable), p. 168.
[2] Ibid., p. 171.

League proposed to amend their constitution, so that it would ally them with Congress in a common demand for 'Swaraj'.

Mohammed Ali Jinnah spoke at this meeting of the Muslim League —from which he had so far kept apart, because of its 'exclusively sectarian' aims. But he no doubt felt justified in supporting the proposed changes in the League's constitution, since it would reconcile the League with the policy of Congress; the policy of the 'greater national welfare' to which he was pledged.

Jinnah's chief work remained with the Congress, and the Imperial Legislative Council. There are records of two speeches he made in 1912, before the Council: the first, in March, was on the subject of Police Administration; the second, in April, was in support of Gokhale's Elementary Education Bill. Half a century before, Syed Ahmed Khan had cried, "Educate! Educate! Educate!", and Aligarh University had been the answer. But Syed Ahmed Khan had relied on his own vision and will, and on a few rich Muslims and Englishmen who patronized his scheme; and he had produced an educated upper class of scholars who could share in the administration of the country. In 1912, Gokhale and Jinnah were pleading for the great sea of illiterates—the masses, for whom they wanted schools and compulsory education, to be controlled and paid for by the State. They asked for elementary education through Government grants, not private patronage. Jinnah's argument against those who opposed the Bill was characteristic: he examined the protests, and answered them, one by one, in a speech presented with the skill of a seasoned advocate. It was a long speech, of almost four thousand words. One passage, dealing with finance, reveals his method—the direct, persistent attack with which he was to wear down so many opponents in the future.

"If you have money, you will get teachers; if you have money, you will get school buildings. The real point is whether you have got the money or not. . . . Now, Sir, this is a very, very old story that you have no money, and all I can say is this—Find money! Find money! Find money! . . .

"I ask, is it such an insurmountable difficulty to get three crores of rupees from the Imperial Exchequer? Is it such a great, gigantic feat to be performed for a country like India, with its three hundred millions of people? I say, Sir, that there is nothing in that argument.

I ask the Government, I say 'find the money—if necessary, tax the people.' But I shall be told that the people are already taxed; I shall be told that we shall be facing great unpopularity. . . . My answer is that you must remove the reproach that is justly levelled against British rule, namely, the neglect of elementary education. My answer is that it is the duty of every civilized Government to educate masses, and if you have to face unpopularity, if you have to face a certain amount of danger, face it boldly in the name of duty. . . ."

Jinnah was not ungenerous : he admitted India's debt to Britain, for existing educational benefits, and said, " . . . let me tell you that you have no better friends in this country—I mean the friends of the Government—than the educated classes of this country . . . we know the blessings of education; we have learnt that from the British Government. They have been the first to open our eyes to it. They have brought us up to this level when we can stand in the Council and deliberate upon the affairs of our nation and of our country."

Some time at the beginning of 1913, the Viceroy proved his regard for Jinnah's talents by nominating him, for a second term, to the Imperial Legislative Council. He seemed to flourish immediately : with this encouragement, he made a number of speeches—on the Indian Extradition Bill, in March, and in April, a long address on the Criminal Law Amendment Bill.[1] He still spoke with the technique of the lawer, but also as a stern keeper of the law.

Some years later, the Raja of Mahmudabad said that Mohammed Ali Jinnah was " no apostle of frenzy," a fact that was already apparent in these early debates. During his speech on the Criminal Law Amendment Bill, Jinnah said, "I . . . wish to express that every attempt on the part of my countrymen to undermine the authority of the Government, and to disturb law and order, deserves the strongest condemnation and the highest punishment." Such malcontents were, he said, " the biggest enemies " of his " country " and his " people ". He continued, "I believe in criticizing the Government . . . freely and frankly, but, at the same time, that it is the duty of every educated man to support and help the Government when the Government is right."

Jinnah spoke then of those of his countrymen who were responsible

[1] The full text of the speech is reprinted in *Mohomed Ali Jinnah : An Ambassador of Unity*, pp. 226-43.

for 'political crimes.' "Let those men who still have these misguided ideas; let those men who still have these hallucinations, realize that, by anarchism, by dastardly crimes, they cannot bring about good government : let them realize that these methods have not succeeded in any country in the world, and are not likely to succeed in India. . . ."

Early in 1913, Jinnah achieved another success, with his gift for argument, with the Mussalman Wakf Validating Bill, which he had first introduced in March 1911.

This measure, which received the Viceroy's Assent on March 7, 1913, was of cardinal importance to the Muslims of India. As early as 1871, Mr William Hunter [1] had prepared a report on the subject, 'Our Indian Mussalmans : are they bound in conscience to rebel against the Queen.' He wrote of the 'chronic sense of wrong' which the Muslims suffered 'under British rule,' and of the sad fate of the once rich and educated Muslim aristocracy—the poor heirs of the princes who had long ago enjoyed the roses and fountains of Delhi and Lahore. '. . . in every district the descendant of some little line of princes sullenly and proudly eats his heart out among the roofless palaces and weed-choked tanks. . . . Their houses swarm with grown-up sons and daughters, with grandchildren and nephews and nieces, and not one of the hungry crowd has a chance of doing anything for himself in life. They drag on a listless existence in patched-up verandahs or leaky outhouses, sinking deeper and deeper into a hapless abyss of debt, till the neighbouring Hindu money-lender fixes a quarrel with them, and then, in a moment a host of mortgages foreclose, and the ancient Mussalman family is suddenly swallowed up and disappears forever.'

The only way of saving the property of these bewildered and feckless Muslim landlords, was by introducing, into the law of British India, the right of a Muslim to make a *Wakf*—a form of trust known in Mohammedan law, by which the beneficiaries would be safe against the folly of any one member of the family ; and which would provide security and an income to succeeding generations, in perpetuity.

Sir Syed Ahmed Khan had tried to introduce *Wakfs* for Muslims some years before, but he had failed. Mohammed Ali Jinnah took

[1] Then Director-General of the Statistical Department of India. Created Sir William Hunter, 1887.

up the cause : he pleaded for the rights of the oppressed minority, arguing as a dispassionate lawyer, rather than a Muslim protesting on behalf of his own people. There was not a phrase that betrayed religious prejudice : he said, " The one objection which has been urged against this Bill is the question of public policy. Now the answer to that, Sir, is a very simple one . . . what we have got to do is to administer the Muhammadan Law to the Mussalmans ; and therefore, to introduce the question of public policy, which is foreign to Islamic jurisprudence, to my mind is outside the question ; and there is no such thing as public policy of any kind—so far as Muhammadan jurisprudence is concerned—to which the provisions of this Bill are in any way opposed. I therefore give that simple answer to that point."

The legal pattern of Jinnah's speech makes some of it obscure to the lay mind, but the force of his words is apparent all the way through. When the Bill had been passed and received the Viceroy's Assent, one of the first to congratulate him was Mrs Sarojini Naidu : she wrote of this, his first private and personal success as a legislator,

> His admirable skill and tact in piloting through such an intricate and controversial measure—the first instance of a Bill passing into legislation on the motion of a private member—won him not only the appreciation of his colleagues but also his first meed of general recognition from his co-religionists all over India, who while still regarding him a little outside the orthodox pale of Islam were so soon to seek his advice and guidance in their political affairs.

★   ★   ★

AN ESSAY IN FRIENDSHIP

THERE was little of the disciple in Mohammed Ali Jinnah. Up to 1913, when he was thirty-six years old, he had never attached himself to any human being, in love or friendship. He liked to relax in the drawing-rooms of the rich Parsees in Bombay ; he could bow and make extravagant compliments to ladies ; and he liked laying down the law to the young, when they came to him for advice. But he discouraged intimacy, and was still a celibate introvert, timid of human relationships.

In 1913 he seemed to emerge from this chill armour, for the first time, in his devotion to Gopal Krishna Gokhale, the Hindu leader : a man who was as faultless as Jinnah, in both ethics and virtue.

Gokhale had been born in 1866, of a humble Brahmin family. He must have been a fascinating, as well as a strong character : he graduated from Elphinstone College, Bombay, and in 1884 he dedicated his talents to a long venture—he agreed to become professor of history and political economy at Ferguson College, Poona, at a nominal salary, for a term of twenty years. After 1902, he began his splendid political career ; and two years later Lord Curzon honoured him with the C.I.E., in recognition of his selfless patriotism. In 1906 John Morley wrote of him, ' He has a politician's head ; appreciates executive responsibility ; has an eye for the tactics of practical common-sense. He made no secret of his ultimate hope and design— India to be on the footing of a self-governing colony.' The article on Gokhale, in the *Encyclopædia Britannica*,[1] fortifies these judgments of his character : ' Gokhale's intense patriotism, powerful grasp of facts and great industry, raised him head and shoulders above his contemporaries ; and his moderation, invariable courtesy and lofty personal character marked him out as one of the last and greatest of the old school of Congress politicians before the age of non-co-operation.'

Jinnah the Muslim, and Gokhale the Hindu, had liked each other from the beginning : there was no conflict between their minds and they were not held apart by suspicion. Gokhale said of Jinnah, " He has true stuff in him, and that freedom from all sectarian prejudice which will make him the best ambassador of Hindu-Muslim unity." And Jinnah said that it was his " one ambition to become the Muslim Gokhale."

They both needed a holiday from their ideals, and their labours, so, in April 1913, they sailed for England. Gokhale was then almost forty-seven years old : Jinnah was thirty-six. There are neither letters nor diaries to tell what these two men talked about as their ship carried them towards England : Mrs Naidu vaguely estimated that ' the Arabian stars and Egyptian waters kept record, doubtless,

[1] Supplementary Volumes to the 13th ed., Vol. II, p. 240.

of their mutual hopes and dreams for the country of their devoted service.'

The word 'holiday' was alien to Jinnah's busy mind. During the visit to London, he added two important chapters to his story: he helped to create the London Indian Association, and he made a surprising decision by agreeing to join the Muslim League, on the eve of his return to India.

The problems of the Indian students in England, in 1913, were more complicated than they had been when Jinnah was studying law at Lincoln's Inn, twenty years before. In the 1890's, there was but a small Indian colony—mostly sons of noble, rich or privileged families—and it had been easy to admit them to the English universities and Inns of Court. Being few, they were an innovation, but not a problem. By 1913, Indians were migrating to England in big numbers, and they were beginning to use English education to sharpen their temper against British rule. These cryptic subjects of the King-Emperor brought their politics into the silence of England's ancient places, and the intrusion was resented. With their politics, they brought also their caste-system: instead of meeting socially and enjoying their adventure in scholarship, they divided themselves into many little groups, each with its own hobby-horse.

There were grievances on both sides, and, to avert folly, some Indian leaders, and their English friends, met and formed the London Indian Association. Their aim was to remove restrictions imposed upon Indians wishing to enter the universities and Inns of Court; also to acquire a central club-house in which the students could meet, for debates and social pleasures.

The Association lasted only a few years: it perished for want of support from the Indians themselves. But the failure of the plan does not lessen the interest of Jinnah's speech—his first in England—at Caxton Hall, on June 28, to an audience of several hundred Indian students.

He recalled his own years of study at Lincoln's Inn and then reminded his listeners that "the caste system—the bane of India", was to blame for the lack of friendliness among the students themselves. He was, as ever, coldly honest. He told them that one of the first tasks of the proposed association should be to "get rid of the exclusiveness" that was spoiling their chances of learning the best from England. After scolding the students for their "isolationism", he upbraided them for meddling in politics. Instead of behaving as students and learning all they could " of the civilization which the British people had taken centuries to build up," some of them had resorted to "strong language" and "strong action" in political issues.

Jinnah reminded the students that, in India, the men most active in politics were those " who had been educated in England " and who " returned home to serve their country." But he warned them that politics were dangerous fireworks in the hands of the young ; and that only by avoiding " strong language and hysterical ideas " could they " hope to go back home as great missionaries in the cause of progress." The moral of the speech was conventional enough : the phrases did not shine, but they confirmed Jinnah's regard for what England could teach, and his belief that scholarship should come first and politics after. " To take part in politics," he said, " will simply injure your position as students."

The rest of the summer was spent in leisure : Gokhale and Jinnah may have travelled to Europe, or they may have wandered through England. Little is known of these months, except that, since they remained together, they must have continued to enjoy each other's company. The conciliatory tone of their political conversations is suggested in Jinnah's last action before he sailed home to India, with Gokhale, in the autumn.

Two Muslim leaders, Maulana Mohamed Ali and Syed Wazir Hassan, who were in England at the same time, were among the many who regretted that Jinnah had always refused to join the Muslim League. They called on him and reminded him of the decision, made on March 22, to bring the policy of the League into line with the progressive and national aims of Congress. They argued that Congress and the League now spoke with the same voice and they pleaded with Jinnah to join. He agreed. There is no record of the scene, except a short half-page by Mrs Naidu, who wrote : [1]

> . . . Jinnah formally enrolled himself as a member of the All-India Muslim League, to whose expanded outlook he had already contributed so signally by his example. Typical of his exquisite, if somewhat exigent sense of honour, is it to find that even so

[1] *Mohomed Ali Jinnah : An Ambassador of Unity*, p. 11.

simple an incident partook of something like a sacrament. His two sponsors were required to make a solemn preliminary covenant that loyalty to the Muslim League and the Muslim interest would in no way and at no time imply even the shadow of disloyalty to the larger national cause, to which his life was dedicated.

The year ended in a unique victory for Mohammed Ali Jinnah. He returned to India, with Gokhale, and in December they went to Karachi for a meeting of Congress. Jinnah allowed himself to be sentimental at the beginning of his speech : he said, " You do not know what pleasure it gives me to stand on this platform in the city of Karachi where I was born. . . ." The members interrupted him with cheers : then he went on, ". . . where I have found by me . . . personal friends with whom I played in my boyhood. I am delighted to see so many of my Sindhi friends who are here."

At the age of thirty-seven he was back in his home-town, with the glow of success ; but also with the rewards of wisdom. His decision in London, to join the Muslim League, was justified in one of the resolutions of Congress during the session. The members ' placed on record' their ' warm appreciation of the adoption by the All-India Muslim League of the ideal of Self-Government for India, within the British Empire ; and of the belief which the League had so emphatically declared at its last session " that the political future of the country depends upon the harmonious working and co-operation of the two great communities."'

On his way from the meeting Mohammed Ali Jinnah may have walked along the street where, as a boy, the astrologer was said to have told him that he would grow up to be a ' king '. But the astrologer no longer scratched prophetic patterns in the dust with a stick : he was not able to stop Jinnah again and make the alarming prophecy —" Your pledges of harmony will be of no avail : thirty-four years from now you will come back to Karachi, as a king ; but, to achieve this, your countrymen will divide themselves against each other. In the process, hundreds of thousands of Muslims and Hindus must perish."

Neither Gokhale nor Jinnah could envisage any of this : they returned to their hotel in perfect accord of heart and mind. Gokhale had said that Jinnah would become the " ambassador of Hindu-

Muslim unity," and this day in December 1913 made the phrase seem almost true.

Jinnah's position was now trebly secure : he was a member of the Imperial Legislative Council, a member of Congress, and of the Muslim League, ' to whose expanded outlook ' he had ' contributed so signally by his example.'

Writers of the future may argue, according to their temper, whether good fortune, or brilliant political planning, had brought Jinnah to this happy state, of being trusted by the leaders of both communities. Had he designed a safe political career, over the years ; or was he really sincere in his belief, that the Hindus and Muslims, together, might still make a united and free India, of their own ?

One of his oldest friends in Bombay, Sir Cowasjee Jehangir, who had known Jinnah when he was twenty-five years old, has answered this question : he has said, "I knew him when he first arrived in Bombay : he was more of a peacock then than in later years, when he was successful. I can assure you that he was sincere about Hindu-Muslim unity : it was no political trick. Indeed, I can say that, whatever faults he had, political trickery was not one of them."

★ ★ ★

A GENTLEMAN 'OF RECOGNIZED POSITION'

EIGHT months after the session of Congress, in Karachi, the first World War began : in the meantime, Mohammed Ali Jinnah led a delegation to England, to lay before the Secretary of State the views of Congress on the Council of India Bill, due for its first reading in the House of Lords on May 25.

Jinnah had already prepared a resolution regarding the Bill, which had been adopted by Congress during the Karachi session. He repeated and explained its terms to members of both Houses of Parliament, at a breakfast-party given by Sir William Wedderburn,[1] at the Westminster Palace Hotel.

Sir William's speech of welcome was consoling and hopeful : he

[1] 1838–1918. Formerly a judge of the High Court, Bombay, and acting Chief Secretary to the Government of Bombay; and twice President of Congress.

assured his guests that if there had been "unrest in India," it had "proceeded from misunderstanding"; and he claimed that the British desired " to establish an atmosphere of sympathy and brotherly kindness between the two great branches of the Aryan race." Jinnah, who once described himself as "a man of cold-blooded logic," was more factual: he ignored the "atmosphere of sympathy", and, as he spoke, he counted his points of argument on the fingers of his left hand.

His first demand was that the salary of the Secretary of State for India "should be placed on the English estimates". In his earlier speech, in Karachi, he had said that the existing constitution of the Council of India made the Secretary of State "a greater Moghul than any Moghul that ruled in India"; that he could "come to any conclusion" he liked, and that he was "responsible to nobody." This would be remedied if his salary were paid by Britain: then his decisions and actions would be controlled by the British Parliament.

Another important demand concerned the composition of the Council of India. In 1907, John Morley had appointed a Hindu and a Muslim to his Council, but this had been little more than a gesture: these Indians, nominated by the Secretary of State, enjoyed neither an effective voice in the Council, nor the support of their countrymen at home. Jinnah wished to change this: he proposed that one-third of the Council (which should have a minimum of nine members) should be Indians, elected by those Indians who themselves had been elected by their peoples to serve on the Imperial and Provincial Legislative Councils in India. Of the remaining, British, members of the Council of India—nominated as before by the Secretary of State —Jinnah demanded that half their number (i.e. one-third of the total Council) should be "men of merit unconnected with Indian administration." The "men of merit" would thus be able to "hold the balance between the two other sections"—the elected Indians and the nominated "Anglo-Indians"—and would, he said, "bring to bear upon the deliberations of the Council that independent judgment which was so characteristic of public men" in England.

At the time of Jinnah's visit to London, the 'public men' were concerned with the terrible affairs in Ireland, following the incident at Curragh Camp, where fifty-seven British officers had refused to take part in 'active operations' in Ulster. The fortunes of India were relegated to second place, in Westminster, as news from Ireland arrived each day, still threatening civil war. Jinnah had perhaps chosen an unfortunate hour in which to plead for India. While Ireland was attracting the attention of British leaders to the west, in the east an assassin was busy with the morbid plan that culminated in the revolver shot, at Sarajevo, in June.

Against this background of alarms and danger, the Council of India Bill was read a first time in the House of Lords. Jinnah thought the "concessions" defined in the Bill were "most disappointing," and on June 3, he stated his views in the better part of a column in *The Times*. The opening sentence was emphatic. He wrote: 'India is perhaps the only member of the British Empire without any real representation, and the only civilized country in the world that has no system of representative government.' Then he repeated his arguments, and his objections to the tame concessions.

The Bill was rejected—or rather, 'postponed'—after its second reading; not because the Lords considered the proposed reforms too revolutionary, but because several of them believed that the Bill was inopportune and unsuited to the needs of the Indian people. Lord Ampthill said, "A bad mistake has been made, and it would be far better for all concerned to make a fresh start in a better way and at a better and more convenient time."

So Mohammed Ali Jinnah returned to India, empty-handed; and the reforms he advocated had to wait, while the war in Europe quickly assumed its horrible shape. His compensations for failure were personal: he had been listened to by officials in Westminster, for the first time; he had been described by Sir William Wedderburn as one of the "gentlemen of recognized position in the public life of India," and, for history's sake, his opinions had been recorded, at good length, in the columns of *The Times*.

* * *

THE LUCKNOW PACT

A GLOW of nobleness comes into the story of Indian affairs with the beginning of the 1914 war. Leaders of both Congress and the Muslim League rested their differences and promised to help the Government. Rulers of Native States pledged their support, in arms and money; and within a month of war being declared, 70,000 Indian troops embarked, to serve overseas. Before hostilities ended, in 1918, more than a million men were to sail from India, to the various theatres of war.

Congress put a price on this co-operation: in December 1914 the members resolved that 'in view of the profound and avowed loyalty the people of India have manifested in this present crisis' the Government should take 'such measures as may be necessary for the recognition of India as a component part of a Federated Empire, in the full and free enjoyment of the rights belonging to that status.'

Jinnah no doubt agreed to these demands, but the war did not divert him in his quest for Hindu-Muslim unity. When he spoke to the Bombay Muslim Students Union, on February 13, 1915, he directed the boys to the virtues of " discipline " and " self-reliance ": he deplored racial discrimination and urged them to co-operation, unity and goodwill " between the Mohammedans and other communities of the country." He appealed to them to " do away with dissensions " with all their " might ".

Six days later, Gopal Krishna Gokhale died—Jinnah's only close and dear friend. In later years, Jinnah recalled his " liberal and broad-minded statesmanship," and spoke of him as " a great Hindu," and as a " tower of intellect." When he referred to Gokhale, three months after his death, he confessed his " sorrow and grief "—words that were unusual in his cold vocabulary.

From this time, Jinnah's story can be told without mere conjecture, and without having to hunt for elusive clues. He was now a maker of history, and the facts of his political life, from 1915 to the end, are told in newspapers and many books. He remained what he had always been—logical and honest [1]; and forceful to an extent

---

[1] The degree of this honesty is revealed in the story of Jinnah, talking one day to an important member of the firm of Tata. Jinnah complained that Tatas gave opportunities to young men of every faith except Muslims. The representative of Tatas answered, " But there are no educated Muslims whom we can take into the firm." Jinnah scoffed at this and said that there were many worthy of the opportunity. The representative said, " Then choose me six and I will take them."

It would have been a feather in Jinnah's cap, among the leading Muslims, had he named six of their sons. He refused, and answered, " No, I won't select them just to catch their favour. You choose them yourself."

that intimidated people when they came near him. His only faults were his parsimony and the sharpness of his tongue : in all else he belonged to the great tradition of political leadership.

Mrs Naidu wrote that the death of Gokhale had ' brought Hindus and Mussalmans close together in a bond of common loss and sorrow.' She believed that the time was ' ripe ' for a ' more direct and definite *rapprochement* between the two great communities.'

In December 1915, Congress was due to hold its annual session, in Bombay. Jinnah, with the approval of leading local Muslims, sent a letter inviting the members of the All-India Muslim League to hold their annual session in the same place and at the same time. This brave move was in line with his own liberal political creed. Twenty-eight years after,[1] he recalled his aims at this time : he said, " undaunted, hope sprang eternally in my heart and soul . . . I was not going to give up. . . ." He wished neither to absorb the League into the Hindu-dominated Congress, nor to weaken Congress by exposing it to the sectarian character of the League. He wished only for unity, and he was supported in this by a number of moderate leaders in both communities ; enough for him to hope that the dream might come true.

Jinnah had to endure cynical and violent opposition, from extremists in both Congress and the League ; also from those few Britons who still believed in the motto, ' Divide and Rule ' ; who thought that Britain's strength in India depended greatly on the political differences between the two communities. Now Jinnah had to turn aside, momentarily, from the big issue of unity, and try to reconcile the antagonized elements within the League. Their load of prejudices might have made him despair : some believed that as the League was pledged to self-government within the Empire, they should not marry with Congress, which was anti-British at heart ; others argued that the League should disband, because Turkey—the home of the Caliphate—was now allied to Germany, in the war against England.

Jinnah appealed [2] to them—' We are bound by our constitution. Reverence for and obedience to that constitution, and discipline, are absolutely necessary qualities to enable us to say that we are fit for real political franchise, freedom and self-government. At this juncture

[1] In a speech at Delhi, April 1943.
[2] A written appeal, issued on November 11, 1915.

we are watched not only by India but by the whole of the British Empire, of which we aspire to be an independent, free and equal member.' He asked, 'Can we not bury our differences—show a united front? . . . It will make our Hindu friends value us all the more and will make them feel, more than ever, that we are worthy of standing shoulder to shoulder with them. . . .'

The Muslim League met in Bombay on December 30, 1915. In support of Jinnah's appeal, that differences should be buried, three Congress leaders, Dr Annie Besant, Mrs Sarojini Naidu, and Mr Gandhi, sat with him on the platform. Gandhi had lately returned from South Africa, greatly satisfied by his success as a reformer in having removed injustices against the Indian colony in Natal.

This first attempt at showing 'a united front' might have been discouraging for Jinnah. Long before the meeting began, fifty police officers took up their places within the hall, and outside—in case there was disorder. There were a few hooligan outbursts at the beginning of the session, but the audience settled down and listened. On the second day there was uproar, and, in Jinnah's words, the meeting was broken up under the "very nose of the police". He believed, he said, that it was with their "connivance" that the trouble began. Jinnah and his supporters had to make their way from the bedlam within the hall, and conclude the meeting in a room in the Taj Mahal Hotel.

Mrs Naidu wrote a record of the incident; of Jinnah as the 'dauntless soldier of unity,' risen ' to the heights of an invincible patriotism '; of his ' proud and splendid indifference to all personal suffering and sacrifice, heedless alike of official dissuasion or favour.' She referred also to the ' aggressive machinations of his opponents.'

The enthusiasm with which the Indian leaders had committed themselves, and their people, to the war, had now begun to wane. The 'postponed' Council of India Bill—for which Jinnah had visited England in 1914—had emerged the following year as the 'Government of India Act of 1915,' to which the Royal Assent had been given on July 29. Almost every reform that had been hoped for was omitted from the Act, and the arguments presented by Jinnah when he was in London had been ignored. He remained loyal to the British cause, but, after these disappointments, his plan for unity and reform became more lively than ever.

In April 1916—the month when Lord Chelmsford replaced Lord Hardinge as Viceroy—Jinnah had the satisfaction of seeing a joint Congress and Muslim League committee formed to discuss the 'irreducible minimum' of reforms they should demand from the Government. He continued to grow in stature and power : in the autumn he was again 'elected' to the Imperial Legislative Council, and in October he made a long speech at Ahmedabad, which revealed more statesmanlike ways of argument. He summed up India's part in the war, he repeated his views on reform, and he spoke of the demand for separate Hindu and Muslim electorates, which was another hurdle in the path of unity between the two communities. He said :

> As far as I understand, the demand for separate electorates is no a matter of policy but a matter of necessity to the Muslims, who require to be roused from the coma and torpor into which they have fallen, for so long. I would therefore appeal to my Hindu brethren that in the present state of position they should try to win the confidence and trust of the Muslims, who are, after all, in the minority in the country. If they are determined to have separate electorates, no resistance should be shown to their demands.

Then Jinnah returned to his chief crusade—self-government for a united India. "A new spirit is abroad," he said. "It is young India, who—to put it in the words of Lord Morley—'leave our universities intoxicated with the ideas of freedom, nationalism and self-government,' and have to be satisfied."
Then he said :

> Among the many benefits that have been conferred upon India by British rule, perhaps the greatest of boons, albeit, an indirect one, which India has received at the hands of the English people, has been the birth of a genuine spirit of patriotism. . . .
> But for a real, New India to arise, all petty and small things must be given up. She is now India *irredenta*, and, to be redeemed, all Indians must offer to sacrifice not only their good things, but all those evil things they cling to blindly—their hates and their divisions, their pride in what they should be thoroughly ashamed of, their quarrels and misunderstandings. These are a sacrifice that God would love.

THE LUCKNOW PACT

Jinnah yielded to neither the heroic compliments of Mrs Naidu, nor the 'machinations of his opponents.' In December 1916, he succeeded once more in prevailing upon both Congress, and the Muslim League, to hold their annual sessions in the same place, at the same time. They met at Lucknow, with Jinnah presiding over the League and achieving his first great victory as the 'Ambassador of Hindu-Muslim unity.'

During his long speech, he said, ". . . amid the clash of warring interests and the noise of foolish catchwords, no cool-headed student on Indian affairs can lose sight of the great obvious truism, that India is, in the first and the last resort, for the Indians." Of the separate cause of the Muslims, Jinnah said, " We want no favours, and crave for no partial treatment. That is demoralizing to the community and injurious to the State. The Mussalmans must learn to have self-respect." Then—" Towards the Hindus our attitude should be of goodwill and brotherly feelings. . . . India's real progress can only be achieved by a true understanding and harmonious relations between the two great sister communities."

There was no reason for Jinnah to suppose that this was a pipe-dream. The sessions of Congress, and the League, closed in warm assent : both agreed as to the 'irreducible minimum' of reforms, first discussed by the joint committee in April, and this decision was passed on to the Government of India. The chief domestic problem, of separate electorates, was also overcome. Congress heeded Jinnah's appeal : they won the 'confidence and trust of the Muslims' by agreeing that in 'certain provinces' in which the Muslims were a minority, they should be 'guaranteed a proportion of seats in the future Legislative Councils in excess of the number they could otherwise hope to win.'

Mohammed Ali Jinnah was given credit for these harmonious decisions, and, from this time, his name was proudly associated with what came to be known as the 'Lucknow Pact.' He had reached the first peak of his ambitions : Dadabhai Naoroji's disciple had become a leader of united India.

* * *

GANDHI, ANNIE BESANT, AND EDWIN SAMUEL MONTAGU

MOHAMMED ALI JINNAH had rivals, with different aims, in this awakening of India during the 1914–18 war : other, conflicting, streams of political theory were gaining strength, so that they would overwhelm him, temporarily, in a few years' time. The first of the rivals was Gandhi, who had established his influence in India within two years of returning from South Africa. The two men could not have been less alike : they clashed in mind, temperament and method. Gandhi, with what Jinnah later described as his " vague philosophical absurdities," was a humanist : he had fought for the rights of the Indians in South Africa, but he had also served in a Red Cross unit in the Boer War ; he had organized a plague hospital and he had been a stretcher-bearer in Natal, during the revolt of 1908. His heart and his ' soul-force ' usually governed his actions and his reason. Jinnah shunned emotion, and sentimentality : yet, in the end, he was to hasten his own death in a cause to which he gave his will and his logic, as passionately as Gandhi led his disciples, with his zeal and his intuition.

The difference between them was revealed on an occasion, in the far future, when Jinnah considered that Gandhi had broken a promise. Gandhi claimed that his " inner light " had ordered his change of mind. Jinnah turned to his secretary and said, " To hell with his ' inner light ' : why can't he be honest and admit that he made a mistake ? "

In 1907, the extremists in Congress had been expelled : by 1916, Gandhi's influence was such that they had been brought back again. It was this unity among the Hindus, under Gandhi, that ultimately destroyed Jinnah's ' larger national cause.'

There was another formidable and persistent fighter who shared the scene. At the beginning of 1916, Dr Annie Besant had begun her ' Home Rule League ', which soon spread throughout India, so that she was able to enlist considerable forces to embarrass the Government and hasten ' Swaraj '. In June 1917, Dr Besant was interned, and, out of sympathy for her, Jinnah joined the Bombay branch of the Home Rule League and became its President. He protested against the internment, " not only on principle," but also because it was " an attempt to intern the Home Rule or self-government scheme framed and adopted conjointly by the Indian National Congress and the All-India Muslim League at Lucknow." He resented " the methods adopted " and the " attempts " that were being made " to silence the people of India from carrying on their constitutional agitation."

In Westminster—still engaged in the struggle of war—these events in India were overshadowed by issues of deeper significance. On July 11, 1917, Mr Austen Chamberlain, Secretary of State for India, resigned, following the report of the Mesopotamia Commission, and Mr Edwin Samuel Montagu was appointed in his place. The new Secretary of State was already informed, and aware of India's problems, for he had been Under-Secretary from 1910 to 1914. In 1911 he had visited India, and declared his opinions on the subject of British ' prestige '. He had said : " We do not hold India by invoking this well-mouthed word : we must hold it by just institutions, and, more and more as time goes on, by the consent of the governed."

Jinnah welcomed the new appointment, and said that the " selection " gave " the people " of India " great satisfaction." But he added a condition—" . . . before Mr Montagu sets to work at his task, there should be, in my opinion, a general amnesty declared and all those interned as political prisoners released."

Edwin Samuel Montagu had inherited from his predecessor in office a document of great importance, on which Mr Chamberlain had been working for some time, with the help of Lord Curzon. On August 20, 1917, Mr Montagu revealed the terms of this document to the House of Commons, in a Declaration of the Indian policy to be adopted by the Government. He said :

> The policy of His Majesty's Government is that of increasing the association of Indians in every branch of the administration and the gradual development of self-governing institutions with a view to the progressive realization of responsible government in India as an integral part of the British Empire. . . . Progress in this policy can only be achieved by successive stages. The British Government and the Government of India, on whom the responsibility lies for the welfare and advancement of the Indian peoples, must be the judges of the time and measure of each advance, and they must be guided by the co-operation received from those upon whom new opportunities of service will thus

be conferred and by the extent to which it is found that confidence can be reposed on their sense of responsibility.

There is no record of Jinnah having made any public comment on these proposals for gradual administration by Indian Ministers. He was, at the time, concerned with a personal equation. He had been on amiable terms with Lord Hardinge, the previous Viceroy, but he did not like Lord Chelmsford, who had succeeded in April 1916. He thought him 'cold'—a fault he could scarcely damn in anyone. This dislike influenced his conduct and his speeches. Before a big audience in Bombay, in July 1917, he chided Lord Chelmsford for his apparent apathy, and said that he hoped his words would " penetrate the rarefied atmosphere of Simla " (the Viceroy's summer headquarters), where he was maintaining " a studied silence," at a time when " India was stirred to its very depths."

Lord Chelmsford was observing the awakening of young India with conscientious and sympathetic concern, as he worked in ' the rarefied atmosphere of Simla.' Little more than a year after Jinnah had complained of his 'studied silence,' he wrote to the King [1]:

> We have here an educated class, 95% of whom are inimical to us, and I venture to assert that every student in every University is growing up with a hatred of us. These are, of course, at present a mere fraction of the population, but each year sees the numbers augmented, and it may well be imagined that their potentialities for mischief are infinite. If we can win these men over to our side, I am convinced that we can only do it by inviting and enlisting their co-operation.

This was the view of the Viceroy, who collaborated with the Secretary of State in drawing up the Montagu-Chelmsford Report, which became the basis of the Government of India Act, passed in 1919.

In November 1917, Mr Montagu travelled to India to make his own observations, and to meet the leaders of the various political parties, whom he ultimately extolled in his diary. He wrote of Dr Annie Besant—who had been released from internment two months before—' in her white and gold embroidered Indian clothes, with her

[1] October 4, 1918. *King George V. His Life and Reign*, Harold Nicolson, p. 503.

short, white hair, and the most beautiful voice' he had ever heard. He thought her 'very impressive', and he wrote, 'It is her activity and her [Home Rule] League which has really stirred the country up into a condition in which it is no longer true to say that political interest is confined to the educated classes.'[1]

He wrote also of 'the renowned' Gandhi, as a 'social reformer' with 'a real desire to find grievances and to cure them, not for any reasons of self-advertisement, but to improve the conditions of his fellow men.' Mr Montagu added, 'He dresses like a coolie, forswears all personal advancement, lives practically on the air, and is a pure visionary. . . .'[2]

His description of Mohammed Ali Jinnah was the most penetrating of the three. He wrote:

> They were followed by Jinnah, young, perfectly mannered, impressive-looking, armed to the teeth with dialectics, and insistent upon the whole of his scheme. All its shortcomings, all its drawbacks, the elected members of the Executive Council, the power of the minority to hold up legislation, the complete control of the Executive in all matters of finance—all these were defended as the best makeshifts they could devise short of responsible government. Nothing else would satisfy them. They would rather have nothing if they could not get the whole lot. I was rather tired and I funked him. Chelmsford tried to argue with him, and was tied up into knots. Jinnah is a very clever man, and it is, of course, an outrage that such a man should have no chance of running the affairs of his own country.[3]

[1,2,3] *An Indian Diary*, Edwin S. Montagu, edited by Venetia Montagu (Heinemann, 1930), pp. 57, 58.

PART THREE

M. A. JINNAH, ABOUT THE TIME OF HIS SECOND MARRIAGE

JINNAH'S SECOND MARRIAGE: 1918

TWENTY-SIX YEARS had passed since Mohammed Ali Jinnah's boyhood marriage, in the modest house in Karachi. The celebrated advocate and politician of 1918 seemed remote from this episode; from the girl wife, in purdah, who had died before she could influence his mind, or his affections.

Jinnah was forty-one years old, and he had lived for some time, alone, in a bungalow in Mount Pleasant Road, on the cooler heights above Bombay. From his terrace he could see the ocean, framed between big, rich trees that sheltered him from the brazen light, and the noise of the city. In a small office within the bungalow he wrestled with his problems, in politics and the law: he was able to live simply, but comfortably, and to dress faultlessly, for he had already made a considerable fortune at the Bar.

The first World War was not yet over: battles were still being fought in all the areas of conflict. German troops had penetrated the Caucasus, and the Turks were invading Persia: the weakening defences of the Russians were opening up a way for the enemy into Afghanistan—the way by which so many conquerors had come to India.

Jinnah does not seem to have been aware of these terrible alarms: he devoted his energies and his speeches to his one absorbing plan for Hindu-Muslim unity, despite frequent signs that might have discouraged him. In 1918, there were anti-Muslim riots and acts of terrible cruelty in many parts of India, inspired by the old problem of cow-killing, by Muslims and Christians, which was so deeply offensive to the religious scruples of the Hindus. While Jinnah was writing hopeful speeches, planned to awaken India to the virtues of unity, he had to contend with Gandhi's different view, and his declaration that the Hindus " would not mind forcing, even at the point of the sword, either the Christians or the Mohammedans to abandon cow-slaughter." Jinnah was present at the Calcutta meeting of the All-India Muslim League in December 1917, when the British were blamed and condemned for their ' failure . . . to obtain timely information of the huge organization set on foot by a large section of the Hindu population . . . to plunder the houses of the Mussalmans, defile and destroy mosques and the holy Quran. . . .'

* * *

There is a story told in Bombay, in varying forms, of a day in the Taj Mahal Hotel when an Irishwoman, who was a clairvoyant, asked Mrs Naidu if Jinnah ever suffered any pain in his arm. (It was true that he had sought cures for an ailment, which he had kept secret.) Mrs Naidu went over and asked him : he answered, " Why do you wish to know ? Who told you ? Yes, I do have pain in my arm sometimes."

Mrs Naidu went back and told the Irishwoman, who said, " Yes, I knew. And I know also that this man will some day create a state of his own."

Jinnah could not have plucked much comfort from this prophecy in 1918, as he contemplated Gandhi's growing power over the Hindus, and the riots between the races he sought to unite. Also, at this time, he was engrossed in the startling episodes of his courtship and second marriage.

Among Mohammed Ali Jinnah's friends was Sir Dinshaw Petit, one of the proud, self-confident Parsees who had helped to make Bombay into a prosperous city. Jinnah liked to escape from his desk, and his duties, now and then, to dine with the Petits in their elegant house, or to stay at their country place in Poona.

Sir Dinshaw Petit had a daughter named Ruttenbai, twenty-four years younger than Jinnah. She was an enchanting girl : today— a quarter of a century after her death—there are gallant old gentlemen in Bombay who recall her, and say, " Ah, Ruttie Petit ! She was the flower of Bombay." Then, " She was so lively, so witty, so full of ideas and jokes."

The staid bachelor advocate, sitting on the terrace in Poona, watched Sir Dinshaw Petit's only daughter running in and out of the house : he paused and put his briefs aside. His heart was awakened, the first and only time in his life.

Jinnah and Ruttenbai Petit were betrothed, in secret. When her father was ultimately told, he was furious : he would not tolerate a marriage between his seventeen-year-old Parsee daughter and a

JINNAH AND LORD WILLINGDON

Muslim almost twice her age, so he took out an injunction, forbidding Jinnah to see her.

Jinnah waited, and Ruttenbai remained devoted. When she was eighteen, her father had to reconcile himself to the cold announcement in *The Statesman*, on April 19, 1918, that 'Miss Ruttenbai, only daughter of Sir Dinshaw Petit, yesterday underwent conversion to Islam, and is to-day to be married to the Hon. Mr. M. A. Jinnah.'

The lovely young bride moved into the sombre bachelor house, with her books, her ornaments, and her multitude of pretty dresses. She went to her husband's musty rooms in the Law Courts and enlivened them with bright paint, elegant furniture, and flowers. The first exciting weeks passed in pleasure and harmony: the husband of forty-one came home in the evening, with his talk of the law courts: the wife of eighteen waited, eager for him to see the jade figure she had bought during her idle day, and placed on a window-sill so that it caught and multiplied the sunlight coming in from the garden. But old cronies called and interrupted them, with talk of politics that did not amuse her: she had to listen to their long stories when she wished to be out, singing and dancing.

* * *

At first, Mohammed Ali Jinnah succumbed to his wife's eager charm: he enjoyed her spontaneity and allowed her to influence his behaviour as a politician. The Governor of Bombay at this time was Lord Willingdon, for whom Jinnah began with a good opinion. In October 1916 he had said, to the delegates at the Bombay Provincial Conference, that Lord Willingdon was "all kindness and courtesy," and that he knew "personally" that the Governor was "in full sympathy" with their "ideals and aspirations."

One alleged episode, soon after Jinnah's marriage, may have helped to change this view. He was invited, with his wife, to dine at Government House. The story is that Mrs Jinnah wore a low-cut dress that did not please her hostess; that, while they were seated at the dining-table, Lady Willingdon asked an A.D.C. to bring a wrap for Mrs Jinnah, in case she felt cold. It is reported that Jinnah rose, and said, "When Mrs Jinnah feels cold, she will say so, and ask for a wrap herself." Then he led his wife from the dining-room; and, from that time, he refused to go to Government House again.

JINNAH'S SECOND MARRIAGE

There was a political background to this alleged incident. Five days after his marriage, Jinnah had put his name to a manifesto in the *Bombay Chronicle*, answering an appeal from the Viceroy for increased recruiting and war effort in India. The manifesto repeated the demand that, in return for this war service, Britain should give India the 'responsible government' she had been promised. The signatories described the promise as 'indefinite,' and they asked :

> Let England pledge herself definitely to redeem the promise by accepting here, as in Ireland, that which our leaders have asked for in the Congress and League Pact, and we will work heart and soul to save Britain, India and the Empire. We will triumph with her or we will go down with her in world ruin . . . we cannot forget the ties of many years. . . .
> But, if Britain refuses us our place in the Empire, we shall try as leading a forlorn hope ; whereas, if Britain welcomes us as a nation whose freedom depends upon the issue of the war, the popular enthusiasm will rise to fighting point. . . . Trust us and we will not fail you. . . . But let us fight under the banner of liberty, for nothing less than that will nerve our men to fight and our women to sacrifice.

Six days later, the Viceroy's War Conference sat in Delhi, where Jinnah personally repeated this plea for rewards and benefits in return for India's service. He moved a resolution, based on the Bombay manifesto, but he was ruled out of order. Some six weeks later, on June 10, Lord Willingdon presided over a meeting of the Bombay Provincial War Conference. Jinnah attended, and he had to endure a stern reprimand : the Governor complained that the " activities " of " a certain number of gentlemen, some of whom have considerable influence with the public ; many of them members of the political organization called the Home Rule League "—to which Jinnah belonged—" had been such of later years " that he could not " honestly feel sure of the sincerity of their support." Lord Willingdon continued :

> . . . From reading their speeches, the position of these gentlemen seems to be this. 'We quite realize the gravity of the situation, we are all anxious to help, but unless Home Rule is promised within a given number of years . . . we do not think

we can stir the imagination of the people, and we cannot hope for a successful issue to the recruiting campaign.' . . .

To doubt Mohammed Ali Jinnah's 'sincerity' was to question the law of his life. In the argument that followed, Jinnah said to Lord Willingdon, " If you wish to enable us to help you, to facilitate and stimulate the recruiting, you must make educated people feel that they are citizens of the Empire and the King's equal subjects."

The meeting ended with recriminations, and Jinnah returned to Mount Pleasant Road with the feeling that he, and his colleagues, had been insulted. His resentment did not fade during the remaining six months of Lord Willingdon's term as Governor. Mrs Jinnah's young spirit may have helped to keep her husband's anger alive : she was certainly beside him as an ally in the dramatic scenes that preceded Lord Willingdon's departure from Bombay.

On December 11, 1918, a meeting was called to arrange the customary farewell to a retiring Governor. There were many people who shared Jinnah's anger against Lord Willingdon, and they began to gather on the steps of the Town Hall at ten o'clock on the evening before the meeting. Their protests had been anticipated and there was already a strong force of police, standing near by.

At ten o'clock next morning, when the hall was to open, Jinnah arrived, with his colleagues, and they immediately moved to the head of the queue, to take places held during the night by their supporters.

Then began a battle for seats, and a scene wholly alien to Jinnah, who had always preached to the young about ' order ' and ' discipline '. Outside the hall stood Mrs Jinnah—a pretty young rebel—marshalling her husband's followers as they pressed forward into the hall.

The struggle apparently lasted until five o'clock in the evening, when the Sheriff arrived and stood up to speak. There was further uproar, and cries of " Shame." A Parsee—Sir Jamsetjee Jijibhoy—was elected chairman, but this formality was drowned in cries of " No ! No ! ", while the 'supporters of the platform shrieked and yelled in derision, hurling challenges and epithets' at the anti-Willingdon faction.

It was claimed afterwards that a resolution of loyalty and appreciation of Lord Willingdon had been passed, but it was lost in the clamour. The Commissioner of Police ended the farce by ordering his men to clear the hall. Mohammed Ali Jinnah was among those who were assaulted during the confusion. The 'cold logician' was cold no longer: with his wife beside him, he led a noisy crowd to Apollo Street, where he became a tub-thumper for the only time in his life. He stood up above the crowd and said:

> Gentlemen, you are the citizens of Bombay. You have today scored a great victory for democracy. Your triumph has made it clear that even the combined forces of bureaucracy and autocracy could not overawe you. December the 11th is a Redletter Day in the history of Bombay. Gentlemen, go and rejoice over the day that has secured us the triumph of democracy.

Mr Matlub Saiyid [1] has written that, after this incident, Jinnah 'was at once a hero.' Public addresses were presented to him, and garden parties were given in his honour. For the first time in his lonely career, Jinnah was a popular figure—a leader of the people. His admirers contributed thirty thousand rupees to build a Memorial Hall in his honour and, in spite of the ravages of Partition, it is still called Jinnah Hall. On the wall is a marble plaque recalling the 'historic triumph' of the Citizens of Bombay, 'under the brave and brilliant leadership of Mohamed Ali Jinnah.'

* * *

THE YEARS OF DISILLUSIONMENT

DURING the second and third years of his marriage, Mohammed Ali Jinnah made three remarkable decisions: he resigned from the Imperial Legislative Council, the Home Rule League, and the Indian National Congress. For some time after this he was overshadowed by other leaders, especially Gandhi. The graph of Jinnah's career showed a downward trend; but, as his story unfolded, the three decisions were proved to be honourable, wise and right.

On July 8, 1918, the joint recommendations of the Secretary of

---

[1] The author is indebted to Mr Saiyid, and to his book, *Mohammed Ali Jinna, A Political Study* (pp. 194–217), for most of the facts in this report of the conflict between Lord Willingdon and Jinnah; and of the meeting in the Town Hall.

State and the Viceroy were published, as the Montagu-Chelmsford Report. Jinnah was cautiously favourable: in a statement to the press he suggested 'vital changes,' but he ended his criticisms by advising his 'countrymen' to 'treat the Report . . . with due respect and serious consideration.' He tried to influence other leaders towards this 'serious consideration'—among them Dr Annie Besant, who had said of the Report that it was 'unworthy of England to offer and unworthy of India to accept.' Mr Kanji Dwarkadas has recorded his version of the meeting between Jinnah and Dr Besant, who 'came down to Bombay' to see him. 'Jinnah wanted her to tone down her criticism of the proposals, and he had a two hours tête-à-tête conference with Dr Besant. As he came out of her room almost half dead at about 8 in the evening, I asked, " Well, Jinnah, what happened ? " With his hand on his head he answered, " My dear fellow, never argue with a woman." ' [1]

The next move was during the September session of the Legislative Council, when a committee of non-official members approved the suggested Montagu-Chelmsford reforms, 'with certain qualifications.' In November the war ended and a semblance of peace came to Europe, but not to Indian politics. Within a few weeks of the happy news of the armistice, the annual sessions of both Congress and the Muslim League met in Delhi. During eleven years, since the split at Surat in 1907, there had been no deep differences of policy within Congress, but, in December 1918, the Extremists—since described as Nationalists —dominated the debates and 'wholly condemned' the proposed Montagu-Chelmsford reforms.

Jinnah had to look close at his political chess-board: for many years he had enjoyed the increasing support of the Moderates in Congress, in his idealistic policy of Hindu-Muslim unity. They had applauded all his peaceful intentions, but they were now outnumbered by the Nationalists, with their demand for immediate self-government. Jinnah was among the outnumbered. Gandhi—in prison or out— was to catch the eye and raise the fervour of the people, with his gift for emotional leadership, which Jinnah lacked.

Any sympathy for British policy that had been awakened in India by the Montagu-Chelmsford Report was killed by two alarming events, early in 1919. In January, the draft of a bill, that was later

[1] *Gandhiji, Through my Diary Leaves*, Kanji Dwarkadas, p. 14.

passed as the Rowlatt Act, came before the Legislative Council. The bill—the outcome of recommendations of a committee presided over by Mr Justice Rowlatt—sought to curb seditious crime by giving the Government power to detain and try insurgents and active enemies of its policy, without a jury. Although these powers were safeguarded 'by elaborate protection against abuse,' and although they were never enforced, thoughtful Indians became anxious as to the possible, dangerous effects of such a new shackle on the freedom of the people. Jinnah shared this anxiety : he enumerated his objections, on his fingers, in the Legislative Council, and said, at the end :

> . . . it is my duty to tell you that, if these measures are passed, you will create in this country from one end to the other a discontent and agitation the like of which you have not witnessed ; and it will have, believe me, a most disastrous effect upon the good relations that have existed between the Government and the people.

In the third week of March, the repugnant Rowlatt Act became law, and, on March 28, Jinnah wrote to the Viceroy, accusing the Government of India of having 'ruthlessly trampled upon the principles for which Great Britain avowedly fought the war.' He considered that the passing of the Act 'clearly demonstrated' that the Imperial Legislative Council was 'a legislature but in name— a machine propelled by a foreign Executive.' As a 'protest' he tendered his resignation, and ended his letter with the hope that 'this Black Act' would be annulled.

Gandhi's protest was less personal : he commanded a day of 'humility and prayer' and, remembering the success of his policy in South Africa, he ordered a similar campaign of non-violent civil disobedience in India. But Gandhi did not sense the peril in releasing a thoughtful policy among millions of untutored, superstitious people. Also, he further bewildered them by announcing the beginning of his campaign for March 30, and then changing it to April 6. In many parts of India the day of 'humility and prayer' became one of riots and blood-lust : when Gandhi made a tour of the big cities, he succeeded only in awakening the passions he dreaded most.

On April 7, Gandhi was forbidden entry into the Punjab, and the police escorted him back to Bombay. On the 9th, in Amritsar, two

THE CALIPHATE MOVEMENT

Hindu leaders, who had been making rebellious speeches, were arrested for deportation. These two acts led to cruel rioting in the city. Three European bank managers were murdered, their safes were looted, and a crowd of insurgents tried to fire the railway station. On the 11th, the British commander of the Jullundur Brigade, Brigadier-General R. E. H. Dyer, was ordered to quell the disturbances. Public meetings were declared unlawful, but, on April 13, several thousand Indians gathered within the Jallianwala Bagh—a walled area, from which there were only two narrow ways of escape. Then followed an act of terrible folly : General Dyer ordered his troops to fire on the defenceless throng. Almost four hundred were killed, and twelve hundred wounded.

Martial law was declared throughout the Punjab, and enforced with humiliating ruthlessness. Then Gandhi realized the savage consequences of his civil disobedience movement, and he called off the campaign. But sullen resentment remained, long after calm was restored to the Punjab, and the memory of Amritsar soured Indian politics for many years to come.

Jinnah had no part in these terrible acts and decisions. He remained aloof, watching Gandhi use his dangerous talent for influencing the Hindus. He was their *Mahatma*, or ' Great Soul ', and his power over them went deeper than politics—into subconscious instincts that were fused with their mysticism and their worship of many deities. But he also came to enjoy influence over the Muslims, for a different reason. They were monotheists, and there were no religious implications in their regard for Gandhi's leadership. His appeal to them succeeded only when it was purely national and non-sectarian, or when he chose to espouse a cause of particular concern to the Muslims. In this matter, events served him well.

The scene widens, to include Britain and her relationship with the vanquished Turks, at the end of the 1914-18 war. The punishment of Turkey was defined in the Treaty of Sèvres, on August 10, 1920 : contrary to all assurances made by Mr Lloyd George to loyal Indian Muslims during the war, the Sultan's empire was to be divided and shared, and his powers as Caliph ignominiously reduced. The Muslims in India were indignant against Britain for this offence to their spiritual overlord, and they formed a Caliphate Movement to defend their religious rights. Gandhi acted quickly and assumed the rôle of their champion. In August, a few days after the signing of the Sèvres Treaty, he wrote to the Viceroy and deplored the ' unscrupulous, immoral and unjust' treatment of the Caliphate. He wrote also that he had ' neither respect nor affection ' for the Government that had failed to punish the officials guilty of the ' wanton cruelty and inhumanity' in the Punjab ; and he announced his decision to begin a campaign of complete non-co-operation.

Jinnah waited a month before he made his protest against the humbling of the Caliphate. (Was he being wise : had he any premonition of what was to happen, in November 1922, when the Sultan—' the Shadow of God on Earth '—was deposed by his own people, and in March 1924, when the Ottoman Caliphate was abolished for ever ?) Jinnah was cautious : he had not joined the Caliphate Movement—a crusade that demanded the renunciation of titles, office and appointments in Government service, and the boycott of all British goods and enterprises. This was not his way : he sat back and observed Mahatma Gandhi, seducing into his fold a number of powerful Muslim religious leaders, some of whom even agreed to form societies for the ' protection of cows,' as a reciprocal gesture to those Hindus who had agreed to be indignant over the British treatment of the Caliphate.

In September, Jinnah at last stated his view, at a meeting of the Muslim League in Calcutta. He denounced the post-war reforms of the British Government : he again rebuked the " self-satisfied Viceroy " who sat " in Olympian Simla," and then, referring to the Rowlatt Act, the Punjab atrocities, and the " spoliation " of the Caliphate, he said :

> One degrading measure upon another, disappointment upon disappointment, and injury upon injury, can lead to only one end. It led Russia to Bolshevism. It has led Ireland to Sinn Feinism. May it lead India to freedom.

Despite his indignation, Jinnah remained reasonable. When he spoke of Gandhi's campaign of non-co-operation, at the same Muslim League session in Calcutta, he was not dictatorial : he advised his listeners patiently, as if they were students at Aligarh :

> It is now for you to consider whether or not you approve of its principle, and, approving of its principle, whether or not you

approve of its details. The operations of this scheme will strike at the individual in each one of you, and therefore it rests with you alone to measure your strength and to weigh the pros and cons of the question before you arrive at a decision. But once you have decided to march, let there be no retreat in any circumstances.

The advice seemed ambiguous; but there was no ambiguity within himself, and Jinnah soon showed that he approved of neither the principle nor the details of Gandhi's plan.

In October 1920, Jinnah resigned from the Home Rule League Dr Besant, its creator, had already departed because, she said, the League had "become so intertwined with Religion." Gandhi had been elected in her place and, most cleverly, he had suggested that the title be changed to *Swaraj Sabha*—the Hindi equivalent of Home Rule League. He thus enlarged its appeal beyond the English-speaking few, to the Hindi-speaking many. He also extended the aim of the League. Under Dr Besant—with Jinnah as a member—the slogan had been, ' Self-government *within* the British Empire.' Gandhi appealed for complete Swaraj—freedom from all ties with Britain. Jinnah's reaction to this change was typical: the lawyer in him—the absolute tidiness of his mind—urged him to speak again of " constitutional methods " and of " responsible " government. When he protested that the meeting was not competent to change the constitution of the League, the Chairman answered that it was " open to any member . . . to resign his membership " if he could not abide by the " altered constitution." It was then that Jinnah, with nineteen other members, decided to leave.

The episode demonstrated not only Jinnah's independence, and stubborn devotion to ' constitutional methods ' : it finally revealed his deep, instinctive dislike of the Mahatma's mind. Gandhi wrote and asked him to return to the Home Rule League ; to take his share in the ' new life ' that had ' opened up before the country.' Jinnah refused, in a letter that states, clearly, his thoughts at the time. He wrote :

> I thank you for your kind suggestion offering me ' to take my share in the new life that has opened up before the country.' If by ' new life ' you mean your methods and your programme, I am afraid I cannot accept them, for I am fully convinced that

it must lead to disaster . . . your methods have already caused split and division in almost every institution that you have approached hitherto . . . people generally are desperate all over the country and your extreme programme has for the moment struck the imagination mostly of the inexperienced youth and the ignorant and the illiterate. All this means complete disorganization and chaos. What the consequences of this may be, I shudder to contemplate.

Jinnah's thoughts and words grew out of his proved experience: he believed that emancipation could come only through the education of the people—a conviction that had not wavered since he fought for Gokhale's Elementary Education Bill, eight years before; and he believed that to stir the masses by way of their emotions was a sin. This was the wedge driven between himself and Gandhi—whom he described as ' that Hindu revivalist '—at this time and for ever.

In future years, Jinnah was to share many talks with Gandhi, but the cleavage remained, and revealed itself in facetious exchanges of mockery and sharp answers. One day Gandhi said to Jinnah, " You have mesmerized the Muslims." Jinnah answered, " You have hypnotized the Hindus." Another day, when they appeared together before an attack of reporters and press photographers, Gandhi said to Jinnah, " You like this, don't you ? " Jinnah answered, " Not as much as you do."

In support of this amusing petulance between them, there is a story told by Mr Mohammed Noman,[1] the first secretary of the All-India Muslim Students Federation. He said, " One day I went to see Jinnah, early in the morning. He was sitting up in bed, reading a speech that Gandhi had made—it was some time in January or February 1940. Jinnah said to me, ' You know, I have not slept a wink, reading this and trying to find out exactly what is in his mind.' "

*   *   *

Jinnah's disillusionment became complete during the session of Congress at Nagpur, in December 1920. Fourteen thousand delegates met, and agreed, under Gandhi's spell, to support the decision of the Home Rule League—to abandon all compromise and demand absolute

[1] Author of *Muslim India* (1942).

freedom for India. Almost to a man—Jinnah excepted—they agreed to employ Gandhi's weapons of non-co-operation and boycott to achieve this freedom.

There is no verbatim report of Jinnah's protest against what he regarded as political anarchy. The focus was on the Mahatma, gazing into his crystal, and even prophesying an actual day—September 30, 1921—for India's deliverance.

Among the delegates at Nagpur was Diwan Chaman Lall, the distinguished Indian barrister. He has said of Jinnah—whom he first knew in 1918—" He was a lovable, unsophisticated man, whatever may be said to the contrary. And he was unpurchasable."

Diwan Chaman Lall has recalled [1] the scene during the Congress meeting at Nagpur when Jinnah protested against Gandhi's extreme measures. Jinnah said, " Your way is the wrong way : mine is the right way—the constitutional way is the right way."

At this, one of the leaders of the Caliphate Movement, Maulana Mohamed Ali, leapt up and said, " You talk too much of the constitutional way. It reminds me of a story—of a young Tory who came out of the Carlton Club one evening and walked up to Piccadilly Circus, where there was a Salvation Army meeting in progress. The speaker was saying, ' Come this way—it is God's way.' The young Tory interrupted him and said, ' How long have you been preaching this ? ' ' Twenty years,' said the Salvationist. ' Well,' was the answer, ' if it's only got you as far as Piccadilly Circus, I don't think much of it.' "

Diwan Chaman Lall then said, " Jinnah sat down, with a hurt look on his face. He just lapsed into silence."

There is one paragraph, in Sir Chimanlal Setalvad's *Recollections and Reflections*, that adds, but little, to this picture of Jinnah on the edge of the wilderness. Sir Chimanlal wrote, 'Jinnah strongly opposed this change and boldly stood his ground in spite of violent opposition from a large part of the audience. After this, Jinnah parted with Congress.'

Thus he abandoned all public office—except for his membership of the Muslim League ; and even there, he met antagonism from the many members who were swerving towards Gandhi's opinions. Many years were to pass before any observer could decide whether

[1] To the author.

1921-1928

Mohammed Ali Jinnah's stubbornness—his consistency—was the hobgoblin of a little mind, or the mark of a great strategist who was content to bide his time.

*   *   *

1921-1928

THE tangled political arguments of the 1920's are important here only in so far as they help to clarify the picture of Mohammed Ali Jinnah. The question is, ' How was he influenced by these arguments ? What part did he enact in the interplay between Gandhi and the other leaders, who seemed more in love with the conflict than with any solution that might be bred of it ? ' Dr Annie Besant's view was that Gandhi believed 'in suffering,' and that he was 'not happy' if he achieved his object 'through normal evolutionary methods.'[1] In this also Jinnah was his opposite, for he was devoted to 'normal evolutionary methods,' and he remained so, to the end.

There are records of these years, 1921-28, in many books published in India, but they are prejudiced, and seldom detached. There are no diaries, and few letters from which to trace the progress of Jinnah's mind ; no painted portrait into which one might search for the look on his face. It is therefore difficult to keep the light on him during these years of lull, between his resignation from the Imperial Legislative Council, the Home Rule League, and Congress—and his ultimate decision, in 1931, to settle in England and abandon Indian politics for ever.

These were the years of his brief marriage, of which he was always reluctant to speak. His only child, Dina Jinnah, was born on August 15, 1919. For Jinnah, married life was a solemn duty : for his young wife, it was also an opportunity for pleasure. Jinnah had been a recluse for many years, coming home from the law courts, or his political meetings, to his staid bachelor habits. Now he had to adapt himself to a social life that was too merry for his nature. There were holidays in London, where the student who had trudged from

[1] *Gandhiji*, Kanji Dwarkadas, p. 22.

Lincoln's Inn to one gas-lit room on the drab edge of Kensington now had to endure the frivolities of the Berkeley and the Savoy.

Jinnah learned to reconcile these holidays and excitements with his work as a brilliant advocate, receiving the highest fees paid in India. In politics, he had retired to a second place from which he watched Mahatma Gandhi's overwhelming success, achieved by ways that Jinnah despised. He said to a rival politician, in later years, " You try to find out what will please people and you then act accordingly. My way of action is quite different. I first decide what is right and I do it. The people come around me and the opposition vanishes." He continued to believe this true, but, during these years, he had to watch another star enjoying the heavens.

On the sixth anniversary of Gopal Krishna Gokhale's death, Jinnah spoke in memory of his friend : " It is a pity there are so few men like him to be with us in such a critical time as the present." He was " convinced " in his mind that Gandhi's programme was " taking " the people into a " wrong channel." Gandhi had talked of withdrawing boys from Government-aided schools and sending them into the villages to teach the illiterate : he had even tried to induce the students to leave Aligarh—still the chief stronghold of young Muslim scholarship.

Jinnah answered these extravagant ideas with the practical argument that, if Gandhi boycotted the schools founded on the British pattern, he must then build national schools in their place. Of Gandhi's campaign of non-cooperation and boycott of British goods, Jinnah asked, " How many of the twenty thousand delegates at the National Congress " had really " boycotted foreign goods up to now ? " He would accept their principle only when they built their own mills and " competed with the foreigners like men." Always, he dragged Gandhi's dreams back to earth and reality.

The Government of India Act of 1919 had introduced many concessions to the Indian people, and in January 1921 the Duke of Connaught arrived to inaugurate the new constitution, in the King's name. A greater degree of responsibility had been given to the Indians, in almost every department of local government. The details of these reforms are explained in many political histories of this period : a glance at them shows that, in the legislatures of the major provinces, while such departments as finance, land revenue, and police, were ' reserved ' to the Governor and his executive council, the care of education, public health, etc., was ' transferred ' to Indian ministers, chosen from the elected leaders of the Provincial Legislatures. Thus, by a system of ' dyarchy ' or dual-government, the British were trying to keep the internal security in their hands, whilst giving the Indians the opportunity to care for their own social and nation-building services. The change that might have affected Jinnah was the abolition of the old Imperial Legislative Council, and the introduction of a ' two-house ' parliamentary system, with a Council of State and a Central Legislative Assembly. In both houses, the elected members formed the majority. The first polls under the new constitution had been held in November 1920, but Jinnah had not sought election.

In April 1921, Lord Reading succeeded Lord Chelmsford as Viceroy. On November 17, the Prince of Wales arrived in Bombay : he said, " I want you to know me and I want to know you. I want to grasp your difficulties and to understand your aspirations." Then—" I feel some awe at the difficulty which I may experience in getting to know India." In another part of Bombay, at Gandhi's behest, there was a public burning of ' foreign ' clothes, as a protest against the Prince's visit.

Jinnah's social life at this time was mostly with his wife's Parsee friends. It is therefore interesting to read, in the confidential report written by the Political Secretary to the Government of India, after the Prince had departed : ' In Bombay, perhaps the principal political result of the visit has been indirectly to strengthen the traditional loyalty of the Parsee community. . . . The general effect has been that the great bulk of the Parsee community and all their responsible leaders have definitely recognized that their interest as a community lies in opposition to the forces of disorder and non-cooperation.'

Jinnah no doubt shared this belief, that his interests also lay ' in opposition to the forces of disorder and non-cooperation.' Meanwhile, the Mahatma's ' mass awakening,' as he called it, led to ' lust for plunder ' and ' rapine ' ; and, as a measure against further disaster, he was arrested for sedition and sent to prison. Jinnah still waited patiently : he took little part in political affairs until November 1923, when he was elected to the Central Legislative Assembly, unopposed, by the Muslims of Bombay. His plea, before the elections, was moderate : he said, " I have no desire to seek any post or position or title from the Government. My sole object is to serve the cause of the country as best I can." His faith in Hindu-Muslim unity did not weaken, in spite of the terrible evidence that the differences between the two communities were so deep-rooted that no politician could ever hope to dispel them.

In May 1924—three months after Gandhi had been released from prison—Jinnah again stated his enduring belief, at a meeting of the Muslim League in Lahore. He said, " . . . the advent of foreign rule and its continuance in India is primarily due to the fact that the people of India, particularly the Hindus and Muslims, are not united and do not sufficiently trust each other. . . . I am almost inclined to say that India will get Dominion Responsible Government the day the Hindus and Muslims are united."

But these conciliatory words became lost in the widening rift between the two communities. Jinnah pleaded for adequate representation of the Muslims—and of other minorities—in all the legislatures of the country : he called on the Hindus to realize that, unless Muslims were guaranteed separate electorates, with a fixed number of seats in the legislatures, his people would be in constant fear of being dominated and outvoted in every province where they were in a minority. But the promises made by Congress in the Lucknow Pact, in 1916, were ignored and never kept. Jinnah later recalled [1] that "from 1925 onwards . . . many efforts were made for the adjustment of Hindu-Muslim differences." He said, "Every time we were the petitioners, the supplicants standing at the doors of Mr Gandhi and the Congress, with our proposals formulated." He added, "For some reason or other the reply was always 'No'."

In February 1925, Jinnah was appointed to the committee which was to advise on the 'Indianization' of the army and the establishment of a military training college, on the pattern of Sandhurst. This involved a journey, to Europe and England. One episode, during the visits to Sandhurst, proved that Jinnah was still overbearing in his manner ; that experience was not bringing mellowness to his lively spirit. The officer chosen to organize the deputation at Sandhurst was Captain Gracey—now General Sir Douglas Gracey—who has said,[2] "Jinnah's behaviour with the officers who gave evidence before the deputation was so arrogant : it was as if he were dealing with

[1] In his speech before the Muslim League, April 1943.
[2] In a conversation with the author.

hostile witnesses before a judge. I had to protest and point out that the officers were giving evidence voluntarily, with the object of helping him, and that they had a right to be treated with courtesy and consideration." General Sir Douglas Gracey added, " Of course, he calmed down immediately. That was something I always liked about him in later years : once he was challenged, he became reasonable, and he would never bear malice afterwards. The outcome of the deputation was the establishment of the military college at Dehra Dun, and, for me, a touching insight into Jinnah's character. He might have remembered the episode at Sandhurst with bitterness, for I had stood up to him in no mean fashion. But no ! When my name came up before him as Commander-in-Chief of the Army in Pakistan [to follow General Sir Frank Messervy], he accepted me, and welcomed me, with good grace. He remembered me quite well, but never showed resentment."

Jinnah returned to India with the deputation, and continued his weakening campaign for unity. In November 1926, he was again elected to the Central Legislative Assembly. In March 1927, at Delhi, Jinnah and other Muslim leaders set down their proposals for ' representation in the various legislatures in any future scheme of Constitution.' Their good faith towards the Hindus was shown by their willingness—should their proposals be accepted—to give to Hindu minorities in the predominantly Muslim Provinces ' the same concessions that Hindu majorities in other Provinces are prepared to make to Muslim minorities.'

In May, there was a glimmer of hope that Jinnah might have his way, when the Committee of Congress agreed, in the main, to his proposals for Muslim representation. But these local affairs were overshadowed, in November 1927, by the announcement that Sir John Simon and six other members of the British Parliament would proceed to India, to review the progress made under the constitution of 1919, and to advise on further reforms and measures of self-government. There was an immediate outcry, in which Jinnah joined, against the ' all-white ' membership of the Commission. Sir John Simon and his colleagues arrived in Bombay on February 3, 1928 : two months later, Jinnah sailed for England, alone.

★ ★ ★

'THE LONELIEST OF MEN'

Early in 1928, Mrs Jinnah had left the house in Mount Pleasant Road and had gone to live in the Taj Mahal Hotel. Husband and wife had come to a crisis in their relationship where the difference in their ages, and their habits, made harmony impossible. Once, after they parted, an old Parsee friend tried to reconcile them: Jinnah said to him, " It is my fault : we both need some sort of understanding we cannot give."

Mrs Jinnah had already sailed for Europe, with her parents, when her husband left Bombay in April 1928 ; his political career in dark confusion, and his one experiment in private happiness apparently wrecked for ever.

One of Jinnah's companions on his voyage was his friend, Diwan Chaman Lall, who wrote of him :

> Today he is, unfortunately, frankly disgusted. . . . He said . . . " The first problem to solve and settle is the problem of Hindu-Muslim unity. This is not a mere phrase. It is a concrete proposition. . . . And suppose we did settle the problem. I say that, then, the united voice of the nation would be irresistible." . . .
>
> Jinnah is frankly in a despondent mood. He is one of the few men who have no personal motives to nurse or personal aims to advance. His integrity is beyond question. And yet he is the loneliest of men.

When they came to Suez, Diwan Chaman Lall induced Jinnah to go ashore. While the ship was creeping through the Canal, Jinnah, in his immaculate clothes, mounted a camel, Diwan Chaman Lall mounted a donkey, and they went to see the Sphinx.

Diwan Chaman Lall had observed Jinnah's political problems during the voyage : a few weeks' later he was to see past these concerns, into his unfortunate heart.

Soon after the ship arrived in England, Jinnah went to Ireland, and Diwan Chaman Lall to Paris, where Mrs. Jinnah was also staying, alone. Chaman Lall had been in his hotel only a few minutes when he learned that Mrs Jinnah was in an hospital, dangerously ill. He has described the sad story of what followed.[1]

" I went to the hospital immediately. I had always admired

---
[1] To the author.

Ruttie Jinnah so much : there is not a woman in the world today to hold a candle to her for beauty and charm. She was a lovely, spoiled child, and Jinnah was inherently incapable of understanding her. She was lying in bed, with a temperature of 106 degrees. She could barely move, but she held a book in her hand and she gave it to me. 'Read it to me, Cham,' she said.

"I took the book : it was a volume of Oscar Wilde's poems, opened at *The Harlot's House*. She repeated, in a whisper, 'Please read it to me, Cham.' When I came to the closing lines,

> And down the long and silent street,
> The dawn, with silver-sandalled feet,
> Crept like a frightened girl.

I looked up. Ruttie was in a coma. I hurried out and brought the doctor. A few days later, Jinnah arrived from Ireland. I waited in the hospital while he went in to see her—two and a half hours he was with her. When he came out of her bedroom, he said, 'I think we can save her : we'll change the doctor and take her to another hospital. I am sure she will pull through.'

"Ruttie Jinnah recovered, and I left Paris soon afterwards, for Canada, believing they were reconciled. Some weeks passed and I was in Paris again. I spent a day with Jinnah, wondering why he was alone. In the evening, I said to him, 'Where is Ruttie ?' He answered, 'We quarrelled : she has gone back to Bombay.' He said it with such finality that I dared not ask any more."

* * *

THE 'PARTING OF THE WAYS'

SOME of the chief players in the drama of Indian affairs had changed: in April 1926, Lord Irwin [now the Earl of Halifax] had arrived as Viceroy ; in 1924, Lord Birkenhead had become Secretary of State for India, in the Baldwin government. Like Jinnah, Lord Birkenhead had never been intimidated by authority : he also had scored many victories over judges in the law courts. During four years as Secretary of State, he had become impatient with the long delays and arguments of the partisans in India, especially with their boycott of the Simon Commission. He was a pessimist over the future of India: he had written to Lord Reading, on December 4, 1924, 'To me it is frankly inconceivable that India will ever be fit for Dominion self-government.' A month later he had written, 'In ultimate analysis, the strength of the British position is that we are in India for the good of India.' He believed also that the Hindus and Muslims were irreconcilable, and he wrote, 'All the conferences in the world cannot bridge the unbridgeable.' Nevertheless, early in 1928 he challenged the Indians to produce their own scheme for a Constitution, instead of always 'indulging in mere destructive criticism' of the Government.

The challenge led, first, to an All-Parties Conference in Bombay. From this, a committee was appointed, under Pandit Motilal Nehru, father of Pandit Jawaharlal Nehru. The report of the committee was published in August—while Jinnah was still in Paris—and it was then placed before the members of a 'Unity Conference' at Lucknow. A copy reached Jinnah at Aden, on his way home. His comment on landing at Bombay, was cautious: he said that he had not yet "had time enough" to digest the report: he supposed "the signatories . . . and various prominent men who met at Lucknow" had "made an effort towards Hindu-Muslim unity," and added "one cannot help appreciating" their "great endeavour." Then this typical proviso: "However, the Nehru Report and the decisions of the Lucknow Conference are not—like the laws of the Medes and Persians—the last word in the matter."

Jinnah kept his 'last word' for two months. On December 28 —three days after his fifty-second birthday—he spoke before another All-Parties Conference, in Calcutta.

Between the time of the drafting of the Nehru Report, and its presentation at the conference in Calcutta, the Muslim League had drawn up a series of amendments which had been sent to the Nehru Committee. The main proposals were that, under any future Constitution, a minimum of one-third of the elected representatives in both houses of the Central Legislature should be Muslims; also that 'residuary powers' should be vested in the Provinces—thus ensuring that the Muslim-majority Provinces should be autonomous, and not menaced by a Hindu-majority Centre.

THE 'PARTING OF THE WAYS'

These moderate proposals had been ignored by the Nehru Committee, who had instead adopted the 'principle' that, 'wherever such reservation has to be made for the Muslim minority, it must be in strict proportion to its population.'

In a long speech, during which he repeated the demands of the Muslims, with fine emphasis, Jinnah expressed his grief, and disgust, over the short-sighted policy of the Nehru Committee's recommendations, which would oust the Muslims from any fair part in India's political future. Jinnah said, " I am exceedingly sorry that the Report of the Committee is neither helpful nor fruitful in any way whatsoever. . . . I think it will be recognized that it is absolutely essential to our progress, that a Hindu-Muslim settlement should be reached, and that all communities should live in a friendly and harmonious spirit in this vast country of ours."

He then spoke of majorities, " apt to be oppressive and tyrannical," and of minorities, with their " dread and fear that their interests and their rights" might " suffer and be prejudiced." Then, with great skill, which is apparent even in the cold printed record of his speech, he repeated his demands—justice for the Muslim minority, and, above all, unity. He warned the Conference of the dangers of a Constitution under which minorities felt insecure ; of the inevitable result— " revolution and civil war."

This formidable prophecy, which came true nineteen years later, did not impress his listeners. The first speaker to follow him, Sir Tej Bahadur Sapru, dragged Jinnah's appeal and warning into the dust of personalities : although he was for giving him what he wanted, " and be finished with it," he talked of him as " a spoilt child, a naughty child."

Among those who listened to Jinnah's speech was a Parsee, Jamshed Nusserwanjee, who was to become the builder, and the mayor, of the new city of Karachi. This fine old gentleman, who has since died, was an admirer, and a friend of Jinnah. He has said,[1] " Yes, his memory is very beautiful to me. He was never a demonstrative person : he was reserved, dignified and lonely. But I wish to tell you about the day in 1928—and it is a fine thing that I can tell you. Mr Jinnah stood up—wearing the fashionable clothes he had brought back from England—and he pleaded for his people. I knew the

[1] To the author.

greatness of his heart : he *believed* that the Hindus and Muslims could be brought together. There was no hate in him. Some years later, after Partition, he told me how much he wished the Muslims to be tolerant of the minorities in Pakistan. I beg you to believe that Mr Jinnah was a humanitarian. He was never generous with tears—oh, no—but I saw him weep, twice. Once was after Partition, in January 1948, when I went with him to see an encampment of Hindus who had stayed on in Pakistan. When he saw their misery, he wept. I saw the tears on his cheek. His cheeks were very noble.

" The first time I saw him weep was after his amendments had been rejected at the Calcutta meeting to consider the Nehru Report, in 1928. It is a fine thing that he did—pleading, as a great man, for his people. His demands were rejected. One man said that Mr Jinnah had no right to speak on behalf of the Muslims—that he did not represent them. He was sadly humbled, and he went back to his hotel.

" About half-past eight next morning, Mr Jinnah left Calcutta by train, and I went to see him off at the railway station. He was standing at the door of his first-class coupé compartment, and he took my hand. He had tears in his eyes as he said, ' Jamshed, this is the parting of the ways.' "

* * *

During the days of struggle that led to this ' parting of the ways,' Mrs Jinnah was dangerously ill at the Taj Mahal Hotel in Bombay. Two months later, she died—not yet twenty-nine years old. Jinnah was away from Bombay, but he hurried back for the long burial service in the Muslim cemetery, and he sat behind the mourners, with Kanji Dwarkadas beside him. After a tense silence, he began to talk, hurriedly, of his political worries. Kanji Dwarkadas did not answer. When the body was lowered into the earth, Jinnah abandoned his defences : he bowed his head and sobbed.

Jinnah went back to his house on Malabar Hill ; to the chill comfort of being alone. He had to endure two griefs at once : his belief in Hindu-Muslim unity was shattered, and his marriage had ended in tragedy. In time, he was to ascend to greatness and power ; but, in 1929, there was no light to encourage him in such a hope. He remained in his bachelor house, increasing the solitariness from which he was never to escape. When an old friend called, to describe his wife's last hours, he saw a cold, discouraging look in Jinnah's eye and did not dare broach the subject. The pretty objects Mrs Jinnah had bought for the house were packed away : every photograph, every souvenir of the desperate years was removed. The only sign of mourning was the correct black band on the sleeve of Jinnah's coat.

* * *

At a time when public failure and private grief might have overwhelmed him, a touching letter was written by the wife [1] of a British officer who met Jinnah at a dinner-party at Viceregal Lodge in Simla, towards the end of May 1929. She wrote to her mother, on the 29th, " . . . 75 covers were laid. All the gold plate was out, & the big gold bowls were filled with bright scarlet sweet peas. . . . After dinner, I had Mr Jinnah to talk to. He is a great personality. . . . He talks the most beautiful English. He models his manners & clothes on Du Maurier, the actor, & his English on Burke's Speeches. He is a future Vice Roy, if the present system of gradually Indianizing all the services continues. I have always wanted to meet him, & now I have had my wish. . . ."

* * *

EXILE: 1930–1934

ON the morning of June 5, 1929, Mr Ramsay MacDonald kissed hands as Prime Minister. Thus King George V received his second Labour Government, with Mr Wedgwood Benn [2] as Secretary of State for India. Indian nationalists were greatly encouraged : eleven months before, Mr MacDonald had said,[3]

> I hope that within a period of months rather than years there may be a new Dominion added to the Commonwealth of ou

[1] Mrs Freeth, wife of the late Major-General G. H. B. Freeth, Deputy Adjutant-General.
[2] Afterwards Viscount Stansgate.
[3] July 2, 1928, at the British Commonwealth Labour Conference, in London.

nations; a Dominion of another race, a Dominion that will find self-respect as an equal within this Commonwealth. I refer to India.

Mohammed Ali Jinnah wrote to Mr MacDonald on June 19, damning the Simon Commission and informing him that India had 'lost her faith in the word of Great Britain.' He then suggested 'a solution' which 'would most probably be acceptable'; that His Majesty's Government 'should invite representatives of India, who would be in a position to deliver the goods . . . to sit in conference with them, with a view to reaching a solution which might carry, to use the words of the Viceroy, the "willing assent of the political India."' Jinnah claimed that 'such an invitation,' coming 'directly from the Prime Minister,' would be 'irresistible.'

On October 16, Sir John Simon, still in the throes of preparing his report, made a similar suggestion to the Prime Minister. He wrote:

> It seems to us that what would be required would be the setting up of some sort of conference . . . [in which] His Majesty's Government would meet both representatives of British India and representatives of the States . . . for the purpose of seeking the greatest measure of agreement for the final proposals which it would later be the duty of His Majesty's Government to submit to Parliament. . . .

These representations led to the first Round Table Conference, in London, which was opened by the King in St James's Palace on November 12, 1930. Mohammed Ali Jinnah was one of the fifty-eight delegates from British India. The first sessions lasted through December, and into January, and the conclusions were encouraging. Future development was to be on a Federal basis : 'certain safeguards regarding defence and financial stability' were still to be controlled by the British, but, otherwise, 'full responsibility' for government was to be 'in Indian hands.'

In the later Conferences, Jinnah was to be overshadowed by the Aga Khan, as leader of the Muslim delegation, and by Gandhi. The Mahatma had refused to attend the first Conference,[1] but he became a dominant figure when the delegates met again, in September 1931.

It is interesting to compare the two men at this time : Jinnah,

---

[1] He was subsequently imprisoned, from April 1930 to January 1931.

disillusioned and silent, walking over Hampstead Heath, in search of a house in which he could live, as an English gentleman, retired from the fury of Indian politics; and Gandhi—the "seditious fakir", as Sir Winston Churchill once called him—assuming the language of a constitutional politician and saying to the Viceroy, in March 1931, "I want to see India established in her own self-respect and in the respect of the world. I therefore want to see India able to discuss with Great Britain on terms of equality. . . . I know perfectly well that we want British help in many things for a long time yet. . . ."

Lord Irwin [1] was impressed: he wrote of this interview, to the King: 'I believe it, Sir, to be definitely untrue to suggest . . . that he is out to break the unity of Your Majesty's Empire.' [2]

The second Round Table Conference failed: the harmony in which the delegates had met in 1930 was shattered in 1931. The rival leaders merely transplanted their fierce domestic squabbles from India to London, and they stirred up unreasonable scenes whenever the communal problem was discussed. The closing sessions met in an atmosphere of suspicion and contempt: the suspicion of the Indians for each other, and their common contempt for Britain. The Conference ended with a rebuke from Mr Ramsay MacDonald. He said:

> We shall soon find that our endeavours to proceed with our plans are held up—indeed they have been held up already—if you cannot present us with a settlement acceptable to all parties as the foundations upon which to build. In that event, His Majesty's Government would be compelled to apply a provisional scheme, for they are determined that even this disability shall not be permitted to be a bar to progress.

The delegates went home, with their angers, leaving the British Government to apply their own provisional scheme' for communal representation, later included in the Government of India Act of 1935.

* * *

One of the delegates to the Round Table Conferences was Sir Muhammad Iqbal, the greatest Muslim philosopher and poet of his

---

[1] In April, Lord Irwin was succeeded by Lord Willingdon, as Viceroy.
[2] The Viceroy, to the King, March 13, 1931. *King George V. His Life and Reign*. Harold Nicolson, p. 508.

SIR MUHAMMAD IQBAL

time. Iqbal, who was born in 1876, had been educated in Lahore, Cambridge and Munich : his politics had grown out of scholarship and a deep sense of history. He was a philosopher—never a fanatic—and his influence over the fortunes of the Muslim people, and on Mohammed Ali Jinnah, was profound and enduring.

Iqbal had already studied the miserable dilemma of the Muslims in India, and he had dismissed as impossible the unity that Jinnah had believed in, and argued for, during more than twenty years. He said,[1] in 1930, " To base a constitution on the conception of a homogeneous India, or to apply to India the principles dictated by British democratic sentiments, is unwittingly to prepare her for a civil war."

Iqbal advocated partition : he even demanded, and defined the frontiers of a proposed " consolidated Muslim State ", which, he believed would be " in the best interests of India and Islam." He said, " I would like to see the Punjab, the North-West Frontier Province, Sind and Baluchistan, amalgamated into a single state . . . the formation of a consolidated North-West Indian Muslim State appears to me to be the final destiny of the Muslims, at least of North-West India."

Jinnah met Sir Muhammad Iqbal many times in London, and they were good friends. But, despite his disillusionment, Jinnah did not yield to Iqbal's arguments. Almost a decade was to pass before he admitted that he had " finally been led to Iqbal's conclusions, as a result of careful examinations and study of the constitutional problems facing India."

*   *   *

It seems that, by the end of the second Round Table Conference, Jinnah had retired into a state of stubbornness and eclipse. He had made no important speeches during either of the first two sessions, and he was not included in the third Conference because he was not thought to represent any considerable school of opinion in India. He stayed in England, haunted by the memory of his unfortunate marriage, and discouraged as a politician. All that remained to him out of this disorder was his talent as an advocate. Abandoning all other interests, he decided to make his home in London and to practise at the Privy Council Bar.

There are vague claims, in newspapers, and in contemporary

[1] At the Muslim League session in Allahabad.

reminiscences published in India, that Jinnah wished to become a Labour member of the House of Commons, so that he could ' fight India's battles ' in Westminster, as Dadabhai Naoroji had fought them, thirty-nine years before. At the time of his death in 1948, the *Sunday Chronicle* (Manchester) recalled that Jinnah had ' addressed the Selections Committee of the Yorkshire divisional Labour party, but was turned down because of his immaculate dress. " We don't want a toff like that," one of the Labour men remarked ! '

There is no proof in any letters, nor any record in the archives of the Trades Union Congress, to support this story ; nor did Jinnah ever refer to such a wish in his subsequent speeches. There is only a report, in *The Yorkshire Post*, of April 18, 1932, of a speech which he made to the members of the Leeds Luncheon Club, to whom he said : ' If the British Government wishes to bring peace and good-will in India, its best policy would be to introduce at once a bill giving India self-government, and to leave out the idea of a federation of all India . . . the federation is a golden illusion, a mirage, to my mind.'

Jinnah gave his own reasons for remaining in England, in a speech to the students of Aligarh in 1938—when he had again settled in India. He said :

> I received the shock of my life at the meetings of the Round Table Conference. In the face of danger, the Hindu sentiment, the Hindu mind, the Hindu attitude led me to the conclusion that there was no hope of unity. I felt very pessimistic about my country. The position was most unfortunate. The Mussalmans were like dwellers in No Man's Land : they were led by either the flunkeys of the British Government or the camp-followers of the Congress. Whenever attempts were made to organize the Muslims, toadies and flunkeys on the one hand, and traitors in the Congress camp on the other, frustrated the efforts. I began to feel that neither could I help India, nor change the Hindu mentality ; nor could I make the Mussalmans realize the precarious position. I felt so disappointed and so depressed that I decided to settle down in London. Not that I did not love India, but I felt so utterly helpless.

It was in this state of mind that Jinnah began his exile in England.

* * *

PEACE IN HAMPSTEAD

One day in June 1931, when Jinnah was walking in Hampstead, he paused before West Heath House, in West Heath Road. It was a three-storied villa, built in the confused style of the 1880's, with many rooms and gables, and a tall tower which gave a splendid view over the surrounding country. There was a lodge, a drive, and eight acres of garden and pasture, leading down to Childs Hill.

All are gone now, and twelve smaller, modern houses occupy the once-pretty Victorian pleasance. Nearby lives Lady Graham Wood, from whom Jinnah bought the house; and she remembers him, on the day when he first called, as " most charming, a great gentleman, most courteous."

Jinnah accepted Lady Graham Wood's terms with grace: he asked her to recommend a school to which he could send his daughter, and he agreed to take over Bradbury, the chauffeur. All that he begged was that he might be allowed to move into the house as soon as possible.

In September 1931 Jinnah took possession of West Heath House, and he assumed the pattern of life that suited him. In place of Bombay, with the angers of his inheritance for ever pressing upon him, he was able to enjoy the precise, ordained habits of a London house. He breakfasted punctually and, at nine o'clock, Bradbury was at the door with the car, to drive him to his chambers in King's Bench Walk. There he built up his new career, with less fire of words, and calmer address, than during the early days in Bombay. In later years, Lord Jowitt was to recall this period of Jinnah's practice at the Bar: he wrote, ' We all had a great admiration for his legal skill and the judgement with which he conducted his cases before the Privy Council.'

Jinnah's life was now dignified and secure: his fortune was growing and he could enjoy the pleasant luxuries he had learned to accept—carefully chosen dinners at the Carlton Grill, and talks with calm, intelligent lawyers, in the still security of their London clubs. Also, he enjoyed the constant companionship of his sister, Miss Fatima Jinnah, who had resigned from her work in Bombay, to travel to England and be with her brother. From this time, to his death, she abandoned all other interest, to his care, and his career.

On Saturdays and Sundays, Jinnah liked to walk across Hampstead Heath to Kenwood—past *Jack Straw's Castle*, the inn before which

EXILE: 1930-1934

Karl Marx used to sit during his exile, drinking ginger beer with his children. Jinnah seemed to enjoy leisure, for the first time in his life: the harmony of this high landscape, where Constable's trees still framed the distant view of St Paul's, and Keats's nightingales still sang, within earshot of *The Spaniards*. These were Jinnah's years of order and contemplation, wedged in between the time of early struggle, and the final storm of conquest.

* * *

One morning in November 1932, Mohammed Ali Jinnah read a review of H. C. Armstrong's *Grey Wolf, An Intimate Study of a Dictator*, in the Literary Supplement of *The Times*. After breakfast he walked—past the pond and down the hill at Hampstead—and bought a copy of the book. For two days Jinnah was absorbed in the story of Kemal Ataturk: when he had finished, he handed the book to his daughter—then aged thirteen—and said, " Read this, my dear, it is good."

For many days afterwards he talked of Kemal Ataturk; so much that his daughter chaffed him and nicknamed him ' Grey Wolf '. She was then on holidays from her English school, and their companionship had become a delight to both of them. She alone could tease her father—a fond treatment he had lacked, all his life: she alone could extend her hand—slim and expressive as his—and cajole him into putting a brief aside, with the plea, " Come on, Grey Wolf, take me to a pantomime; after all, I am on my holidays."

It is interesting to read the story of Kemal Ataturk again and imagine the influence the book must have had on Mohammed Ali Jinnah's mind. Like ' Grey Wolf ', Jinnah was to create a nation out of a perplexed multitude of Muslim people; but, in character—one a libertine, and the other a puritan—they were as different as any two men could be.

Mustafa Kemal was born in 1881, so he was more or less Jinnah's contemporary. His mother also had lived in purdah and had been ' quite uneducated ', and ' ignorant of all the ordinary affairs of the outside world.' Jinnah might have recognized himself in the description of MustafaKemal as an ' abnormally self-sufficient boy ' who ' rarely made friends with other children.' He might also have comprehended the protest Mustafa Kemal made to his companions at school: "I don't mean to be like the rest of you; I mean to be somebody." Other cries, from the rebellious young Turk, indignant under the iniquities of Abdul Hamid, find echoes in the development of Mohammed Ali Jinnah, equally indignant under the apparent harshness of British rule in India. We read, in *Grey Wolf,* 'All the young men cried out for reform;' and of Mustafa Kemal seeing himself 'always the centre, the leader, the ruler obeyed and respected by all.' Jinnah also had been 'a brilliant, difficult youth' with whom it was impossible 'to be intimate.'

But there, the personal parallels end. There could be no recognition between Mustafa Kemal, at twenty, plunging 'wildly into the unclean life of the great metropolis of Constantinople,' and the immaculate Jinnah who, at the same age, had played a game of forfeits with some English friends and refused to pay *his* forfeit—a kiss for one of the girls in the party—because he thought it wrong to kiss a woman unless he was in love with her.

Jinnah read of Mustafa Kemal 'in the full flood-light of his great prestige, high up alone on a pinnacle of greatness.' It would not have occurred to him that he was to enjoy similar prestige and eminence, and achieve them, not by ordering 'two thousand of his cavalry to advance towards the English lines,' but with the lone sword of his own argument, over a conference table.

There are passages in *Grey Wolf* that must have recalled Jinnah from the safe habits of his exile, back to the passions of Indian politics; back to his 'cause'. He read of Mustafa Kemal: 'Now he repeated publicly the terms on which Turkey would make peace. . . . Turkey must be an independent sovereign state, within its own frontiers, and free from all foreign interference.' Then the broader vision—'I am neither a believer in a league of all the nations of Islam, nor even in a league of the Turkish peoples. Each of us has the right to hold to his ideals, but the Government must be stable, with a fixed policy grounded on facts, and with one view and one view alone—to safeguard the life and the independence of the nation within its national frontiers. . . . Neither sentiment nor illusion must influence our policy. Away with dreams and shadows! They have cost us dear in the past.'

Jinnah might have read this important statement a second time, and repeated aloud, "Away with dreams and shadows! They have cost

EXILE: 1930-1934

us dear in the past." He was himself coming to the end of a dream : the illusion of peace, in Hampstead, was not to last much longer.

One evening in July 1933, Liaquat Ali Khan and his wife arrived at West Heath House and begged Jinnah to return to India.

* * *

Nawabzada Liaquat Ali Khan, born in 1896, was Jinnah's junior by twenty years. His education had been broader, and richer : he had graduated from Aligarh in 1918, and had then gone to Exeter College, Oxford, where his political ideas began to stir. He took part in undergraduate debates, and was secretary of the Indian Majlis. He was called to the Bar in the Inner Temple in 1922, and returned to India in the same year. But he did not practise the law : he became a politician, immediately, and in 1926 he was elected to the Legislative Council of the United Provinces.

Liaquat Ali Khan was the ally Jinnah needed. Jinnah's appeal had always been to the ' educated ' Indians—the phrase occurs often, in his speeches. He described himself as a proletarian, but he had never made himself, or his ideas, known to the masses. It was part of Liaquat Ali Khan's talent that he could charm vast, illiterate audiences, and that he was not over-ambitious. In the years that followed, when Jinnah enjoyed his own omnipotence, Liaquat Ali Khan did not mind : indeed, it was part of his nature that he enjoyed the subtle rewards of second place. He was to become the brilliant administrator ; the builder of Jinnah's architectural design. Jinnah was to find in him the complement to his own talents : together, they were to become inviolable, because they formed one mind, and the trust between them remained absolute, to the end. A great part of the fortunes of Pakistan were decided on the day, in July 1933, when Liaquat Ali Khan crossed Hampstead Heath, to talk to his exiled leader.

* * *

Begum Liaquat Ali Khan has spoken [1] of the friendship between Mohammed Ali Jinnah and her husband, and of their meeting at Hampstead. "They had known each other from 1928—at the Calcutta Conference where Jinnah was so humiliated. You will remember how he was cried down as not being in any sense an

[1] To the author.

accepted leader of the Muslims. Liaquat was one of those who stood by him : he had always admired Jinnah, and believed in him as much then as he did at the end.

"We were married early in 1933 and we decided to go to Europe for our honeymoon. You must remember the circumstances of Muslim politics at that time. The Muslim League was in a degraded state ; the finances were being misused and the League had neither dignity nor power. The cause had gone downhill—seemingly beyond recall. Liaquat had the belief that Jinnah was the one man who could save the League, and the Muslims. But Jinnah was in England : it was believed that he would never come back and that he was disgusted with his own people.

"Liaquat and I arrived in London and we met Jinnah at a reception. Liaquat immediately began his appeal to Jinnah to return. I remember him saying, 'They need someone who is unpurchasable.' It was a word my husband liked. And it was true : Jinnah *was* unpurchasable. He listened, but he did not answer at first : he talked of his life in England, and of his contentment at Hampstead. But Liaquat was not to be denied. He said, 'You must come back. The people need you. You alone can put new life into the League and save it.'

"Jinnah suddenly said, 'Well, come to dinner on Friday.'

"So we drove to Hampstead. It was a lovely evening. And his big house, with trees—apple trees, I seem to remember. And Miss Jinnah, attending to all his comforts. I felt that nothing could move him out of that security.

"After dinner, Liaquat repeated his plea, that the Muslims wanted Jinnah and needed him.

"I had hero-worshipped Mr Jinnah for a long time. I chirped in, 'And I'll make the women work for you ; I'll bring them back into the fold.' He smiled at me and said, 'You are young ; you do not know the women ; you do not know the world.' But he listened to Liaquat, and in the end he said, 'You go back and survey the situation ; test the feelings of all parts of the country. I trust your judgment. If you say " Come back," I'll give up my life here and return.'

"Liaquat was a very happy man as we drove back to London. We sailed for India and, for some months, my husband devoted every day to his journeys and his enquiries. You know, he was the most thorough man I have ever known. He amassed his evidence—talked to a hundred people—and only when he was convinced, he wrote to Jinnah and said ' Come '."

* * *

Jinnah returned to India, to prove to himself that he was needed. At first, he was reluctant: one evening, at the Willingdon Club, in Bombay, he said to Diwan Chaman Lall, " Politics ! I am finished." Then—" But if you could only get six people like yourself to support me, I would come back."

Diwan Chaman Lall has told the story.[1] " I sent telegrams to six of the honest and stalwart ones, asking them if they would support Jinnah if he returned. They all replied ' Yes.' He already had the whole-hearted devotion of Liaquat Ali Khan, to strengthen these encouraging signs. As you know, Jinnah returned to England again and gave up his practice before the Privy Council ; he sold his house at Hampstead and he came home, to Bombay. The house in Mount Pleasant Road was opened again and the re-awakening of the Muslims began."

Mr T. W. Ramsay, who still practises at 10 King's Bench Walk, had been Jinnah's neighbour in Chambers during the years in London. He has described their farewell. " I remember the day when he came in and said he was returning home. Several other lawyers had their eye on his beautiful office furniture and they wished to buy it. There were some lovely mahogany pieces. One of my colleagues said to Jinnah that he would buy it all, but he answered, ' It is yours. I don't care about these chattels. I am going on a grand mission to India '."

[1] To the author.

PART FOUR

RETURN TO INDIA: 1935-1937

THE 'grand mission' did not begin immediately. Liaquat Ali Khan had written 'Come,' but there was still some torment in Mohammed Ali Jinnah's mind; some reluctance to return to the open seas of conflict he would have to endure. He did not act with his usual quick determination.

During 1934 and 1935, Jinnah was a restless traveller. In April 1934 he was back in India, denying his own belief that there was 'no hope' of unity. At a meeting of the Muslim League Council, in April, he said, "Nothing will give me greater happiness than to bring about complete co-operation and friendship between Hindus and Muslims." He returned to London, still caught up in the strange conflict between his old ideal and his reason. In October, while he was in England, the Muslims of Bombay elected him an Independent member to the Central Legislature, without seeking his consent. The news, that he was needed by his own people, reached him within the untroubled comfort of a London hotel. In January 1935 he sailed for India once more, to attend the first session of the new Assembly, but, in April, he returned to England, where he remained until October.

While Jinnah was in London, the King gave his Royal Assent to the Government of India Act of 1935, which remained unaltered, in its principles, until the 'transfer of power' to India and Pakistan, in 1947. The 'benefits' of this Act are described [1] by the Australian statesman, Mr R. G. Casey, who was Governor of Bengal from 1944 to 1946. He wrote:

> The Government of India Act of 1935 was a big step towards self-government, and it went considerably beyond the recommendations of the Simon Commission. In the Provinces, responsible government was established over virtually the entire field of subjects ordinarily falling to a province in a federation. In nearly all matters the Governor was bound to act on the advice of his Ministers. In a few matters he could legally act against advice. In still fewer matters he could act even without advice.

[1] In his book, *An Australian in India* (1947), pp. 49-50.

These 'safeguards' were very few, and the Governors were particularly enjoined not to exercise their powers so as to relieve Ministers of proper responsibility. In fact the over-ruling powers were very little used.

The second part of the Government of India Act 1935 was designed to secure the federation of the whole of India, and to introduce responsible government at the Centre. But it has never come into force, because the Princes refused to join a federation. So the Centre carried on as before.

The Provinces—now increased to eleven—were given almost complete autonomy, and were made secure from central interference in the exclusively Provincial field. Each was to have its own elected Ministry, with all the portfolios in the hands of Ministers elected by the people and chosen by the leader of the majority party. In the structure of such elections, the several minorities—whether Muslim, Christian, Parsee, European, Depressed Classes—or Hindu—were to be safeguarded by the just apportioning of seats, voted for in separate communal electorates. It was implicit in the new Constitution that, so far as possible, each Provincial Ministry should include Ministers selected from the minority parties.

The pattern of representation, described as the Communal Award, had been devised by Mr Ramsay MacDonald's government after the Round Table Conferences, as an attempt to satisfy the minorities —the Muslims in particular.

Mohammed Ali Jinnah was 'not satisfied' with the Award. But, in a speech made in the Assembly, in February 1935, he said that he was prepared to accept it, because—having 'done everything . . . to come to a settlement '—no ' scheme of Constitution ' would otherwise be ' possible.'

* * *

Early in 1936, Jinnah played his part in an act of conciliation that was significant for two reasons. In the city of Lahore was a mosque, once the property of the Muslims. The Sikhs had usurped it, and, after much wrangling, there was one more cruel explosion between the Muslims and Sikhs of the Punjab, ending in riots and the imprisonment of the leaders. Jinnah went to Lahore to cool the belligerents with reason. Here was an opportunity to prove that unity between communities was possible. He brought the contestants together: he used the words, "constitutional methods," like a bludgeon, and induced them to accept legal arbitration.

The Governor of the Punjab recorded his official thanks: he wrote,

> I am greatly indebted to the efforts of Mr Jinnah for this improvement and I wish to pay an unqualified tribute to the work he has done and is doing. Mr Jinnah succeeded in his first task, namely, bringing the Muslim agitation to strictly constitutional and legal lines, and has thus made it possible for Government to take action for which they had been awaiting an opportunity. . . .

The episode was important because it had obliged Jinnah to apply his theories to a specific incident; important also because it revealed Liaquat Ali Khan's influence on his leader. Up to this time, Jinnah had never stepped down, to mingle with the people in their troubles: he had usually theorized over them, from afar. But, within twelve months of the first elections under the new Constitution, Jinnah was learning to come closer to the voters who were to decide the shape of India's political affairs, and his own destiny, in the next decade.

★ ★ ★

The elections were to be held in the first weeks of 1937. As early as 1934, the 'high command' of the Congress party had begun their preparations: their own Parliamentary Board—comparable to Labour's Transport House, or the Conservative Central Office, in England—was formulating policy and briefing the selected candidates. The 'opposition', of whom Iqbal wrote:

> I shed tears of blood at the indolence of Muslims;
> Your carpets are Persian, your sofas Western!

were almost two years late in beginning their campaign. Early in 1936, the Muslim League met in Bombay and decided to form their own Central Election Board, with Jinnah as President.

The Muslim League was indolent no longer: with Liaquat Ali Khan at hand, to interpret Jinnah's orders and wishes, the League came alive again. In March, Jinnah spoke to some of the members, in Delhi, he said:

> We must think of the interests of our community. Unless you make the best efforts, you will fail and will command no respect and nobody will bother to consult you. Organize yourselves and play your part.
> The Hindus and Muslims must be organized separately, and once they are organized they will understand each other better, and then we will not have to wait for years for an understanding. . . . I am helping eighty million people, and if they are more organized they will be all the more useful for the national struggle.

*　　*　　*

It is folly to think of the Muslims and Hindus as if their differences were as clearly defined as those of two armies on a battlefield; one bearing the standard of 'the League' and the other the standard of 'Congress'. The error comes easily to those who are used to such simple devices as 'Tory' and 'Labour', 'Republican' and 'Democrat'. Behind the fronts of League and Congress were spread a multitude of people, strangely divided and opposed. Not all the Hindus belonged to the Congress Party: many of them were Liberals and Independents, who disliked the revolutionary policy of the Mahatma and his disciples. Nor did the eighty million Muslims march as one man. In the Punjab, especially, where they were in a majority, and in no danger of Hindu domination, there were popular parties of Muslims, led by Muslims, that had flourished long before Jinnah awakened the moribund League to contest the 1937 elections. They were not likely to leave their proven parties, to join the 'revived' League, which was still weak, and young.

Some groups of the Muslims were ardent supporters of Congress: the North-West Frontier Province, where the Muslims were ninety per cent of the population, was a Congress stronghold. In this part of the country—the home of the stalwart Pathan highlanders—not a single Muslim League candidate had been returned to the Legislative Assemblies. The Muslims in the province of Sind had openly 'disowned the League': they allied themselves with Congress, and opposed any suggestion of partition. Jinnah was therefore attempting a prodigious task, in asking these Muslim communities—unaware of each other and scattered over thousands of square miles—to 'organize' and regard themselves as one undivided army.

The cast of leaders in India had changed during the years of Jinnah's absence in England. By 1937, Gandhi, who had made boycott and mass civil disobedience into a sullen and terrible force, was sixty-seven years old: he was now something of an oracle, clothed in mysticism, and he left the laborious tasks of Congress to a younger man, Pandit Jawaharlal Nehru, aged forty-seven. Mr Nehru called the Mahatma *Bapu*, or 'father'. Eight years before, in a speech opposing the Round Table Conference, Nehru had said,

> We have not the material or the training for organized violence, and individual or sporadic violence is a confession of despair. The great majority of us, I take it, judge the issue not on moral but on practical grounds, and if we reject the way of violence it is because it promises no substantial results. But if this Congress, or the nation at any future time, comes to the conclusion that methods of violence will rid us of slavery, then I have no doubt that it will adopt them. Violence is bad, but slavery is far worse.

Nehru was less challenging during the campaign for the 1937 elections: he did not talk of violence, but of the value of constitutional opposition, from within the Congress. Jinnah was to say of him, "He is a Peter Pan; he will never learn anything, or unlearn anything." Nevertheless, Nehru led the army of Congress workers to victory at the polls. Out of 295 millions in British India, 30 millions held the vote: of these, 30 per cent were Muslims. The League candidates recorded less than five per cent of the Muslim votes that were cast. Nehru was naturally confident after this heartening victory: early in March 1937, shortly after the elections, he said that there were "only two parties" in the country—"Congress and the British." Jinnah replied, "There is a third party . . . the Muslims," and he added,

> We are not going to be dictated to by anybody. We are willing to co-operate with any group of a progressive and independent character, provided its programme and policy correspond to our own. We are not going to be camp-followers of

any party. We are ready to work as equal partners for the welfare of India.

Pandit Nehru and Congress remained scornful and Jinnah's offer 'to work as equal partners' was ignored. Sir Percival Griffiths, a former Leader of the European Group in the Indian Central Legislature, has written [1] of this 'grave tactical blunder':

> The Congress High Command refused to sanction Congress-League coalitions and in the Hindu majority provinces ministries consisting only of Congressmen were formed. In the United Provinces, for example, Muslim representatives were invited to join the ministry, but only on condition that they became members of the Congress Party and that the Muslim League ceased to exist. In other provinces, similar conditions were imposed, and with one exception members of the Muslim League were rigorously excluded from office.
>
> The Congress party was fully within its rights in adopting this exclusive policy and may even have felt that it was following normal parliamentary practice. There can be little doubt, however, that it made a grave tactical blunder. There was no difference in social or economic policy serious enough to make Congress-League coalitions unnatural or unworkable, and the Muslims therefore felt, rightly or wrongly, that they were excluded from office merely because the Congress was essentially a Hindu body.

* * *

Jinnah returned to his desk in the house in Mount Pleasant Road, discouraged, but not in despair. He worked alone, with no personal staff and not even a secretary to copy his letters and keep his papers tidy. But there was one bundle of letters, in a drawer, to which he could turn for consolation: they had been written to him by Sir Muhammad Iqbal, after their meeting in England in 1932. On May 28, 1937, Iqbal had recorded his belief that, 'to make it possible for Muslim India' to solve her problems, it would be 'necessary to redistribute the country and to provide one or more Muslim states with absolute majorities.' And he had asked, 'Don't you think that the time for such a demand has already arrived?'

[1] *The British Impact on India* (Macdonald, 1952), p. 340.

PANDIT JAWAHARLAL NEHRU AND M. A. JINNAH,
AT SIMLA, IN 1946

There is no record of Jinnah's reply to this letter. On June 21, Iqbal wrote again, ' I know you are a busy man, but I do hope you won't mind my writing to you so often, as you are the only Muslim in India today to whom the community has a right to look up for safe guidance through the storm which is coming. . . .'

Jinnah heeded this letter : in a speech at Lucknow, on October 15, he said, " . . . the majority community have clearly shown their hand that Hindustan is for the Hindus." He warned his listeners that the ' present Congress Party policy ' would result in ' class bitterness ' and ' communal war.'

Mahatma Gandhi considered Jinnah's words ' carefully,' and wrote to him, ' As I read it, the whole of your speech is a declaration of war. This . . . is written in all good faith and out of an anguished heart.'

* * *

1937–1939

WITH the speech at Lucknow, Mohammed Ali Jinnah had begun his ascent towards final power. There was no longer any confusion in his mind as to the aims of Congress, or the possible fate of the Muslims in India. He referred to the programme of ' mass contact ' among the Muslims, and the ' stupendous undertaking ' it had been ' to contest the elections in the provinces,' among the people who were ' numerically in a minority and weak, educationally backward, and economically nowhere.' He talked of the ' suffering and sacrifice ' and the ' fire of persecution ' through which deliverance would come ; of the ' nation ' that would ' emerge ', and of the ' eighty millions of Mussalmans ' who had ' nothing to fear '. Then the characteristic sentence, " Think one hundred times before you take a decision, but once a decision is taken, stand by it as one man."

On November 5, Jinnah answered Gandhi's letter of protest and ' anguish ' over the Lucknow speech. He wrote that he was ' sorry ' if Gandhi considered he had made ' a declaration of war,' and pleaded that it was ' purely in self-defence.' He asked, ' Kindly read it again and try to understand it ' ; and added, ' Evidently you have not been following the course of events of the last twelve months. . . .'

1937–1939

Gandhi waited three months before he replied :

You seem to deny that your speech was a declaration of war, but your later pronouncements too confirm the first impression. . . .

In your speeches, I miss the old nationalist. When in 1915 I returned from the self-imposed exile in South Africa, everybody spoke of you as one of the staunchest of nationalists and the hope of both Hindus and Muslims. Are you still the same Mr Jinnah ? If you say you are, in spite of your speeches, I shall accept your word.

Jinnah was more prompt, and abrupt, with his answer : he wrote, twelve days later,

. . . you say that in my speeches you miss the old nationalist. Do you think that you are justified in saying that ? I would not like to think what people spoke of you in 1915 and what they speak and think of you today. Nationalism is not the monopoly of any single individual, and in these days it is very difficult to define it ; but I do not wish to pursue this line of controversy any further.

It has been said that Jinnah was not alone in his study of Burke's speeches ; that volumes of them, in the libraries, were so tattered with use by young political aspirants, that new copies had to be sent out to India each year. But the example of Burke's address was perhaps neglected by the leaders of Congress and the League, during the season of argument in 1937 and 1938. About the time when Jinnah and Gandhi were engaged in their recriminations, Pandit Jawaharlal Nehru and Jinnah were exchanging equally acrimonious letters.

On February 25, 1938, Nehru wrote to Jinnah :

I am afraid I must confess that I do not yet know what the fundamental points of dispute are. It is for this reason that I have been asking you to clarify them. So far, I have not received any help in this direction. . . .

Six days later, Jinnah replied :

. . . I am only amazed at your ignorance. This matter has been tackled since 1925 right up to 1935 by the most prominent leaders in the country, and so far no solution has been found. I would beg of you to study it, and ... not take up a self-complacent attitude ; and if you are in earnest I don't think you will find much difficulty in realizing what the main points in dispute are, because they have been constantly mentioned both in the press and public platform, even very recently.

On April 6, Nehru wrote, in the name of Congress :

... Obviously, the Muslim League is an important communal organization and we deal with it as such. But we have to deal with all organizations and individuals that come within our ken. We do not determine the measure of importance or distinction they possess. ... Inevitably, the more important the organization, the more the attention paid to it, but this importance does not come from outside recognition but from inherent strength. And the other organizations, even though they might be younger and smaller, cannot be ignored.

Six days later, Jinnah replied to Nehru :

It seems to me that you cannot even accurately understand my letter. ...

Your tone and language again display the same arrogance and militant spirit, as if the Congress is the sovereign power. ... I may add that, in my opinion, as I have publicly stated so often, that unless the Congress recognizes the Muslim League on a footing of complete equality and is prepared as such to negotiate for a Hindu-Muslim settlement, we shall have to wait and depend upon our 'inherent strength' which will 'determine the measure of importance or distinction' it possesses. Having regard to your mentality, it is really difficult for me to make you understand the position any further. ...

On September 30, Mr Neville Chamberlain and Adolf Hitler conferred in Munich, and the Prime Minister returned to Downing Street with the piece of paper which he believed to be a guarantee of ' peace in our time.' The threats of world upheaval drew the attention of the Indian leaders away from their personal conflict, and their game of taunts had to stop.

On October 8, in his speech to the Muslim League Conference in Karachi, Jinnah referred to the behaviour of the British to the Arabs in Palestine. He claimed that Great Britain had ' thrown her friends to the wolves' and had 'broken her solemn promises.' He then said, " Only those succeed with the British people who possess force and power and who are in a position to bully them." He then referred to the Germans in Sudetenland, and compared their plight with that of his own people. He said :

> . . . I would draw their [the British] attention—and here also of the Congress High Command—and ask them to mark, learn, and inwardly digest the recent upheaval and its consequent developments, which threatened . . . world war. It was because the Sudeten Germans were forced under the heels of the majority of Czechoslovakia, who oppressed them, suppressed them, maltreated them and showed a brutal and callous disregard for their rights and interests for two decades—hence the inevitable result that the Republic of Czechoslovakia is now broken up and a new map will have to be drawn.
>
> Just as the Sudeten Germans were not defenceless, and survived the oppression and persecution for two decades, so also the Mussalmans are not defenceless, and cannot give up their national entity and aspirations in this great continent.

Jinnah was now the leader of these aspirations. During the eleven months preceding September 3, 1939—when war was declared—his power over the Muslims was established, with Liaquat Ali Khan as the adept organizer behind him. Iqbal had died on April 21, 1938, having sent a final warning to Jinnah : he had written, ' I believe that a political organization which gives no promise of improving the lot of the average Muslim cannot attract our masses.' At last, Jinnah learned the difference between aloof, academic leadership, and popularity with a multitude. In the month that Iqbal died, Jinnah was able to say, ". . . the League has been growing stronger and stronger every day. Before the Lucknow session, the membership . . . ran into several thousands, but today there are hundreds of thousands of Mussalmans who are under the banner of the League."

★   ★   ★

The 'hundreds of thousands' who had been attracted to the 'banner of the League' were not all drawn from the adult masses : Jinnah was also becoming a considerable force among Muslims in the universities.

This awakening of political interest among the Muslim students, and their willingness to follow him, came at a time of almost wistful loneliness in Jinnah's private life. He was then fifty-eight years old, and he still lived quietly with his devoted sister. His daughter had made her home with her mother's Parsee relatives in Bombay : she was ultimately to marry a Christian, and become estranged from her father for many years. Jinnah had endured all he wished of emotional relationships, and he permitted no one to disturb his disciplined, celibate, recluse habits. But he was slowly learning to unbend with the young, in a way that psychiatrists might describe as a manifestation of the frustrated father instinct in a solitary, ageing man.

One summer, the son of a friend came, with a school companion, to stay with Jinnah in his house. On the last night of their visit, they went to bed and were almost asleep when the door was opened. The boy, who became one of Jinnah's ardent followers in later years, has described what followed. 'The light was switched on and we saw Mr Jinnah in his pyjamas and dressing-gown. He apologized for disturbing us ; then he said, "I could not sleep because you are going away tomorrow." He sat down and talked to us for a long time—not about politics, but about his life in England, and of the earlier years when he was a boy in Karachi. When he got up to return to his room, he said he was sorry he had kept us awake. As he turned out the light, he said, "I wish that I had a son."'

One of the first young men to break past Jinnah's defences was Ibrahim Habibullah, who had just come down from Oxford when he went to hear both Jinnah and Pandit Jawaharlal Nehru speak at a meeting. Ibrahim Habibullah walked away from the hall with Jinnah, who said to him, "Don't you think that Nehru was talking nonsense ?"

"No," answered Ibrahim Habibullah, "I agree with all his views."

Jinnah then said, referring to some point in Nehru's speech, "The laws of the jungle must always prevail. Unless you understand that, you are a madcap."

Habibullah replied, "We call ourselves human beings because we have emancipated ourselves from the jungle. If you do not appreciate that, then, sir, you are the madcap."

1937-1939

Jinnah was delighted with this challenge from someone less than half his age : he said, " Oh, I need young men like you. Come and join me."

Slowly, Jinnah was gathering his young army about him ; among them, Mohammed Noman, who was ultimately secretary of the All-India Muslim Students Federation. He was still a student at Aligarh University, in February 1935, when he went to Delhi to hear Jinnah speak in the Assembly and became his devoted and lively follower. At the end of the day, Mohammed Noman was walking with another student when they came to the house where Jinnah was staying : on a board by the gate was the name, *Mr M. A. Jinnah*. Mohammed Noman wrote ' Two Aligarh Students ' on a card and gave it to the servant. Within a few minutes they were with Jinnah in his study, and he talked to them, and enthralled them, for an hour.

Mohammed Noman went back to his studies at Aligarh, and almost a year passed before he saw Jinnah again. He has described the meeting.[1] " It was at the first session of the All-India Students Conference, in Lucknow—inaugurated by Pandit Nehru and presided over by Mr Jinnah. I think it was the last time they ever appeared on a platform together. Mr Jinnah spoke splendidly, to a big audience of students—but there could not have been more than half a dozen Muslims amongst them. Yet Mr Jinnah had the courage, before that almost entirely Hindu gathering, to accuse Congress of being a Hindu body. There were some protesting voices, but Mr Jinnah silenced them. I saw and felt that he was so disgusted by the fact that there were so few Muslims present.

" I was very young and enthusiastic—I was attending the session as delegate from Aligarh. A few days later I asked if I might see Mr Jinnah : I went to him and suggested the formation of a student organization entirely for the Muslims. He agreed and gave me his blessing. Out of that impulse grew the All-India Muslim Students Federation, with more than fifty thousand members—all working ceaselessly to attain Pakistan.

" I became secretary of the Federation, and because of this I saw Mr Jinnah two or three times a week during more than two years. He was no fanatic : his approach to our problems, as students, was

---

[1] To the author.

never sentimental. He liked reality and reason. Muslim Student Associations were formed—in one city after another. You must realize what this means—that the *younger* generation of educated Muslims became his followers. Mr Jinnah presided over our first session, in 1937, at Calcutta. There were three hundred delegates, and he told them that they were a wonderful generation. That was good for them; it increased their self-respect. And when they cheered him he said, ' Well, many Jinnahs will arise from among you —I have no fear of the future in your hands.'

"In 1938, I wished to go to England to complete my education. I had spent much of my time travelling from one college to another, trying to stimulate the students; but I had much to learn. I told Mr Jinnah that I had applied to the Hyderabad Government for a grant, so that I could travel to London. He said, ' No—you must do it out of your own strength.' He suggested that I should write the history of the Muslim League, which I did. I remember him saying, ' Then you can educate yourself on the royalties from the book.'

"He worked with me; he gave me all the papers that I needed. Hour after hour he sat with me, until the book was finished. His patience with me was incredible."

Among Mohammed Noman's talents is mimicry. His imitation of Jinnah was delightful—the raised finger, slicing the air with emphasis; the voice, and the solemn look. But the talent—which he perfected when still at college—once led him into alarming embarrassment. One day Jinnah sent for him and said, "I am told that you mimic me with great skill. Show me how you do it."

Mohammed Noman had to stand before him and do his best. At the end of the impersonation, Jinnah took off his astrakhan hat and monocle, and said, " Very good. Take these; they will make it more authentic in future."

Another young Muslim League member of the late 1930's, Captain Saied Abbas, described Jinnah's power over the students: he wrote,[1] ' It was during 1937–1938 that I first saw Mr Jinnah, when he visited Allahabad. For us Muslim students, he represented the spear-head of the Muslim renaissance, all over India. For the Hindu students, he was an incorruptible fighter for freedom. At that time, they

---

[1] To the author.

seemed to think that he might still be won over—there was still some uncertainty about his so-called communalism. He was met with the biggest reception ever given to a political figure—including Gandhi. The Delhi-bound Calcutta mail train, by which he arrived, had to wait two hours while the platform and the tracks were being cleared of the crowds.

'None of us—the Muslim students—had ever seen Mr Jinnah. We had all heard stories of his Western clothes; that he was very English. As the train steamed in, we rushed to receive and garland him. We opened the door of a carriage and saw a smartly dressed man, in a blue serge suit and stiff white collar. We crowded about him with our garlands. The gentleman protested, "I am not Mr Jinnah!" but I shouted, "You are trying to be modest."

'Suddenly we heard shouts of "Mohammed Ali Jinnah, Zindabad." We had chosen the wrong man: we were just about to carry the baffled gentleman on our shoulders. We turned and saw the real Mr Jinnah: there was no mistake about the thin, elegant, gentle frame after that; it left everlasting imprints on our minds.

'I remember two parts of the great speech that he made to us, at Allahabad University. He said, "Gentlemen—if for bettering the conditions of the teeming millions of this country; if for uplifting the social, economic and political standards of the Mussalmans of India, I am branded as a communalist, I assure you, Gentlemen, that I am proud to be a communalist."

'There was thunderous applause. Only once was there an interruption, when some Hindu students cried out, "Gandhiji-ki-Jai!"

'Mr Jinnah paused and there was a pin-drop silence. Then he said, in a quiet voice, "Yes, by all means. Gandhi is a great Hindu leader." After that, the students—Muslims and Hindus—listened to him, without interruption.'

*   *   *

During these years of political campaigning, which took him all over the country, Mohammed Ali Jinnah seems to emerge as a happier man—as much as it is possible to judge someone who wrote and said so little that was self-revealing. For twenty-five days during 1939, he stayed at Quetta, in a house and garden where he could rest, between the vigorous tours and speeches among the tribesmen of Baluchistan.

His hostess during this time has said: "I loved and respected Jinnah very much. He was always sympathetic and courteous to me. Only once was he at all angry: it was before a meeting of the tribal chiefs at which he was to preside. There was a strong prejudice against unveiled women in Baluchistan—purdah was strictly observed. My husband suggested that, because of this, Miss Jinnah should not sit on the platform with her brother. She, of course, did not observe purdah, and neither did I. I protested and said, ' Why not ! You have to start breaking down their prejudices some time.' Jinnah was quite angry: he said to me, ' You are trying to ruin four years of work among these people.' He meant, of course, four years of building up sympathy for the Muslim League, among the tribesmen. Next morning, he spoke to me alone: he was most tender, and said he was sorry.

" My little son was then two years old: he would run into Jinnah's room in the morning, calling, ' I want Dada Jinnah.' Then he would sit on his knee and they would gossip together. Whenever I tried to take my little boy away, Jinnah would say, ' No, leave him.' He showered him with presents—a silver mug, with a replica of his hand-writing on it ; an ivory ring with three little silver dogs that rattled. One day he drove into Quetta, alone with the chauffeur— we did not know what for. You must realize that he was then a great figure and people gathered wherever he went. We heard the story afterwards. Making his way through a crowd, he walked into a toy shop and said, ' I want a rocking-horse.' You may imagine the surprise of the man in his humble little shop when the celebrated Mr Jinnah asked for a rocking-horse ; and my surprise when he walked into the house and gave it to my son."

* * *

On September 3, 1939, Mr Neville Chamberlain declared to the British people, over the air, " . . . consequently this country is at war with Germany." Almost immediately, Lord Linlithgow, who had been Viceroy since 1936, announced that India also was " at war with Germany." When Gandhi saw the Viceroy on September 5, he ' broke down ' as he pictured the destruction of the Houses of Parliament and Westminster Abbey. ' I am not thinking just now of India's deliverance,' wrote the Mahatma. ' It will come, but what will it be worth if England and France fall, or if they come out victorious over Germany, ruined and humbled?' On September 8, Pandit Nehru promised that Congress did not aim to take advantage of 'British difficulties': he said, "In a conflict between democracy and freedom on the one hand, and Fascism and aggression on the other, our sympathies must inevitably lie on the side of democracy ... I should like India to play the full part. . . ."

These sympathetic views did not endure. On October 10, the All-India Congress Committee resolved that 'India must be declared an independent nation,' and that 'present application must be given to this status to the largest possible extent.' By November 15, at the behest of the Congress 'High Command', the Congress Ministries, in the seven provinces which they had won in the 1937 elections, had resigned. Four days later, at Allahabad, the Congress leaders reaffirmed their policy of non-co-operation and refused to assist in the war effort unless India was 'declared independent . . . at once.'

This was Mohammed Ali Jinnah's great chance: the majority of the Muslims were now his supporters and his hand was strong. He called on his followers to observe the coming December 22 as a "Day of Deliverance and Thanksgiving, as a mark of relief that the Congress regime has at last ceased to function." To the surprise of Congress, December 22 became not merely a Muslim celebration: Parsees, Christians, Hindus opposed to Congress, and hundreds of thousands of the 'Untouchables', joined in the demonstration.

This was a day of private retribution for Jinnah. In 1928, when he had spoken before the All-Parties Conference in Calcutta, he had been called 'a spoilt child', with no right to speak on behalf of the Muslim people. The right had now come, adding a new meaning to the phrase, 'the parting of the ways.'

* * *

1940: 'PAKISTAN'

> *Pakistan is both a Persian and Urdu word. It is composed of letters taken from the names of all our homelands—'Indian' and 'Asian'. That is, Panjab, Afghania (North West Frontier Province), Kashmir, Iran, Sindh (including Kutch and Kathiawar), Tukharistan, Afghanistan and Balochistan. It means the land of the Paks—the spiritually pure and clean. It symbolizes the religious beliefs and ethnical stocks of our people; and it stands for all the territorial constituents of our original Fatherland.*
>
> From *Pakistan*, Choudhury Rahmat Ali.

THE remarkable events of 1940, leading to the absolute decision of the Muslim League to demand their own nation—Pakistan—were anticipated in two articles published in English journals: one an interview with Mr Jinnah in an English newspaper,[1] the other an article in *Time and Tide*, March 9, 1940, written by Jinnah himself. They reveal what was in his mind at this time.

Jinnah said to the English correspondent, '. . . it has been established beyond doubt . . . that the sole aim of the Congress is to annihilate every other organization in the country, and to set itself up as a Fascist and authoritarian organization of the worst type.' He spoke of 'the thirty-five millions of voters, the bulk of whom are totally ignorant, illiterate and untutored, living in centuries-old superstitions . . . thoroughly antagonistic to each other'; and of the impossibility of working 'a democratic parliamentary Government in India.' He said, '. . . democracy can only mean Hindu *Raj* all over India.' Then this challenge—'This is a position to which Muslims will never submit.' Jinnah reminded English readers that Muslims would not be the only victims of such absolute government by Hindus: there were also 'sixty millions of "Untouchables," six million Christians, Jews, Parsees, and the domiciled British.' He also asked that, in envisaging the political future of India, the English should 'dismiss' from their minds the examples of federal government in Canada and Australia, where British democracy had planted natural and thriving roots; and he quoted Lord Morley's dictum that the 'fur coat of Canada' would not do for the 'extremely tropical climate of India.'

---

[1] *Mohammed Ali Jinnah (A Political Study)*, M. H. Saiyid, pp. 663–7.

1940: 'PAKISTAN'

In his article in *Time and Tide*, Jinnah wrote:

> What is the political future of India? The declared aim of the British Government is that India should enjoy Dominion Status in accordance with the Statute of Westminster in the shortest practicable time. In order that this end should be brought about, the British Government, very naturally, would like to see in India the form of democratic constitution it knows best and thinks best, under which the Government of the country is entrusted to one or other political Party in accordance with the turn of the elections.
>
> Such, however, is the ignorance about Indian conditions among even the members of the British Parliament that, in spite of all the experience of the past, it is even yet not realized that this form of Government is totally unsuited to India. Democratic systems based on the concept of a homogeneous nation such as England are very definitely not applicable to heterogeneous countries such as India, and this simple fact is the root cause of India's constitutional ills.

Mr Jinnah then quoted from the Report of the Joint Select Committee on Indian Constitutional Reforms, which had been conducted by the British Parliament in 1933-34:

> India is inhabited by many races ... often as distinct from one another in origin, tradition and manner of life as are the nations of Europe. Two-thirds of its inhabitants profess Hinduism in one form or another as their religion, over 77 millions are followers of Islam, and the difference between the two is not only of religion in the stricter sense but also of law and culture. They may be said, indeed, to represent two distinct and separate civilizations. Hinduism is distinguished by the phenomenon of its caste, which is the basis of its religious and social system, and, save in a very restricted field, remains unaffected by contact with the philosophies of the West; the religion of Islam, on the other hand, is based upon the conception of the equality of man.

Jinnah added, 'Perhaps no truer description of India has been compressed into a paragraph.' Then:

> The British people, being Christians, sometimes forget the religious wars of their own history and today consider religion as a private and personal matter between man and God. This

can never be the case in Hinduism and Islam, for both these religions are definite social codes which govern not so much man's relation with his God, as man's relation with his neighbour. They govern not only his law and culture, but every aspect of his social life, and such religions, essentially exclusive, completely preclude that merging of identity and unity of thought on which Western democracy is based. . . .

At the end of his article, Jinnah used the significant phrase, 'two nations': he wrote, '. . . a constitution must be evolved that recognizes that there are in India two nations, who must both share the governance of their common motherland.' This was possibly the last time that he spoke of a 'common motherland'. Two weeks later, he presided over the All-India Muslim League session at Lahore, where, on March 23, the 'Pakistan Resolution' was passed.

A few days before, Sir Percival Griffiths dined with Mr Jinnah. During dinner, Jinnah 'declared that at the stage of imperial rule where self-government was not in sight, the British were the finest administrators known to history, but when politics and national feeling had begun to count, they completely failed to understand the mentality of subject races. "You talk," he said, "of the unity of India, but you ought to know that it is a chimera, existing nowhere except in your minds and in the external unity which you wisely forced on the country. You go on to talk of parliamentary democracy and you fail to realize that the assumptions on which it depends have no application at all to Indian conditions."'

Sir Percival Griffiths wrote that Jinnah 'went on to develop, cogently and impressively, his two-nation theory and to expound the full Pakistan demand. . . . The writer and others present raised all the obvious objections—economic dangers, frontier problems, military and administrative difficulties. Mr Jinnah brushed them all aside and completely refused to discuss details. This capacity for adhering to a clearcut idea and ignoring all difficulties of detail and procedure was perhaps Mr Jinnah's greatest source of strength. From this time onwards, he who had for long been the apostle of the unity of India set his face steadfastly towards partition and would not be deflected either by blandishments or by threats.'[1]

In Lahore, during these days, the earth wrestling-ring on the edge

[1] *The British Impact on India*, pp. 342-3.

1940: 'PAKISTAN'

of the city was being prepared for the Muslim League session. An immense tented enclosure was to shield the delegates from the sun, and from their opponents. Within the city was the nucleus of a riot : the Khaksars, a Muslim group founded on Nazi lines—anti-Jinnah, anti-Muslim League, and led by a malcontent educated at Cambridge—were fired on by the police. Thirty persons were killed during the episode, and many were wounded.

Three days later, on March 22, Jinnah arrived in Lahore and he immediately visited the wounded Khaksars in hospital. This tactful act of charity calmed some of the bewildered people, but when the Muslim League session opened, on the same day, there were disturbances, and shouts of protest from a few of the crowd. One man who was present has described the scene : " Mr Jinnah stood up to speak. There were some murmurs, but he stood calmly ; and while the crowd settled into silence, he lit a cigarette and looked over them with his compelling eye. From then, they listened and did not utter a word."

In his Presidential Address, Jinnah repeated the arguments already described, but he also introduced one new theme : he recalled that " a committee of ladies " had been appointed at the previous session, and he said :

> . . . I believe that it is absolutely essential for us to give every opportunity to our women to participate in our great struggle of life and death. Women can do a great deal within their homes, even under purdah . . . if political consciousness is awakened among our women, remember, your children will not have much to worry about. . . .

Jinnah waited some years before he spoke frankly of the ' crime against humanity ', that Muslim women should be ' shut up within the four walls of houses as prisoners.' In 1940, at Lahore, where the majority of Muslims kept purdah, he was cautious ; but he believed, as he said many times later, that " no nation can rise to the height of glory unless its women are side by side with the men."

Next day, March 23, the Muslim Premier of Bengal, ' Sher-e-Bangla A. K. Fazlul Huq,' moved the resolution that was to divide India. Its chief provision was :

> . . . that it is the considered view of this session of the All-India Muslim League that no constitutional plan would be work-

THE LAHORE RESOLUTION

able in this country or acceptable to Muslims unless it is designed on the following basic principle, namely, that geographically contiguous units are demarcated into regions which should be so constituted, with such territorial readjustments as may be necessary, [and] that the areas in which the Muslims are numerically in a majority, as in the North-Western and Eastern zones of India, should be grouped to constitute 'Independent States' in which the constituent units shall be autonomous and sovereign.

Some time after this meeting, Jinnah turned to Matlub Saiyid, who had been present at the Lahore session, and said, "Iqbal is no more amongst us, but had he been alive he would have been happy to know that we did exactly what he wanted us to do."

The Indian newspapers coined the phrase, 'Pakistan Resolution' for their headlines next morning. Jinnah adopted it ; and in a speech that he made later in the year, he said, " No power on earth can prevent Pakistan."

PART FIVE

A BIRTHDAY PRESENT

ON December 25, 1940, Mohammed Ali Jinnah was sixty-four years old. A startling white lock showed in his grey hair, but he was still as slim, erect, and quick in his movements as when he was young. His name was now the one light of hope for most of the Muslims in India : not merely the educated classes, but also the wide-eyed, illiterate masses, called him *Quaid-i-Azam*, the Great Leader.

His heart might have warmed a little at the reception given him on his birthday : eighty-three eminent men, of all religions, paid tributes to him. Dr C. R. Reddy, a Hindu, Vice-Chancellor of the Andhra University, wrote, ' He is the pride of India and not the private possession of the Muslims. . . .' Sir Frederick James, a Christian, wrote of Jinnah's ' unique parliamentary gifts,' and then—' He is a powerful debater and a first class strategist . . . a leader of men, fearless and incorruptible.' Sir R. K. Shanmukhan Chitty, another Hindu, wrote, ' Mr Jinnah is a realistic patriot . . . he yields to none in his enthusiasm to obtain the political emancipation of his country.' Sir Cowasjee Jehangir, a Parsee, who had known him in the first days of his briefless struggle in the Law Courts, recalled Jinnah's ' sturdy independence,' and ' courage and tenacity.' He added, " He has never put self or his own interests before those of his country." Rao Bahadur M. C. Rajah, a Hindu, and a leader of the Depressed Classes —the ' Untouchables '—contributed a thoughtful message that should be read at length :

> All religions hold the belief that God sends suitable men into the world to work out His plans from time to time, and at critical junctures. I regard Mr Jinnah as the man who has been called upon to correct the wrong ways into which the people of India have been led by the Congress, under the leadership of Mr Gandhi. The Congress did a great service to the country so long as it followed the lines of critical co-operation and co-operative criticism towards the British Government, as laid down by Dadabhai Naoroji and Gokhale. But it took a wrong

turn when it adopted wholesale the non-cooperation programme of Mr Gandhi and assumed an attitude of open hostility towards Britain, and tried to infuse in the minds of the people a spirit of defiance of law and civil disobedience, more or less thinly veiled under a formula of truth and non-violence. Moreover, by Mahatmafying Mr Gandhi, it appealed to the idolatrous superstitions of the Hindus, thus converting the religious adherence of the Hindu section of the population to the Mahatma into political support of his non-cooperation programme. While this strategy was of some avail in hustling the British Government to yield more and more to the demands of Congress, it divided the people into Hindu and non-Hindu sections.

In these circumstances, a man was needed to stand up to Congress and tell its leaders that their organization, however powerful numerically and financially, does not represent the whole of India.

I admire Mr Jinnah and feel grateful to him because, in advocating the cause of the Muslims, he is championing the claims of all classes who stand the danger of being crushed under the steam roller of a [caste-] Hindu majority, acting under the inspiration and orders of Mr Gandhi. . . .

These birthday tributes to the Quaid-i-Azam came about the time that he moved into a new, splendid house that had been designed and built for him. The old house in Mount Pleasant Road, where he had lived, first as a bachelor and then during the years of his marriage, had been a Goanese bungalow. Perhaps its ghosts had become oppressive, for, in 1939, he had ordered that it should be pulled down ; and above its dust he built a mansion. In the meantime, he had made his home in Little Gibbs Road, higher up on Malabar Hill.

Nothing remains of the temporary house in Little Gibbs Road : in May 1952, a block of apartments was rising from the rubble, and there were few signs that anyone had ever lived there—only twelve cracked white bathroom tiles, leaning against a pile of new red bricks. But the view from the eminence was one for a conqueror to enjoy : the Arabian Sea, framed between the scarlet mohur trees, and the noise of the waves beating on the rocks below ; the waves that beat on the shores of India and Pakistan alike.

Next to the rubble and new bricks is a big house with a lawn and garden. On the day in May 1952 there were three Parsee ladies on the lawn, like fabulous butterflies, in their lovely saris, taking the evening air. When one of them was asked, " Do you know in which house Mohammed Ali Jinnah lived ? " she answered quickly, " Oh, they have pulled it down. It was up *there*. I remember him ; I knew him well. I used to see him almost every day. So erect— and such charm. He always took off his hat and said 'Good morning.' "

The grand house, into which Jinnah moved about the time of his sixty-fourth birthday, is now the residence of the British Deputy High Commissioner, and his name is on the gate. But the Hindu taxi-drivers, scorning the prejudice of partisans, still say, " You mean the Jinnah house," when the traveller asks to be taken there. At the end of a short drive stands the mansion that celebrated the first year of Jinnah's unbridled success ; an edifice of wide balconies, broad, high rooms, and a marble portico leading on to a marble terrace.

In another part of Bombay lives the architect, Mr Claude Batley, who designed the new house for Jinnah. He has recalled that Quaid-i-Azam asked for " a big reception room, a big verandah, and big lawns, for garden parties," and that he appointed a Muslim clerk of works, an English builder, a Hindu plumber, and Italian stonemasons. Jinnah " insisted on choosing the colours of the marble for the terrace and standing by when the pieces of stone were fitted, much to the annoyance of the Italian who was doing the work." " He was most correct in his ideas," added Mr Batley. " His standard was a building that did not leak. Unfortunately, as so often happens with a new house, there was a leak, and he was furious."

The leak was mended and Quaid-i-Azam and Miss Jinnah moved in. The pattern of life they assumed was very different from the old days, when the advocate, at the timid beginning of his political career, sat alone in his study, with neither secretary nor clerk to help him. Now that he had become The Great Leader, he had to build up a little court, so necessary for a man who was about to create a nation.

Jinnah's relations with his staff were revealing : he was an exacting master, but the young men who worked for him were devoted, and their character was fertilized by the example of his integrity. One of them, who worked with Quaid-i-Azam in later years, has described this influence, in an incident from his own experience : he has said, " I was tantalized by the Quaid's aloofness and silence. I was never able to make him relax with me. I suppose that I was piqued because of this, and I wished very much to know what was in his mind. He kept no diary, but there was a little book in which he made occasional entries. He kept it locked in a drawer. One day I found it on his desk, and, being alone, I turned over the pages. 'Here,' I thought, 'are the innermost thoughts none of us are allowed to know.' I stole the book; I took it to my room, and I kept it for two hours. Then my conscience began to talk to me, because he was not the sort of man one would ever wish to deceive. So I took the book back again, and put it on the desk where I found it."

* * *

1940-1942

SIR PERCIVAL GRIFFITHS wrote of the 'blandishments' that the Quaid-i-Azam had to resist after he decided to fight for the partition of India. The first of these came in June 1940, when the Viceroy, Lord Linlithgow, asked Jinnah and Gandhi to visit him in Simla: he hoped that they might inspire both Congress and the League to more lively support of Britain's war.

Diwan Chaman Lall and other non-partisan friends believed that India's cause would be strengthened if the two leaders met and talked amiably together, before they were received by the Viceroy. Unfortunately, their pride made this co-operation impossible. Diwan Chaman Lall has said,[1] "I went to Gandhi and proposed that Jinnah should meet him. I found the Mahatma sitting upon a white sheet, eating from a silver bowl. He looked up when I made the proposal, and gave me the surprising answer, 'Adversity makes strange bedfellows.'"

Diwan Chaman Lall then went to Jinnah, at the Cecil Hotel, in Simla, and 'tried to impress upon him the advantages that might come if only he and Gandhi could meet.' He asked Jinnah, "May I tell Gandhi that you wish to see him?" Jinnah answered, "No. I am willing to see him, if he wishes; but I am not willing that you should say that I *wish* to see him."

Diwan Chaman Lall went back to the Mahatma and asked, "Do

[1] To the author.

THE VICEROY'S PLEDGE

you wish to see Jinnah?" Gandhi answered, "If I were to say that I wish to see Jinnah, it would be a lie. But if Jinnah wishes to meet me, I will walk on bare feet from here to the Cecil Hotel."

The Mahatma and the Quaid-i-Azam did not meet, and the fragile hope of amity, before seeing the Viceroy, was lost.

Lord Linlithgow proceeded with his plan. On July 1, Jinnah gave him his ' Tentative Proposals ', in which he repeated the demands of the Muslims for the division of India, and the terms under which his followers would support the war. (In a private letter to a friend, Jinnah wrote, ' We have not put any difficulty in the way of war efforts . . . our position is that of benevolent neutrality.')

The Viceroy replied to the ' Tentative Proposals ' with a pledge : that His Majesty's Government ' could not contemplate the transfer of their present responsibilities for the peace and welfare of India to any system of government whose authority is directly denied by large and powerful elements in India's national life. Nor could they be parties to the coercion of such elements into submission to such a government.' The long, cautious phrases of the Viceroy's pledge meant, simply, that Britain would not withdraw from India and leave the Muslims to the mercy of the Hindus.

Knowing the end of the drama—that half a million people were to die when India was parted—and three times their number mutilated —the pages of political argument during these years make sad reading. The acres of words—the confusion of good motives and expediency, and spite—lead toward the ultimate phoenix of Pakistan : in the light of this achievement, the words seem like a rubble of dead bones, and over them blows the cold wind of failure.

The political historian will be obliged to consider all these episodes of crisis, conference and disillusionment : for the biographer of Jinnah, the task is less complicated. Quaid-i-Azam was old and tired, and, as was revealed later, already fatally ill. But the way of his mind, and his will, suffered no deviation during the coming years. He had said, at Lucknow, " Think one hundred times before you take a decision, but once the decision is taken, stand by it as one man." He obeyed his own precept : he allowed no argument and none of the tricks of political expediency to interrupt the clear arrow flight of his intentions.

Jinnah's power as leader of the Muslim League was tested and proved in 1941, when the Viceroy appointed the Muslim Provincial Premiers as members of his National Defence Council. Jinnah ' obtained their immediate resignations because the invitations had not come through party channels.' [1] He wrote, in a private letter to Major W. H. Gardiner,[2] on July 26, 1941, '. . . I must say that it was highly improper on the part of the Viceroy, holding the position he does, to have canvassed the Muslim League Premiers and other Muslim Leaguers. . . . I feel that the Viceroy's conduct in approaching them behind the back of the leader and the Executive was most deplorable.'

The next lamp of hope was waved by Sir Stafford Cripps, who arrived in India with his Mission, in March 1942. Jinnah had already talked to Sir Stafford during his previous visit to India, in 1940, and he had been disappointed by the results of the meeting. He wrote to Major Gardiner, on December 26, '. . . I had a frank talk with Sir Stafford Cripps on his recent visit to India, explaining the Muslim point of view. His expression of agreement with me appeared genuine, but even had he disagreed I feel there was no justification for the complete misrepresentation of my views, amounting to nothing less than deliberate falsehood, which he published in a newspaper on his return to England. I am aware that he was not at the time a member of your [Fabian] party, but I thought he occupied an important position in the public, and in his own profession.'

Sir Stafford Cripps landed in Delhi on March 22, and, one week later, he declared that "His Majesty's Government" had "decided to lay down in precise and clear terms the steps which they propose shall be taken for the earliest possible realization of self-government in India." The object was to create "a new Indian Union," which would "constitute a Dominion, associated with the United Kingdom and the other Dominions by a common allegiance to the Crown, but equal to them in every respect, in no way subordinate in any aspect of its domestic or external affairs." All this, "immediately upon the cessation of hostilities."

Without mentioning Pakistan, or the Muslims, the Draft Declaration conceded ' the right of any Province ' that was ' not prepared to accept the new Constitution, to retain its present constitutional position.' And Britain was willing, 'With such non-acceding

[1] *The Making of Pakistan*, Richard Symonds, p. 64.
[2] A Fabian, with whom Jinnah exchanged a long correspondence about this time.

Provinces, should they so desire . . . to agree upon a new Constitution, giving them the same full status as the Indian Union. . . .'

The time chosen for this offer was perhaps inopportune. Britain was still at war, and the fortunes of battle were uncertain in most theatres of conflict. In March, the Japanese had entered Rangoon : it was with them, in the East, that India's chief danger lay. On March 18, Mr Roosevelt had written to Mr Churchill, ' The Japanese may land on the sea-coast of Burma. They might bombard Calcutta.' [1]

The leaders of Congress, and of the League, might have thought more of the Mission if Sir Stafford had arrived at a time when the Allies were marching to victory. But the leaders of both parties seemed to believe that Britain would be defeated : they declined the Cripps offer, which was allegedly described by Gandhi as a ' post-dated cheque on a bank that was obviously crashing.' Mr Casey, who records this episode,[2] wrote that he had ' undisputed and conclusive evidence ' that the rejection ' was greatly regretted in 1943 and 1944, when it was clear that we were going to win the war.'

It is refreshing to turn from the piles of books and documents describing the Mission, to the simplicity of Sir Winston Churchill's record of the events, from the day when Sir Stafford, ' with great public spirit, volunteered for this thankless and hazardous task,' to the day, one month later, when he telegraphed from India, ' I have tonight received long letter from Congress President stating that Congress is unable to accept proposals. . . . There is clearly no hope of agreement and I shall start home on Sunday.'

Later the same day, Sir Stafford sent a further telegram to the Prime Minister : ' My own view is that despite failure the atmosphere has improved quite definitely. Nehru has come out in a fine statement for total war against the Japanese. Jinnah has pledged me unwavering support of the Moslems. . . . We are not depressed, though sad at the result. Now we must get on with the job of defending India.' [3]

Even Sir Winston Churchill's account of the failure of the Mission reveals little awareness of the separate plight of the Muslims ; and Mr Roosevelt's letters at the time show, as Sir Winston admits, that the

[1] *The Second World War*, Winston S. Churchill, Vol. IV, p. 177.
[2] *An Australian in India*, p. 52.
[3] *The Second World War*, Vol. IV, p. 192.

President's mind was ' back at the American War of Independence,' and that he ' thought of the Indian problem in terms of the thirteen colonies fighting George III at the end of the eighteenth century.'[1]

The thoughts of the Congress leaders, on this offer from their British overlords, were naturally confused by the more terrible threat of danger from the advancing forces of the Japanese. Mahatma Gandhi wrote, ' The presence of the British in India is an invitation to Japan to invade India. Their withdrawal would remove the bait. . . . Free India would be better able to cope with invasion.'[2] (At this time, fear of the Japanese was such in Calcutta that Indian servants deserted their posts and escaped inland. British officers, including the military secretary to the Governor, finished their tasks by day and worked in the British soldiers' canteen at night, in place of the Indians who had fled.)

Pandit Nehru said, on the day after Sir Stafford's departure, " We are not going to surrender to the invader. In spite of all that has happened, we are not going to embarrass the British war effort in India."

In his Presidential Address to the Allahabad session of the Muslim League, in April, Jinnah did not relate the failure of the Mission to the perils of the war : he said, " I think I am echoing your feelings when I say that the Mussalmans feel deeply disappointed that the entity and integrity of the Muslim nation has not been expressly recognized. . . . Muslim India will not be satisfied unless the right of national self-determination is unequivocally recognized.

" I trust that in order to give real effect to the principles of Pakistan and Muslim self-determination, His Majesty's Government, and Sir Stafford Cripps, will not hesitate to make the necessary adjustments on their behalf. Let us hope that there will emerge out of these negotiations a settlement that will be just, honourable, and finally acceptable to all."

Elder British statesmen and soldiers who had been in India for many years, were aggrieved over the continuous failure to bring Congress, the League, and Westminster together with one mind. They believed in their own good intentions, and that their service in India was not all for their own selfish sake : they believed also that the Indians had been allowed as many reforms as they could absorb, in view of the

[1] *The Second World War*, Vol. IV, p. 194.   [2] Ibid., p. 196.

racial bitterness, class antagonism and illiteracy that manacled the country and held it back. They knew that concessions towards freedom should be granted, not as demanded by the Indians, but according to their capacity to administer them, with justice and cool reason. This view was shared by Mr Casey : his was not a prejudiced English view ; he had been born in Australia, another land that had 'suffered' under the yoke of Britain, and emerged—like any boy from a good school—proud and independent, but still devoted to his Alma Mater.

Mr Casey wrote of the 'melancholy story' of India— 'a story of hope and sincere endeavour frustrated by fear and suspicion.' Then, 'We have not been dilatory in India by way of constitutional reforms. We have pressed on with all the speed that was wise and practicable —indeed we have pressed on probably in advance of the ability of the country to take advantage of the progressive steps towards self-government that we have made possible.' [1]

* * *

1942-1944: AN ASSASSIN, AND THE DOCTORS

BIOGRAPHERS of great men seldom refer to the medical reports of the doctors who have attended them. A man's ailments are a powerful influence on both his judgments and his acts : his medical history should therefore be considered chronologically, alongside the record of his work, if one is to comprehend the circumstances behind all that he does. This study is sometimes impossible with Mohammed Ali Jinnah, because of the lack of early records, and because he was impatient with ill-health—his own or anyone else's : also, he seemed reluctant to confide in his doctors.

As early as 1941, Jinnah was reported in the newspapers to be 'unwell.' Major Gardiner wrote to him, proposing a diet that would have been more acceptable to Gandhi : he suggested, 'Milk is the best food in the world, but it must be unpasteurized and unboiled. Next, eggs, raw if you can bear them, whipped into some milk, and, finally, lots of fresh fruit and vegetables.'

Jinnah answered, on May 3, 'It is very kind of you. There is

[1] *An Australian in India*, p. 57.

nothing serious the matter with me. It is entirely due to over-work. I intend to have a complete rest, and peace, which is the only prescription for my case.'

But it was not in Jinnah's nature to rest, and he worked on. When Sir Evelyn Wrench talked to him in Bombay, in 1942, he asked the Quaid about his chief recreations—what he did to forget his 'office worries.' Jinnah answered, "My profession is such that it never allows me time for recreation. . . ."

Jinnah worked in the small office, near the front door of his new house, shut off from his private rooms. The office was accessible to callers: on the floor were his papers, in tidy piles. The edges of his desk were his horizon, for most of the day and night—except when Liaquat Ali Khan induced him to go out on great speaking tours in the provinces. The force of his convictions gave a peculiar power to his oratory: his raised finger, admonishing, or accentuating a point, and the thoughtful use of his monocle, compelled big audiences into wonder, and agreement, even if they could not understand all the words he used.

When the tours were ended, he would return to his desk, in memory of the discipline that had begun fifty years before, in the lodging in Russell Road, where the bright lights of Olympia had failed to tempt him to pleasure. As a boy of sixteen he had bent over his books, to pass his Bar examinations in less time than any Indian student before him: the industrious habits endured in the man of sixty-six. He worked out the intricate plans to increase the power of the Muslim League, and he wrote brief, bald notes to his workers, all over India, like a general giving orders in the field. He had even created his own newspaper and named it *Dawn* : it was printed in English, and it helped to fight the propaganda of the British and Hindus, who owned ninety-five per cent of the newspapers in India.

Jinnah had always been indifferent to the value, or the pleasure, of popularity ; and his scorn of pressmen had loosened many crisp anecdotes among the newspaper offices in Bombay. The journalists respected Quaid-i-Azam, but, as one of them recalled, "He never tried to cajole us. He was the most difficult of all politicians to deal with : he was fastidious and proud with us : he would summon us to his house, but he would never offer us a cup of tea or a cigarette. He was above even such trivial bribery as this."

GANDHI'S 'OPEN REBELLION'

"One day in Bombay, at the end of a conference, when Mr Jinnah was about to leave the room, one of my colleagues asked a question. Back came the reprimand, 'The conference is over; you're only wasting time.'"

It was strange that a man who had never employed a press agent and who spurned the favours of journalists, should own, and direct the policy of a newspaper : but it was significant that *Dawn* prospered ; and that, when Pakistan was created, Quaid-i-Azam took his newspaper with him to Karachi, where it became the most authentic and important journal in the capital of the new country.

The year 1942 was horrible with the lawlessness and infamies so alien to Jinnah's 'constitutional methods.' Nehru had said that, despite the failure of the Cripps Mission, the Congress leaders would not 'embarrass the British war effort.' They did not keep their promise : in July, Gandhi warned the British that there was 'no question of one more chance,' and he threatened 'open rebellion.' In August he inaugurated his 'Quit India' movement : the two crisp words were sprawled in white paint, on many walls—in English— by his followers. In the same month the Mahatma spoke before the All-India Congress Committee at Bombay : he said, "Mr Jinnah does not seem to believe in the Congress programme and in the Congress demand. But I cannot wait till Mr Jinnah is converted, for the immediate consummation of India's freedom."

The increasing, ruthless sabotage that followed Gandhi's 'open rebellion' caused Jinnah deep grief. One evening his secretary went into the office, late at night, and found his master bent over the desk with his head in his hands. Before him was a small volume of Milton, on top of the newspapers he had been reading. Might one imagine that the book was open at the lines—

> For what can war but endless war still breed ?
> Till truth and right from violence be freed.

* * *

By mid-August 1942, Mahatma Gandhi, Pandit Nehru, and the other members of the Congress 'High Command', had been imprisoned as a seditious danger to the country. All except Gandhi remained under arrest until the war was over. The Quaid reaped the benefits of his lawful and constitutional ways : he remained at his desk and increased the forces of the Muslim League, throughout the country.

On the afternoon of July 26, 1943, Jinnah was working alone in his room. A new menace to his plans had arisen during June and early July, from the Khaksars [1]—the group of Muslims who had opposed him from the beginning. There had been many letters from them, accusing him of treachery for not aligning the Muslim League with Congress, in a united front against the British. Some days there had been as many as fifty telegrams, letters and postcards, condemning him and threatening his life. On June 27, one of the leading Khaksars had written, 'If your ultimate goal is Pakistan, then in order to bring the stage of its attainment nearer, for God's sake arrive at a compromise with Gandhiji. . . . We request you to see immediately Gandhiji in jail, otherwise [some] of us, risking our lives, shall make you the target of our bullets. . . .'

A few days later, the assassin had been chosen. He was Rafiq Sabir Mazangavi, a young man, about thirty, 'slim and well built, with shaggy black hair and a pointed beard.' [2] Rafiq Sabir arrived in Bombay on July 6 : he got into a tramcar ' with his sparse bedding under his arm,' and went to a hostel where he registered under a false name. On July 24, having bought a knife, he did not ' find the blade sharp enough to his liking,' so he went to ' a knife grinding shop ' and had ' the knife sharpened.'

On Monday, July 26, Rafiq Sabir walked up to Malabar Hill, about 1.15 p.m., when Jinnah had finished his lunch and was already back at his desk. The assassin salaamed the watchman at the gate and said he wished to see Quaid-i-Azam. He was taken to the secretary, who explained that Jinnah was very busy. At that moment, he walked into the room.

In his evidence at the trial of Rafiq Sabir, Jinnah described the next moments. "My whole mind was on my correspondence and, just as I was about to leave the room, in the twinkling of an eye the accused sprang at me and gave me a blow with his clenched fist on my left jaw.

---

[1] See p. 128.

[2] The facts in this story are taken from *Jinnah Faces an Assassin*, by 'A Barrister-at-Law' (Thacker & Co., Ltd., Bombay), and from the account of a police officer, Sheik Abdul Cadir, who was present soon after the attack was made on Quaid-i-Azam and who is now serving in Pakistan.

'DIALOGUE WITH A GIANT'

I naturally reeled back a bit, when he pulled out a knife from his waist."

With 'murderous intent,' Rafiq Sabir had raised his 'huge open knife,' but Jinnah caught the man's hand in his and softened the blow. The only damage was a wound on his chin, and some cuts on his hand, which were bandaged by his sister. During the struggle that followed, many people appeared, among them Jinnah's chauffeur, who snatched the knife from Rafiq Sabir. The Khaksar was ultimately overpowered, taken to gaol, tried, and sentenced by the British judge to 'five years' rigorous imprisonment.'

The pathos of the assassin's act was revealed when he pleaded that he believed it to be his duty to kill Jinnah because he was 'a tool in the hands of British Imperialism.'

Jinnah was attended by a doctor, then he returned to his desk. He wrote to a friend in Quetta, 'I was subjected to a murderous attack, but thank God that I have escaped with minor injuries.' He also telephoned his daughter, still estranged from him and living in another part of Bombay, and said, "I am all right."

* * *

The English newspapers and reviews for these war years contain few articles about Quaid-i-Azam. Perhaps his indifference to publicity, and his brusque reception of pressmen, discouraged visiting writers who might have sought him out and made him into a 'very important person' to English readers. One of the first to enjoy the Quaid's confidence was Mr Beverley Nichols, who wrote a lively, prophetic account of their meeting, in his book on India.[1] He called the chapter, 'Dialogue with a Giant.'

Mr Nichols met Quaid-i-Azam on December 18, 1943, five months after the attempted assassination. He wrote:

> The most important man in Asia is sixty-seven, tall, thin, and elegant, with a monocle on a grey silk cord, and a stiff white collar which he wears in the hottest weather. He suggests a gentleman of Spain, a diplomat of the old school; one used to see his like sitting in the window of the St. James's Club, sipping Contrexville while he read *Le Temps*, which he propped against a Queen Anne toast-rack stacked with toast Melba.

[1] *Verdict on India*, Beverley Nichols (Jonathan Cape), pp. 188-97.

Jinnah leaned over the table, holding his monocle between his busy fingers and said, " The Muslims are a Nation. If you grant that, and if you are an honest man, you must grant the principle of Pakistan." Then, " The Muslims are a tough people, lean and hardy. If Pakistan means that they will have to be a little tougher, they will not complain." Mr Nichols then asked him, " Are the Muslims likely to be richer or poorer under Pakistan ? " and Jinnah answered, " What conceivable reason is there to suppose that the gift of nationality is going to be an economic liability ? . . . How any European can get up and say that Pakistan is ' economically impossible ' after the Treaty of Versailles is really beyond my comprehension. The great brains who cut Europe into a ridiculous patchwork of conflicting and artificial boundaries are hardly the people to talk economics to us. . . ."

Mr Nichols described ' the difference between Jinnah and the typical Hindu politician ' as the difference ' between a surgeon and a witch doctor . . . a surgeon you could trust, even though his verdict was harsh.'

During the talk, Jinnah referred several times to Mahatma Gandhi and his followers : he said, " . . . our outlook is not only fundamentally different but often radically antagonistic to the Hindus. We are different *beings*. There is *nothing* in life which links us together." Then, " The one thing which *keeps* the British in India is the false idea of a United India, as preached by Gandhi."

At this time, Gandhi was still a prisoner, in one of the Aga Khan's palaces, where he was able to enjoy all the refreshments of a contemplative man, in comfort and peace. But he was seventy-four years old, and ill ; so, in May 1944, the Government released him. His aim had not changed during his two years' detention : he still hoped to convert Jinnah to his ' idea of a United India ' ; and on July 17 he wrote to him, addressing him as ' Brother Jinnah '.

> . . . I have not written to you since my release. But today my heart says that I should write to you. We will meet whenever you choose. Don't regard me as the enemy of Islam or of the Muslims of this country. I am the friend and servant of not only yourself but of the whole world. Do not disappoint me.

A DOCTOR'S OPINION

Jinnah answered, from Srinagar, in Kashmir, where he was trying to rest :

> ... I shall be glad to receive you at my house in Bombay on my return, which will probably be about the middle of August. By that time I hope that you will have recuperated your health fully and will be returning to Bombay. I would like to say nothing more till we meet.
> I am very pleased to read in the Press that you are making very good progress, and I hope that you will soon be all right.

The meeting between the leaders was delayed, by illness and doctors. On August 22, after an exhausting tour, Jinnah wrote to a friend, ' I broke down because of the crushing, gushing affection of the people, from the day I started from Srinagar. I had to pay the penalty for having satisfied them to the utmost of my capacity. But I am glad to tell you that I am almost all right and will soon be able to resume my work.'

In September, Quaid-i-Azam was being treated for an ailment in his lungs, and he sought the advice of two doctors. The first of them enjoyed a unique experience : he treated both Jinnah and Gandhi at the same time.

This first doctor recalls Jinnah as ' a good patient.' He has said, " As a politician, he kept his distance. Gandhi was unclothed before his disciples : Jinnah was clothed before *his* disciples : that was the difference between them. Gandhi was an *instrument* of power : Jinnah *was* power. He was a cold rationalist in politics ; a man with a one-track mind, but with great force behind it. That was the fundamental difference between them."

The doctor said that Jinnah was ' potentially kind,' but that he had been ' deeply hurt ' in his life, ' by the years of poverty in Bombay and by the failure of his marriage.' " All this," he said, " made Jinnah guard himself from his potential kindness : it also made him put up defences against close personal relationships."

The doctor then spoke of Gandhi and Jinnah in terms of their personal cleanliness. He said, " Gandhi used to say, ' Cleanliness is not next to Godliness : it *is* Godliness.' He was scrupulously clean in all his physical habits, yet he would perform dirty work and soil his hands, in doing some kindness for the poor. Jinnah was not like that: his cleanliness was a personal mania. He would wash his hands and change his underclothes several times a day. But he did not wish to touch people: it was as if he wished to be immaculate and alone."

Jinnah's second doctor was a Parsee, Surgeon-Commander Jal Patel, now a consulting physician in Bombay and Honorary Physician to the President of the Indian Union. He has provided his own, more realistic account of Jinnah's illness at this time.[1]

" One day Mr Jinnah rang me up—some time in September 1944 —and said, ' I am Mr Jinnah. I want an appointment.' I examined him and found that his blood pressure was about 90. I think he was conducting his difficult meetings with Mahatma Gandhi at that time, working at full pressure. He was very frail and weak and I told him that he needed both rest and a tonic . . . he told me that he had had attacks of dysentery in the past, some pain in his chest, and a cough. There were signs in the base of his lungs of unresolved pneumonia. He showed me an X-ray picture of his chest: it confirmed my diagnosis.

" I gave him calcium injections, tonics, and also short-wave diathermy treatment. The cough subsided, and he went off to the hills for a rest. He came back, having increased his weight by eighteen pounds. The fact got into the newspapers, coupled with my name. I went to Mr Jinnah and said, ' Some fool has done this.' He answered, ' I was the fool: why shouldn't I express my gratitude to the man who served me so well?'"

* * *

1944: JINNAH, GANDHI, AND LIAQUAT ALI KHAN

THE ' difficult meetings with Mahatma Gandhi ' had begun in Jinnah's house on September 9. There is a little book,[2] with an introduction by Liaquat Ali Khan, that tells the story of these talks, during eighteen days, when the two veteran leaders tried

[1] In conversations with the author, in Bombay, during May 1952.
[2] *Jinnah-Gandhi Talks*, published by the Central Office, All-India Muslim League, November 1944.

to reconcile their irreconcilable aims. They were cautious : both insisted that these conversations should be confirmed after each meeting, in an exchange of letters. By September 15, they were already at variance : that evening Gandhi wrote to Jinnah :

> ... In the course of our discussions you have passionately pleaded that India contains two nations, i.e. Hindus and Muslims, and that the latter have their homelands in India as the former have theirs. The more your argument progresses, the more alarming your picture appears to me. It would be alluring if it were true. But my fear is that it is wholly unreal. I find no parallel in history for a body of converts and their descendants claiming to be a nation apart from the parent stock. If India was one nation before the advent of Islam, it must remain one in spite of the change of faith of a very large body of their children.
>
> You do not claim to be a separate nation by right of conquest, but by reason of acceptance of Islam. Will the two nations become one if the whole of India accepted Islam?

Jinnah replied, two days later :

> ... We maintain that Muslims and Hindus are two major nations by any definition or test as a nation. We are a nation of a hundred million, and what is more, we are a nation with our own distinctive culture and civilization, language and literature, art and architecture, names and nomenclature, sense of values and proportion, legal laws and moral codes, customs and calendar, history and traditions, aptitudes and ambitions : in short, we have our own distinctive outlook on life and of life. By all the canons of international Law, we are a nation.

The talks on September 24 and 25 became more realistic : they concerned the actual slicing of the sub-continent, when the hour of partition came.

On the evening of September 24, Gandhi returned to his humble abode, from which he wrote Jinnah a long letter, saying that he was willing to 'recommend to the Congress and the country the acceptance of the claim for separation contained in the Muslim League Resolution of 1940,' on the 'following terms'.

Gandhi began:

> I proceed on the assumption that India is not to be regarded as two or more nations but as one family consisting of many members, of whom the Muslims living in the North-West zones, i.e. Baluchistan, Sindh, North-West Frontier Province, and that *part* of Punjab where they are in absolute majority over all other elements, and in *parts* of Bengal and Assam where they are in absolute majority, desire to live in separation from the rest of India.[1]

Jinnah replied that 'If this term were accepted and given effect to, the present boundaries of these provinces would be maimed and mutilated beyond redemption,' and the Muslims would be left 'only with the husk.'

The Mahatma's second condition was:

> The areas should be demarcated by a Commission approved by the Congress and the League. The wishes of the inhabitants of the areas demarcated should be ascertained through the votes of the adult population of the areas, or through some equivalent method.

Jinnah complained that Gandhi's proposal would mean 'That even in these mutilated areas so defined, the right of self-determination will not be exercised by the Muslims, but by the inhabitants of those areas so demarcated. . . .'

Gandhi presented his third point: he wrote,

> If the vote is in favour of separation, it shall be agreed that these areas shall form a separate state as soon as possible *after India is free from foreign domination*, and can therefore be constituted into two sovereign Independent States.[2]

Jinnah would not agree: he proposed that they should 'come to a complete settlement' of their own, '*immediately*', and by their 'united front and efforts' do everything in their power 'to secure the freedom and independence of the peoples of India *on the basis of Pakistan and Hindustan*.'[3]

The fourth point revealed that, whatever principle of 'separation' Gandhi was willing to concede to the Muslims, 'after' the British

[1], [2], [3] Author's italics.

M. A. JINNAH AND MAHATMA GANDHI, IN 1944

M. A. JINNAH AND LIAQUAT ALI KHAN, IN 1947

departed, he was not prepared to grant to Pakistan the full sovereignty implied in the phrase, 'sovereign Independent States.' He wrote:

> There shall also be a treaty of separation which should also provide for the efficient and satisfactory administration of foreign affairs, defence, internal communications, customs, commerce and the like, which must necessarily continue to be the matters of common interest between the contracting parties.

To this, Jinnah replied:

> ... According to the Lahore Resolution, as I have already explained it to you, all these matters, which are the lifeblood of any state, cannot be delegated to any central authority or government. The matter of security of the two states, and the natural and mutual obligations that may arise out of physical contiguity, will be for the constitution-making body of Pakistan and that of Hindustan ... to deal with on the footing of their being two independent states. ...

From this time, the 'talks' fell to pieces. Jinnah made his complaint, briefly, in an interview [1] with a representative of the London *News Chronicle*. He said, 'The offer made to us is an insult to intelligence;' and he explained, 'There is only one practical, realistic way of resolving Muslim-Hindu differences. This is to divide India into two sovereign parts, of Pakistan and Hindustan, by the recognition of the whole of the North-West Frontier Province, Baluchistan, Sind, Punjab, Bengal and Assam as sovereign Muslim territories, as they now stand, and for each of us to trust the other to give equitable treatment to Hindu minorities in Pakistan and Muslim minorities in Hindustan. We are prepared to trust twenty-five million Muslims to them if they will trust us. ... The fact is, the Hindus want some kind of agreement which will give them some form of control. They will not reconcile themselves to our complete independence.'

Thirteen days after this interview, Kanji Dwarkadas wrote in his diary,[2] '... I had an hour's talk with Jinnah. I found him ill, weak, depressed. Sitting about two feet away from him I could only hear and follow with difficulty what he was saying. He went on whispering, "Why did Gandhi come to see me if he had nothing

---

[1] October 4, 1944.
[2] *Gandhiji, Through my Diary Leaves*, p. 62.

better to offer?" I asked him if he thought Gandhi came to put him in the wrong and to create public opinion against him. Jinnah said: "No, no. Gandhi was very frank with me and we had very good talks.'"

* * *

There was an episode during the talks, when manners and graciousness prevailed, even between such opponents as these. One day when Mahatma Gandhi went to see the Quaid-i-Azam, they ended their arguments and talked, simply, of their daily life. They were weary —a little like expended boxers, finding relief in their parting handshake. Jinnah mentioned that, among his ills, one of his feet was troubled with a nervous rash. The Mahatma sank to the floor and insisted on removing Jinnah's shoe and sock. The scene—of Jinnah in his immaculate clothes, and Gandhi, robed in bare simplicity—is at first amusing, and then touching. The Mahatma held the troubled foot in his hands and said, "I know what will heal you. I shall send it tomorrow morning." Next day, a little box of clay mixture arrived. Jinnah did not use it, but he thanked Gandhi when he came that evening, for one more talk, and told him that the medicine had already relieved the pain.

* * *

During these years, Quaid-i-Azam enjoyed his growing friendship with Liaquat Ali Khan and his beautiful, intelligent wife, Raana. Jinnah and his sister would sometimes join them for an evening at the cinema, or for a game of cards. Once, at the end of a rubber of bridge, Liaquat Ali Khan dared to speak to his leader, of his loneliness: Jinnah smiled at Begum Liaquat and said, "Yes, I might have married again, if I could have found another Raana." When he wrote to them he usually ended his letters, 'My heart is with you both.'

Liaquat Ali Khan had now worked with the Quaid for almost ten years: the affairs and finances of the Muslim League were managed with skill and success, and Jinnah trusted his colleague absolutely. Their friendship, their integrity, and their mutual good humour, had survived all the ethical hazards of public life in the East. The differences between them were perhaps part of this bond: there was perfect amity between the self-made, astringent advocate, raised out of obscurity by his character and talents, and the warm-hearted, devout son of the landed gentry, who had inherited a gift for leadership, without private ambition.

Begum Liaquat Ali Khan has recalled [1] these years when the friendship between Quaid-i-Azam and her husband was being confirmed. "My chief memories of Mr Jinnah are of his immaculate, aloof physical existence, and his incredible honesty. It was not merely honesty as a virtue : it was an obsession. His physical aloofness was shown in the way he would sometimes avoid shaking hands with people. I was told a story of his visit to Baluchistan, when he attended a garden party where he had to meet hundreds of people. Among them was an old chieftain—a Muslim Sirdar—who advanced towards Jinnah and held out his hand. Jinnah, in a sudden mood of aloofness, said, 'If I shake hands with you, I would have to shake hands with all the people here, and for that there is no time.' But it was not rudeness that made him act like that : it was because he existed in a physical world of his own, independent of human contacts. Yet, he could relax, especially with my husband and myself ; and he liked jokes of the schoolboy kind. But his defences were too high for this to happen with strangers.

"Of his integrity—every step he took was on this basis. I remember the time when the Muslim League wished to dispense with annual elections for the Presidency and make Jinnah's appointment permanent. He answered, 'No. Annual elections are important. I must come before you each year, to seek your vote of confidence.'

"People sometimes complained of his brusque manner : this too arose from his honesty and lack of pretence. Once, when some members of the Muslim League told him he should travel third-class on the railway, as Gandhi did, he was furious. He said, 'Do not dictate to me what I should do or should not do. It is not your money I am spending, and I shall live and act as I choose.'"

Begum Liaquat Ali Khan has said of Quaid-i-Azam, "It was his clearness that stirred one's astonishment and admiration—his complete lack of humbug. I seem to remember someone writing about 'twin lamps of truth.' Jinnah's eyes were 'twin lamps of truth.' Only the honest could look him straight in the eye. It was because of this that my husband remained his trusted friend. You will find

[1] In conversations with the author, in Karachi, and London.

people who like dividing the indivisible ; who will suggest that, after Partition, Jinnah would have liked to go his own lonely way, without the allegiance of my husband. This is nonsense : one fact proves this. Back in 1939, when he was still in Bombay, Jinnah wrote his will. Except for one codicil, he never changed it. He appointed my husband as one of his executors, but he never told Liaquat of this trust in him. In all the years till his death, Jinnah never changed his mind. He once described my husband as his ' right hand ' : Liaquat remained so, to the end."

In her final estimate of the Quaid-i-Azam, Begum Liaquat Ali Khan said, " You must remember that Jinnah, apart from his integrity, which was frightening, was a powerful man when he decided to dominate anyone—an individual or a multitude. I have seen him shake his finger at someone and say, ' You are talking nonsense : you do not know what you are talking about.' They always subsided into silence. But his real power was over a great audience. Even with them he would use his monocle ; put it to his eye, remove it, and then speak. All this power over a vast crowd was asserted in spite of the barrier of language. He spoke to them in English— but they listened, bewitched."

PART SIX

1945–1946

WHEN the European War ended in May 1945, the Congress leaders were immediately freed from prison, and the Viceroy, Lord Wavell,[1] presented one more plan, in the long history of plans, with the hope of solving the political impasse between the Muslims and the Hindus. This was discussed at the first Simla Conference, in June.

The British opened their hands a little wider: they proposed that the Viceroy's Executive Council[2] should be wholly 'Indianized', immediately, with only the Viceroy and the Commander-in-Chief as British members; and that the Council should legislate as an 'Interim Government' until the Japanese War ended and a new Constitution could be framed. The negotiations broke down once more: it was accepted that Muslims and Caste Hindus should have equal representation, but neither Lord Wavell, nor the Congress, would agree to Jinnah's demand that the League should be allowed to nominate all the Muslim members. The Quaid was adamant, and the delegates withdrew, having achieved nothing.

Jinnah had not yet brought all the Muslims within the corral of the League: the Prime Minister of the North-West Frontier Province and most of his Ministers were still Congressmen in politics; and the Muslim Prime Minister of the Punjab—Sir Khizr Hayat Khan Tiwana—was opposed to both Jinnah and the League. He led a Unionist Coalition which included Muslims, Hindus and Sikhs. The Quaid had to wait some more months before he could induce responsible Muslim leaders in these areas to join in the cry for Pakistan. He returned to his home in Bombay and his letters to Liaquat Ali Khan became sad: he wrote, 'I am almost all right, but I still need rest badly.'

---

[1] Field-Marshal Viscount Wavell had succeeded the Marquess of Linlithgow as Viceroy in October 1943.

[2] Up to 1941, there was a majority of British members in the Council: in that year it had been expanded to give an Indian majority of three, which, in 1942, was increased to eight.

Jinnah's affairs were suddenly influenced by massive events from the bigger world. In July, the Socialists, under Mr Attlee, were returned to power in Britain; and in August came the unconditional surrender of the Japanese. For the Muslims and Hindus in India, the fear of invasion by a new enemy was thus removed: they were able to devote their energies to their own domestic conflicts, and their indignations against the conqueror already on the field.

The Labour Government in Britain, with many members who were tried friends of India and ardent for reform, hastened the pace of deliverance: one of the early decisions was that general elections should be held in India in January 1946.

The victory of the Muslim League at the polls was overwhelming, both in the Provinces and in the Central Assembly. This was Jinnah's glorious hour: his arduous political campaigns, his robust beliefs and claims, were at last justified. Only the Muslims of the North-West Frontier remained unwilling: but even here, the power of the League was increasing. The votaries of Pakistan were now spread over all India.

Three and a half years before, Nehru had said to an American reporter, 'There is now a demand on the part of some Muslims for partition of India.... Few take it seriously....'[1] The 'few' had become a multitude, and Jinnah was now able to repeat, 'No power on earth can prevent Pakistan.'

On March 1, 1946, Quaid-i-Azam was at a meeting of Muslim League workers in Calcutta. He said, "I am an old man. God has given me enough to live comfortably at this age. Why should I turn my blood into water—run about and take so much trouble? Not for the capitalists, but for you—the poor people." He then recalled the 'abject poverty' of the people in Bengal, when he saw them in 1936. "Some of them did not get food even once a day. I have not seen them recently, but my heart goes out to them. I feel it, and in Pakistan we shall do all in our power to see that everybody can get a decent living."

When Mr S. N. Bakar asked him, "What of the economic situation in Pakistan? There is no iron, no coal, no hydro-electric power, no industries," Jinnah answered, "I am fully aware of this. Our people have had no opportunity to develop these things. I have every

[1] *New York Times Magazine*, July 19, 1942.

faith, and so should you, that, given the opportunity, they will achieve all this. Remember one thing : I am going on, even if it kills me."

*   *   *

It might be said that the body politic in India almost died of a surfeit of conferences. In March 1946, at the behest of the British Cabinet, three of its members sailed for India : they were Lord Pethick-Lawrence—Secretary of State for India—Mr A. V. Alexander, and Sir Stafford Cripps. Their task was to promote, ' in conjunction with the leaders of public opinion, the early realization of self-government in India.' The Viceroy once more summoned the Congress and League leaders, and they met the Cabinet Mission at Simla, on May 5.

The conciliators once more failed to achieve harmony, but the episodes of the next few months must be described, briefly, as they led to the sudden and absolute decision of the British to ' quit India.' When the conference failed, the Cabinet Mission framed and announced their own plan : a central Constituent Assembly was to be formed, with members chosen through communal electorates, on the basis of one member for each million of the population. This Constituent Assembly would frame the new Constitution for the ' Union of India.'

Muslim interests, in this reassembling of political power, were to be safeguarded by a new system of ' grouping ' of the provinces in British India :

Group A : Madras, Bombay, United Provinces, Bihar, Central Provinces, and Orissa—the Hindu-majority group.
Group B : Punjab, North-West Frontier Province, and Sind—the Western, Muslim-majority group.
Group C : Bengal and Assam—the Eastern, Muslim-majority group.

Each of these groups would also have its own constitution, and each would be autonomous in all departments, except Defence, Foreign Affairs, and Communications, which would be controlled by the ' Union of India ' at the centre.

Also, the Cabinet Mission proposed the revival of the Viceroy's plan —rejected at the first Simla Conference—for the formation of an Interim Government, to be in command until the inauguration of the

Constituent Assembly. Here also, Muslim interests were to be cared for. On June 3, Lord Wavell recognized the League's success in the elections by offering them equal representation, with Congress, in the Interim Government. The League and Congress would have five seats each : there would also be one member representing the Sikhs, and one the 'Untouchables.'

On June 6, the Council of the Muslim League met in New Delhi : after many arguments the members agreed, under Jinnah's direction, that 'inasmuch as the basis and the foundation of Pakistan' were 'inherent in the Mission plan, by virtue of the compulsory grouping of the six Muslim provinces,' they would accept the plan 'in the hope' that it would 'ultimately result in the establishment of complete, sovereign Pakistan.'[1]

The League claimed that their support and decision was prompted by an 'earnest desire for a peaceful solution . . . of the Indian constitutional problem.' But Jinnah insisted that the Mission plan was no more than a half-way house to Pakistan ; and he warned the British Government and the Congress that 'the quickest way' to the independence of India was 'to agree to Pakistan.' He raised his inevitable finger, shook it, and said, "Either you agree, or we shall have it in spite of you."

* * *

During these negotiations, Quaid-i-Azam was constantly ill. Soon after the close of the second Simla Conference he was so exhausted that his sister telephoned the doctor in Bombay and asked him to be ready to see her brother when he arrived home.

Dr Jal Patel has described the circumstances of Jinnah's health at this time.[2] "You must consider the weakness of his body when he went to the second Simla Conference in May. While he was there he fell ill again. When he was coming back to Bombay from Simla, some thirty thousand of his followers had prepared to greet him at Central Station. I arranged for him to be taken off at Dadar, a few

---

[1] The 'grouping' plan was acceptable to the Muslims because it recognized the Punjab, and Bengal, as Muslim-majority entities. They achieved less than this in the ultimate partition : both provinces were divided when the frontiers of Pakistan were defined in 1947.

[2] To the author.

miles before the railway terminus in Bombay. When he arrived I saw that he was exhausted, so I induced the stationmaster, who was a Hindu, to allow him to leave by a gate to save climbing the stairs.

"Again it was bronchitis : it was always bronchitis. He had a temperature for ten days. It is possible that he had always had lung trouble : he was completely exhausted, weak and tired."

Dr Patel then related Quaid-i-Azam's medical history to his behaviour at this time : he said, " Let us see what happened to his character—his *moods*—when he was ill in 1946. I remember that he came back from Simla, not only ill, but in a state of depression. He complained that Sir Stafford Cripps had treated him ' shabbily,' and that they were so discourteous to him that he had left the conference in a sulky mood and gone home. Mr A. V. Alexander had telephoned him next morning and said, ' I am sorry, but this climate is not good for our tempers. Lord Pethick-Lawrence says he is sorry ; also that he would like to see you.' Jinnah's answer was, ' Then *he* can come and see me.'

"There," said Dr Patel, " is the petulance that goes with such illness as Jinnah was suffering from."

There is a story told of Quaid-i-Azam's anger, about this time, when he was called to the telephone by the secretary to the Governor of Bombay. He protested, " If His Excellency is too big to come to the telephone, so am I." Then he rang off.

Dr Patel said of this incident, " One must remember how ill he was. The flashes of temper were superficial : in his heart he was a man extraordinarily free of pettiness and small prejudices—especially over racial differences. I went to him once, at the height of the enmity between the Muslims and the Hindus. Jinnah had a Hindu butler, and I said, rather as a joke, ' Aren't you afraid he may do you an injury or something ? ' He answered, ' Oh, no. I like him and I trust him. These days, he seems to be taking an interest in Congress activities, but he's a very good fellow really.' "

★   ★   ★

Pakistani writers accuse Lord Wavell of vacillation and of having broken faith with the Muslims during his last year as Viceroy. Perhaps he made some of his decisions hastily, before he had considered all that they implied : perhaps the maelstrom of changing circumstances was such that no man could have reconciled such opposed factions. On June 3, Lord Wavell had offered the League and the Congress 'equal representation' in the Interim Government, with the addition of two members, one representing the Sikhs and one the 'Untouchables.' Jinnah had agreed to this, but, a few days later, the Viceroy decided to add representatives of the Parsees and the Anglo-Indian community.

On June 16 the Viceroy declared—after conference with the Cabinet Mission—that he hoped 'all parties, especially the two major parties,' would 'co-operate for the successful carrying on of the Interim Government.' Then he promised that, 'In the event of the two major parties, or either of them, proving unwilling' to join, he would 'proceed with the formation of an Interim Government' which would be 'as representative as possible' of those who accepted the plan of the Cabinet Mission.

The Muslims read into this an assurance that, if the members of Congress were 'unwilling' to co-operate, the Viceroy would still form his government without them. Jinnah had been encouraged in this view by a private letter from Lord Wavell, written on June 4, in which he said that he would 'go ahead with the plan,' so far as circumstances permitted, 'if *either* party accepted.' [1]

On June 24, Jinnah learned that Congress had refused to appoint any members to the Interim Government. On the 26th, the Cabinet Mission announced that the plan had been shelved; and the Viceroy —putting his ten-day-old promise aside—formed a 'Caretaker Government' of permanent officials, without reference to the Muslim League, or to the minorities to whom he had promised representation.

With characteristic directness, Jinnah wrote to the Viceroy, 'You have chosen to go back on your pledged word. . . .''

The League nevertheless contested the elections for the Constituent Assembly, early in July. Their success at the polls increased Jinnah's confidence: they won all but three of the 79 Muslim seats. But the elections had been planned on the reformed basis of one member for each million of the various communities: the Hindus, and Congress, were therefore predominant, with 292 seats. Pandit Nehru made it clear that he would exploit this advantage: on July 10, he said there was a 'big probability' that there would 'be no grouping'

[1] *The Making of Pakistan*, Richard Symonds, p. 69.

when the Union of India was formed. Thus he threatened to deny the Muslims the chief benefits promised to them in the Mission plan; the promises Jinnah had accepted, because they offered 'the basis and the foundation of Pakistan.'

The Quaid protested, in a statement to His Majesty's Government,[1] that Nehru had 'made it quite clear' that Congress was 'not going to honour any of the terms of the long-term plan,' and that they were entering the Constituent Assembly only 'to use it as a platform for their propaganda,' in 'utter disregard' of the 'rights and obligations' of the other communities who had agreed to the Cabinet Mission plan.

These arguments, between Jinnah and Nehru, and the Viceroy, were the academic expression of more terrible conflicts that were spreading over most of India. While their masters dallied with law and reason, agitators were already preparing the mass of people for the riots and slaughter that were to come—horror and passions that no form of government could prevent.

During this time, the Viceroy was trying to persuade Nehru to withdraw the Congress decision to boycott the Interim Government. Once more Lord Wavell changed his mind, and he wrote to Jinnah, on July 22, implying that Congress would be appeased if the Muslim League would agree to a revised distribution of seats—six for Congress, five for the League, and three for members representing other minorities.

Jinnah replied, '. . . this is the fourth basis that you are suggesting for the formation of your Interim Government. . . . Every time the Congress turned down the previous three proposals, as you were unable to appease them, or propitiate them; and every time, the departure was prejudicial to the League and in favour of the Congress. . . . Your present proposal clearly destroys the principle of parity . . . and gives a clear majority to the Congress as against the League.'

Jinnah's resentment over the efforts to 'propitiate' Congress was increased when he read the speeches made by Lord Pethick-Lawrence and Sir Stafford Cripps in the British Parliament, on July 18, during the debates on the Mission plan. Sir Stafford Cripps had said, in the Commons, that although " the Muslim League was certainly to be regarded as the major representative of Muslim interests," the Cabinet

[1] *And So To Pakistan*, Altaf Husain, p. 24.

Mission had made it " perfectly clear " to Mr Jinnah that they " could not accept his claim to a monopoly of Muslim appointments " to the Interim Government. In the Lords, the Secretary of State had used the same phrase, that the Quaid-i-Azam had " no monopoly of Muslim appointments."

Thus, not only was Jinnah deprived of the ' equal representation ' which the League had been promised : he was also to be denied his proven right, as President of the League, to leadership of the entire Muslim community in British India—a right which the Viceroy had officially recognized, on June 3, and which had been confirmed by the League's success in the elections for the new Constituent Assembly. In recording these events, Muslim journalists used the words, ' British betrayal.'

During the debates, the Secretary of State had remarked on Jinnah's ' courage and statesmanship ', and said that, " in advance of any pronouncement by Congress," he had induced the League to accept proposals that " differed substantially from the views held and vigorously expressed by his followers until then." In the Commons, Sir Stafford Cripps had also spoken of Jinnah's ' courage and determination ' in accepting the Mission's proposals.

The Quaid was not consoled by these phrases. On July 28, when the Council of the Muslim League met in Bombay, he reviewed the arguments of the Cabinet Mission, and then said, " I feel we have exhausted all reason. It is no use looking to any other source for help or assistance. There is no tribunal to which we can go. The only tribunal is the Muslim Nation."

Then, of the compliment to his own ' courage and statesmanship,' he said, " It is no consolation to me that Lord Pethick-Lawrence and Sir Stafford Cripps have acknowledged that we made very substantial and vital concessions, whereas the Congress has not budged an inch. I wish I could honestly pay a tribute to their courage and statesmanship, which they have so sadly lacked in handling these negotiations."

Late in the evening, after the meeting, a friend called at the house in Mount Pleasant Road. He found Quaid-i-Azam writing the last words of the speech he was to make before the Muslim League Council next day. He has recalled, " My old leader seemed old indeed : he moved away from his desk and we had a drink together.

'DIRECT ACTION'

The glass shook in his hand, and, for the first time in all the years I had known him, he seemed subdued, as if, at last, his burdens were too much."

Next morning Jinnah was refreshed, and he made his startling speech : " I do not think that any responsible man will disagree with me, that we were moved by a desire not to allow the situation to develop into bloodshed and civil war. . . ."

He went on to explain that 'anxiety to try to come to a peaceful settlement' with Congress, had induced the League to accept 'a limited Pakistan,' by leaving the control of Defence, Foreign Affairs, and Communications to the central Union of India. He said, "We offered this unequivocal sacrifice at the altar of Congress," but the compromise had been treated " with defiance and contempt." Jinnah paused and framed his monocle within his curved fingers ; then he lowered his voice and said, ". . . are we alone to be guided by reason, justice, honesty and fair play, when, on the other hand, there are perfidious dealings by Congress ? "

He continued, "I might say that, today, Muslim India . . . is stirred as never before, and has never felt so bitterly. . . . We have learned a bitter lesson—the bitterest, I think, so far. Now there is no room left for compromise. Let us march on."

At this meeting the Muslim League withdrew their acceptance of the Cabinet Mission proposals, and sanctioned 'Direct Action' to force the cause of Pakistan. August 16 was chosen as the day on which, throughout India, the League would explain to the people exactly why its acceptance was cancelled and its policy changed.

The conflict was no longer limited to educated leaders at conference tables : there was already a whisper of distant drums—the rising dust from desperate hordes of refugees—in the decision of the League, ' to achieve Pakistan . . . and to get rid of the present slavery under the British, and the contemplated future of Centre Hindu domination.'

At the end of Quaid-i-Azam's speech, eminent Muslims climbed on to the platform and dramatically renounced the titles and honours they had once accepted from their British rulers.

Miss Fatima Jinnah has since spoken of her brother's state of mind at this time.[1] He expected to be arrested at any moment. The ' cold

[1] Told to the author by Mr Fareed Jafri, former editor of the *Civil and Military Gazette*, Karachi.

logician '—the lover of orderliness and law—revealed the emotions he had always held in check with such exquisite care : before he left the Muslim League meeting, he stood up and declared his willingness to go to gaol. An old man, aged seventy-five, rose and cried, " Quaid-i-Azam shall not go to gaol. We shall offer our lives first. We must form a regiment of *mujahadeen* [holy warriors], and I offer myself to be the first to be fired on by the police, on my bare chest."

Jinnah—one of the few men in India who knew that to die for a cause was easy, but that to live for it called for massive and constant courage—did not answer. He drove home and worked late into the night, on the next move in his campaign.

* * *

About this time Mr R. G. Casey, Governor of Bengal, met Quaid-i-Azam and soon came to appreciate his character and his valour. He wrote :[1]

> It is not too much to say that Mr Jinnah is the only outstanding Muslim of all-India stature in Indian politics today. . . .
> He is tall and very thin. He . . . carries his years well, though he has a look of frailty. . . . He appears to have the legal mind : he holds his cards very close to his chest. He is not a ' warm ' man. . . .
> However, there is something in his eye that hints at a sense of humour and, deeper down, at the memory of human enjoyment. But he is a man of iron discipline, and he has denied himself the luxury of any qualities which might loosen his concentration upon his purpose. He is dogmatic and sure of himself ; I would believe that it does not ever occur to him that he might be wrong. . . .
> Mr. Jinnah's ability and personality are such that it is not much of an exaggeration to say that he *is* the Muslim League. . . . If he says the watchword is to be ' Pakistan', the watchword *is* Pakistan. He is a man whose judgment and authority are not questioned lightly by his colleagues. . . .
> Mr Jinnah is credited with ruling the working committee of the Muslim League with a rod of iron. He is said to tell them what's what, and that they invariably fall into line. At any signs of

[1] *An Australian in India*, pp. 63–6.

MISS FATIMA JINNAH, M. A. JINNAH, LIAQUAT ALI KHAN
AND BEGUM LIAQUAT ALI KHAN

M. A. JINNAH ADDRESSING MUSLIM LEAGUE MEETING,
KINGSWAY HALL, DECEMBER 1946. (See pp. 172-3)

intransigence on what he considers a major point he is said to threaten resignation, after which the argument ceases. . . .

A vast responsibility rests on the shoulders of Mr Jinnah. He is a man well accustomed to authority and responsibility. . . . He is blunt and direct and no one has any doubt what he means when he speaks. A very great deal depends on his handling of affairs over the next year or so—the biggest case he has had.

In a letter [1] recalling his meetings with the Quaid in 1946, Mr Casey wrote, 'I have looked up my personal diary, and I find that I emphasized, in several references, the fact that he looked " very frail." However, he could sustain long periods of active discussion without any sign of tiring—a couple of hours at a time. . . .

' My wife and I dined with him and his sister at Government House in Karachi . . . in March 1948. At this same dinner my wife made some comment about someone or other being " a fanatic." Jinnah said, " Don't decry fanatics. If I hadn't been a fanatic there would never have been Pakistan." '

*   *   *

1946–1947

ON August 8, 1946, following the League's rejection of the Cabinet Mission plan, the Viceroy invited Congress to form an Interim Government, and Nehru accepted. There was a meeting between Nehru and Jinnah, but each of them kept to his lair of stubbornness and their talk came to nothing. Pandit Nehru loved words : Quaid-i-Azam loved the law behind them, and there was no level on which they could meet in harmony. On August 24, the Viceroy announced the names of his Congress-nominated Interim Government, with Nehru as his Vice-President. That evening, without reference to Jinnah or the League, Lord Wavell broadcast an appeal to the Muslims, asking for their co-operation. For Jinnah this was a naïve and extraordinary request : he answered, on August 29, in a speech at Bombay,

The Viceroy has committed a double betrayal in going back

[1] To the author, July 23, 1953.

1946-1947

on his solemn word and in ignoring and by-passing the Muslim League. I do not know whether the British Government or the Labour Party are really in possession of the true facts. But I suspect that there is a move to black out the true facts from the British public and press.

The Viceroy's action today is nothing but a wicked breach of the declaration of August 1940, made by the British Government, to which the Labour Party was committed. . . .[1]

On September 2, when the Congress Interim Government came into power, the Muslim League copied Mahatma Gandhi's old tactics of non-violent protest : every Muslim, from Quaid-i-Azam to the smallest and most frightened little man in his hut, was asked to fly a black flag from his housetop, in 'silent contempt for the Hindu Government.' The millions of black pennants, all over India, only emphasized the differences between Hindu and Muslim neighbours, and excited the enmity that was so soon to lead to slaughter.

Early in October, Jinnah had 'further discussions with the Viceroy and received better satisfaction.' The result of these talks was compromise, in which the Quaid never believed : the Interim Government was reconstituted to admit five Muslim League members. Jinnah appointed Liaquat Ali Khan as leader of these five, and, at the first meeting, he charged his colleagues to work 'for the good of the man in the street, and not for the purpose of party gains.'

Liaquat Ali Khan said, " Nowhere in the world does a Government like the present Interim Government of India exist. It is a novel experiment, and we have come into the Government with the intention of working in harmony with our other colleagues—but you cannot clap with one hand."

The two hands did not clap together, and the Interim Government achieved nothing of enduring value. While the members were repeating their arguments, to so little purpose, the opening of the new Constituent Assembly was being arranged, for December 9. On November 21, Jinnah ordered that no member of the Muslim League was to take his seat : he said, " I deeply regret that the Viceroy and His Majesty's Government have decided to summon the Constituent Assembly on December 9. In my opinion, it is one more blunder of a very grave and serious character. It is quite obvious that

[1] See Chapter *1940-1942*, p. 137.

the Viceroy . . . is entirely playing into the hands of Congress and is appeasing them, in complete disregard of the Muslim League. . . . I want to make it quite clear that no representative of the League should attend. . . ."

★ ★ ★

In the vast spaces of British India the three hundred millions of Muslims and Hindus were already yielding to their deep, ancient hatred : the 'bloodshed and civil war' that Jinnah had dreaded, had already begun.

General Sir Francis Tuker has described these last tragic months of British rule in India, in his book, *While Memory Serves*.[1] The three chapters, 'The Great Calcutta Killing' (August 1946), 'The Butchery of Muslims in Bihar' (October-November 1946), and 'The Garhmukteswar Massacre' (November 1946), reveal the full horror of what happened as the British relinquished control and the Indians took the law into their own hands.

'The Great Calcutta Killing' began on 'Direct Action Day', August 16, 'a warm, sticky, familiar day in the monsoon,' when big numbers of Muslims congregated to listen to the explanations of their leaders. Hindus and Muslims soon turned on each other with their vicious knives. General Sir Francis Tuker describes the 'unbridled savagery, with homicidal maniacs let loose to kill and kill and to maim and burn. The underworld of Calcutta was taking charge of the city. . . . The Market itself was strewn with bodies . . . one room contained fifteen corpses and another twelve . . . we rescued two live children, both wounded and one already gangrenous. As might be expected, they were dazed and half-witted. . . . Most of the dead in the Market had not had the remotest idea of what was happening or why.' Four thousand Muslims and Hindus were killed during this episode in Calcutta.

During October and November, in Bihar, '. . . great mobs of Hindus turned suddenly, but with every preparation for the deed, upon the few Muslims who had lived and whose forefathers had lived, in amity and trust all their lives, among these very Hindu neighbours. . . . The number of Muslim dead, men, women, and

[1] *While Memory Serves* (Cassell, 1950), Lieut.-General Sir Francis Tuker, former G.O.C.-in-C. Eastern Command in India.

children, in this short, savage killing was about seven thousand to eight thousand.' In the United Provinces 'even pregnant women were ripped up, their unborn babies torn out and the infants' brains bashed out on walls and on the ground. There was rape, and women and children were seized by the legs by burly fiends and torn apart....'

This is from the records of a responsible senior officer: not one who lived in a cloud of political unreality, but one who saw these horrors and whose task it was to try to assuage them.

* * *

The scene moves to Whitehall: the reports of the massacres and of the impasse within the Interim Government inspired the British Cabinet to one last effort at reconciliation. The Prime Minister announced that Lord Wavell, Mohammed Ali Jinnah, Liaquat Ali Khan, Pandit Jawaharlal Nehru, and Sardar Baldev Singh—representing the Sikhs—were to arrive in London on December 3, to confer with His Majesty's Government, for the last time, in an effort to save the Cabinet Mission plan.

The Viceroy and the Indian leaders all flew to London in the same aircraft. A reporter from *Time* magazine searched out some crisp details of the journey and of the behaviour of the strangely mixed company, and wrote an article entitled ' Flight to Nowhere ? '[1] In a ' front-row seat ' sat Jinnah, with ' his hawk's head ' buried ' in a book pointedly titled *A Nation Betrayed.*' Behind him sat Nehru, ' wearing Western-style clothes for the first time in eight years.' While flying from Karachi to Malta, ' Nehru breezed through Rosamond Lehmann's *The Ballad and the Source* and Sinclair Lewis' *Cass Timberlaine*, chatted with his good friend, Sikh leader Sardar Balder [*sic*] Singh. In the plane's third row sat Viscount Wavell, Viceroy of India. For three years he had been trying to bring Nehru and Jinnah into agreement, now, with the peace of India hanging by a thread, they were a yard apart in space, politically as remote as ever.'

The party had to wait some hours in Malta, where each went his own way. When they met again, to take off for London, Jinnah made the first amiable move: he went up to Nehru and asked, " Well, what have you been doing all day ? " Nehru answered,

[1] *Time* magazine, December 16, 1946, p. 32.

NEHRU'S DEFIANT SPEECH

"Partly reading, partly sleeping, partly walking." Then the aircraft took off for London, where the leaders were met at the airport by 'Britain's aging, able Lord Pethick-Lawrence', and 'local Indians' who were 'out before dawn in coal trucks, bicycles and buses.'

The detached, American view of this last effort at conciliation, is superficial, but astringent. The writer continued, 'Nehru moved about at receptions with high good humour and grace. At India House, he shook hands with the Dowager Marchioness of Willingdon, whose husband had jailed him; at Buckingham Palace, he ate from His Majesty's gold plate, a delightful change from the tin service he had known as a nine-year guest in H.M.'s prisons. Jinnah was socially crusty, giving the impression of a man deeply aggrieved. When the travellers got down to cases, however, it was the smiling Nehru who proved most stubborn.'

The arguments of the conference tables at Simla were reawakened in London: neither the Congress nor the League leaders were willing to make any concessions, and the meeting fell apart, in three days. Mr Attlee insisted that His Majesty's Government would not withdraw from India unless the Muslims were represented in framing the new Constitution; insisted that the British officials and forces would not quit if this meant leaving all power in the hands of the Congress Party. Pandit Nehru flew back to India, with the Sikh delegate, at the end of the three days, remarking that it was 'silly' to expect a solution, in this time, of 'problems' that had 'been under discussion for months.'

On December 15, Nehru was in Benares, the holy capital of Caste-Hinduism, where he made a defiant speech: he said,

> Whatever form of Constitution we may decide in the Constituent Assembly will become the Constitution of free India—whether Britain accepts it or not. The British Government are thinking that the Constituent Assembly's decisions are not binding on her. But we have not entered the Constituent Assembly in order to place our decisions on a silver plate and dance attendance on the British Government for their acceptance. We have now altogether stopped looking towards London. . . . We cannot and will not tolerate any outside interference. . . .

It was with this prospect that the British prepared, through force or choice, or a mingling of both, to withdraw into the West and leave India to settle her own affairs.

*   *   *

The new Constituent Assembly had met in Delhi on December 9, but not one of the Muslim League members was present: both Jinnah and Liaquat Ali Khan had remained in England.

On December 14, the Muslims living in Britain crowded into the Kingsway Hall to hear Jinnah speak. The setting must have been sadly romantic for him. Near by was Lincoln's Inn, where he had arrived as a student, fifty-four years before; where he had looked up and seen the name of the Prophet over the gate, among the great law-givers of the world. Near also was Finsbury, where Jinnah's first hero, Dadabhai Naoroji, had won his seat in the British Parliament, in 1892.

In eleven days Quaid-i-Azam would be seventy years old: it seemed that he still feared 'the fogs and winter of London,' for he kept his English overcoat closely buttoned about him during the meeting. A Muslim journalist [1] described the scene:

> Pipes of the great organs in the Hall were bannered with silken-flagged slogans—green crescent flags of the Muslim League. . . .
> Leaguers from all over Britain crowded the Hall of the Headquarters of London's Methodist Church to hear their leader. Outside the hall [stamping] their feet to keep out the cold of foggy December were squads of uniformed and plain clothed police.
> The British Press photographers filled the front row of the hall with their cameras loaded and resting on their knees.
> As Mr. Jinnah entered, all the League leaders began to shout, 'Pakistan Zindabad' and 'Quaid-i-Azam Zindabad.'

It was some sign of the reasonableness of the British that no one protested against this demonstration, in the heart of London: a lettered banner hanging in a Methodist church, accusing the Cabinet Mission and the Viceroy of betrayal, and a Muslim audience shouting

[1] Jamil-ud-Din Ahmad, in *Some Recent Speeches and Writings of Mr Jinnah* (Ashraf, Lahore), pp. 497-8.

their claim for Pakistan, within hearing of the posse of policemen outside the hall—symbols of tolerance as well as order.

Jinnah stood up to speak and the Muslims 'roared at him,' *We want Pakistan! Jinnah Zindabad!* His 'pale face worked with emotion' and 'he spoke slowly and haltingly at first.' He said, "I am glad that the British people have awakened a bit. It is a tradition of the British nation that they only wake up when there is something dangerous."

He repeated the arguments of his cause : then, "What is it we want? What are our utmost demands? The answer is Pakistan." There were more shouts of " Zindabad," then Jinnah continued, ". . . we want a separate state of our own. There we can live according to our own notions of life. . . . What would the Hindus lose? Look at the map! They would have three-quarters of India. They would have the best parts. . . .

"What is the objection to these proposals of ours? We should be free . . . is Britain going to stand with its bayonets and hand over authority to the Hindu majority? If that happens, you will have lost every cent of honour, integrity and fair play. . . .

"Democracy is the blood of Mussalmans. . . . I give you an example. Very often when I go to a mosque, my chauffeur stands side by side with me. Mussalmans believe in fraternity, equality and liberty. . . . There is no other way but to divide India. Give Muslims their homeland and give Hindus Hindustan."

* * *

Quaid-i-Azam was ill and exhausted at the close of his visit to London : he returned home by air, and when he landed at Karachi his doctors advised him to rest. He went to Malir, one of the residences of the Nawab of Bahawalpur, where he was not allowed even to listen to the news on the radio. For one month he endured a nervous breakdown, from which he recovered early in March 1947, when he returned to Bombay. During this time, on February 20, Mr Attlee announced in the House of Commons that the British Government would grant complete independence to India; not later than June 1948. The Prime Minister said that the British would transfer their power, either "as a whole to some form of central government for British India or in some areas to the existing provincial governments, or in such other way as may seem most reasonable and in the best interests of the Indian people."

Mr Attlee announced also that the King had approved the appointment of his cousin, Rear-Admiral Viscount Mountbatten, to be the last Viceroy, " entrusted with the task of transferring to Indian hands the responsibility for the government of British India in a manner that will best ensure the future happiness and prosperity of India."

PART SEVEN

1947: PARTITION

THERE is a story that when Lord Mountbatten's task as Viceroy ended—when he had shared out the sub-continent between the Hindus and the Muslims—he remarked, " I don't care what is said about my work in India, during my lifetime : I care only what my grand-children may say and think." This thought perhaps absolves contemporary chroniclers from deciding, too readily, whether the partition of India was a tragedy or a salvation.

In this, his last ' case '—his last battle of wits—Mohammed Ali Jinnah dealt with adversaries sharply different from himself, in mind and character. Lord Mountbatten was an amalgam of minor royalty, cavalier, and valiant sailor : as Supreme Commander, South-East Asia, he had enjoyed victory over the Japanese and he had become one of the heroic figures of the war. The wish to rule dies slowly in royal persons, and he might have been pleased by the prospect of his new appointment ; of being entrusted with political power beyond that of his cousin on the throne. But Lord Mountbatten's ambitions are with the navy : he was reluctant to become Viceroy, and any princely sensations he might have felt must have been tarnished by the knowledge that, while ruling India, his real task would be to divide it and give it away.

The new Viceroy arrived in Delhi on March 22, 1947, with his staff and advisers ; among them, General Lord Ismay, a humanitarian who knew and loved India, and who, when the killing began, sheltered five hundred Muslims in his garden ; and Sir Eric Miéville, also an authority on India, and a wise mediator. Three days later, when Lord Mountbatten received Pandit Nehru, he said, " Mr Nehru, I want you to regard me not as the last Viceroy winding up the British Raj, but as the first to lead the way to a new India." Nehru answered, " Now I know what they mean when they speak of your charm being so dangerous."

Mohammed Ali Jinnah would be at a disadvantage in such company : his cold advocate's manner would not encourage such gallant exchanges. Also, these men, with whom he was to do battle for Pakistan, were younger. Lord Mountbatten was forty-six ; and

Pandit Nehru, who spoke for Congress in place of the aged Mahatma —secure in his refuge of mysticism—was fifty-seven. Jinnah was seventy: already an old man, and slowly dying. But his single-mindedness and persistent integrity still sustained him, so that, in the end, he was able to enjoy considerable victory over his adversaries, both British and Hindu.

As the story of these last months of grinding argument unfolds, it mustbe remembered that even before Lord Mountbatten left England, he had little hope of reconciling Hindus and Muslims within a united India. His initial instructions from the Cabinet, and his own aim, was to establish something like the Cabinet Mission Plan. Congress might have agreed to this, but the Viceroy arrived at New Delhi already aware that the Quaid would fight all attempts to deprive him of Pakistan.

During his first talk with Pandit Nehru, Lord Mountbatten asked the Congress leader for his personal 'estimate' of Jinnah. The Viceroys Press Attaché, Mr Alan Campbell-Johnson, recorded the episode.[1] Pandit Nehru answered that 'the essential thing to realize' was that success came to Jinnah 'very late in life,' when he was 'over sixty.' Then he said, 'Before that he had not been a major figure in Indian politics. He was a successful lawyer, but not an especially good one. . . . The secret of his success—and it had been tremendous, if only for its emotional intensity—was in his capacity to take up a permanently negative attitude.' Nehru said that Jinnah had done this 'with complete singleness of purpose' since 1935— the year when he gave up the seclusion of Hampstead and returned to India. Pandit Nehru claimed, to Lord Mountbatten, that Jinnah 'knew that Pakistan could never stand up to constructive criticism,' and that he had 'ensured that it should never be subjected to it.'

Lord Mountbatten may have sought the Quaid's opinion of Pandit Nehru, but there is no record of such a talk between them. When Jinnah called on the Viceroy, the first time, the journalists who intercepted him thought him 'formal and reserved.' This was a solemn hour in his case for Pakistan and he had prepared his arguments well: having shaken hands with Lord Mountbatten, he began, "I will enter into discussion on one condition only. . . ."

[1] *Mission with Mountbatten*, Alan Campbell-Johnson (Robert Hale, 1915), pp. 44-5.

THE QUAID AND LORD MOUNTBATTEN

The Viceroy trod more softly : he interrupted, " Mr Jinnah, I am not prepared to discuss conditions or, indeed, the present situation, until I have had the chance of making your acquaintance and hearing more about you, yourself."

Mr Campbell-Johnson records that Jinnah was 'completely taken aback,' and that he did not 'respond' but remained 'reserved, haughty and aloof.' In the end his mood 'softened' and he 'duly succumbed to Mountbatten's desire to hear him recount the story of the Muslim League's rise to power in terms of his own career.'

At the close of the talk, Lord Mountbatten 'felt he could not sustain another session' with Jinnah that day. " My God, he was cold," said the Viceroy. " It took most of the interview to unfreeze him."

Next evening, when Quaid-i-Azam and his sister dined with the Viceroy, the conversation was crisp rather than warm. Mr Jinnah 'harped on Muslim massacres and described the horrors at length.' He spoke of the need for a ' quick decision ' and added that it would have to be 'a surgical operation.' Lord Mountbatten answered that 'an anaesthetic' would be required. Before he departed, Jinnah made a last, pathetic protest : he said to the Viceroy, " The Congress want to inherit everything : they would even accept Dominion Status to deprive me of Pakistan."

Quaid-i-Azam returned home, as he was to return from so many meetings in the future, feeling that he had made little access to Lord Mountbatten's heart. His only complaint, to his secretary, was, " The Viceroy does not understand." The legend of antipathy between the Viceroy and Mr Jinnah became dangerous in its effect, especially after Partition, when they were Governors-General of the new, opposed states. Two months after the country was divided, Mr Ian Stephens, editor of *The Statesman*, dined with 'the Mountbattens' and was 'startled by their one-sided verdicts on affairs.' This was in October 1947, when the developing drama in Kashmir was moving towards the Maharaja's accession to India. Mr Stephens wrote [1] that Lord and Lady Mountbatten seemed to have 'become wholly pro-Hindu. The atmosphere at Government House that night was almost one of war. Pakistan, the Muslim League, and Mr Jinnah were the enemy. . . .'

Perhaps these 'one-sided verdicts' were more political and less

[1] *Horned Moon*, Ian Stephens (Chatto and Windus, 1953), p. 109.

personal than contemporary observers realized. Lord Mountbatten often spoke to members of his staff, of Jinnah's 'strong sense of leadership', his 'single-mindedness of purpose', and of his 'standing head and shoulders above all other members of the Muslim League.' And there is the alleviating story of the Viceroy turning to his Press Attaché one day, after a long session with the Quaid, and saying, "You know, I like the old boy, really."

* * *

Lord Mountbatten was not intimidated by Rudyard Kipling's warning that 'it is not good for the Christian's health to hustle the Aryan brown.' He 'tried to hustle the East,' and he succeeded. Mr Wilfred Russell, a business man in India, wrote,[1] '... in Delhi the last Viceroy was working with a speed and determination which fascinated and to some extent terrified both the Indian leaders and the British officials.'

Beyond these hurried scenes, of conferences and reports, the form of the new India was rising, like a group of islands from the sea. That the islands were volcanic, and in eruption, could not be prevented by these dividers of the earth, at their desks in Delhi. While they were deliberating, slaughter spread, frantic and vicious, in almost every part of northern India. The traveller cannot pass through Pakistan or India without being aware of the ghosts of this carnage : before the story of so much death, the living hold their breath.

Mr Richard Symonds has described [2] the 'desperate situation' that Lord Mountbatten had to endure, and try to control :

> ... in the Punjab a Unionist government tottering under the attack of the Muslim League ; in the North West Frontier a a Muslim League civil disobedience campaign ; and all over the country fierce communal clashes, while private armies formed for the final struggle for power. The civil service were bitterly divided by communalism and headed by dispirited Englishmen, anxious to retire. The British troops were already being repatriated, and the morale of the Indian Army was uncertain.

General Lord Ismay, Chief of the Viceroy's Staff, had known the old India, first as a soldier forty years before, and later as Military

[1] *Indian Summer*, Wilfred Russell (Thacker, Bombay, 1951), p. 66.
[2] *The Making of Pakistan*, Richard Symonds, p. 70.

THE PEACE APPEAL

Secretary to the Viceroy, in Lord Willingdon's time. He has spoken [1] of the changes that had come; of the awakening of nationalism, and the social hatred that had multiplied, so tragically, during the five years of wrangling since the Cripps Mission. "The communal feeling I found, I just did not believe possible. It tore at you, all the time. There was slaughter everywhere. We British had all the responsibility and none of the power. The police force was already undermined, and the civil service were frustrated and madly anxious. They were blamed by both Nehru and Jinnah for everything that went wrong.

"This was one reason why, to delay partition, would be to increase the disasters. There was another reason: the Viceroy's Executive Council, which had been composed of six or eight wise men, had disappeared. We had instead a Cabinet of nine Congress leaders and five Muslim League leaders who could agree on only one thought—that the British should quit India."

Lord Ismay has said [2] it was obvious that June 1948, instead of being too early for the transfer of power, would be too late. It would not be possible to achieve an orderly hand-over, to a government that barely existed, a civil service torn by internal strife, and many millions of people intent on killing each other. The perils were inevitable: with delay, they would only increase.

On the one hand was Pandit Nehru, who said to the Viceroy, "This cannot go on. If you do not produce a plan, I shall resign." On the other hand was the Quaid, with his simple, inviolate demand for Pakistan. Lord Ismay reminded him, on behalf of the Viceroy, that if India was to be divided, Bengal and the Punjab would also have to be split in two, 'according to the will of the people.' Jinnah's answer was, "Better a moth-eaten Pakistan that no Pakistan at all."

By April 14, the riots and cruelties were so terrible that Lord Mountbatten induced the Quaid and the Mahatma to agree in the last concerted action of their lives: they signed a 'Peace Appeal,' drawn up by the Viceroy, to be printed and broadcast, and shown in cinemas throughout India. The appeal was particularly aimed at the Punjab, where Hindus, Sikhs, and Muslims were attacking each other so violently that the Governor had been obliged to take over

[1] To the author.   [2] In frequent lectures on the subject.

the administration; and at the North-West Frontier, where the rising strength of the Muslim League had led to open revolt against the Congress Ministry—where, as Mr Wilfred Russell wrote,[1] the 'vote catching power of Congress money' was fast melting 'before the fires of Islam.'

The time for peace appeals had passed: in the Punjab, Master Tara Singh, the Sikh insurgent leader, was inciting his followers to destroy the Muslims and form their own state. The plan—organized with officers, arms, ammunition and vehicles—was reported to Jinnah. The Muslims begged him to release funds and approve the formation of a volunteer corps to fight the Sikhs. His answer was in harmony with his long story of honest dealing: he said, "How can you expect me to approve of such a scheme: I am not a hypocrite. I have just signed the Peace Appeal and I expect the Mussalmans to observe the spirit of the Appeal."

Jinnah's secretary, who worked with him in Delhi at this time, has said, "He would return from his meetings with the Viceroy, solemn and weary. But he would not discuss what had happened during the day; not with me, or other members of the staff. He would work late over his papers, tense and silent."

* * *

Towards the end of April, the hatred and cruelty that raged throughout India forced the Viceroy to admit the folly of further acrimonious negotiation. There were but two alternatives: to send troops out from Britain and resume Imperial control of India, or to hasten withdrawal. After more than five years of impotent conferences, most of the British officials and army officers were disillusioned and only wished to return home. And the Indians themselves were for final settlement, at any price. To reinstate the old *Raj* in India, with the support of an army, would be an impossible act: Lord Mountbatten realized the frightening necessity of immediate partition, and complete withdrawal, as soon as possible. With the help of his advisers he drafted the first form of what came to be known as 'the Plan,' which was to end British rule in India.

On April 23, the Viceroy 'had a three-hour session with Jinnah,' who was 'friendly.' Mr Campbell-Johnson wrote in his diary,[2] of

[1] *Indian Summer*, p. 77. [2] *Mission with Mountbatten*, p. 70.

the Quaid : ' Sometimes he is deliberately rude, but today his mood was to be accommodating. He seemed to be resigned to the partition of the Punjab and Bengal. He did not ask what the boundaries would be, and Mountbatten did not tell him. . . . He told Mountbatten, " Frankly, Your Excellency, the Hindus are impossible. They always want seventeen annas for the rupee." '

From this time, ' the Plan ' grew quickly, and on April 26, Lord Mountbatten decided that Lord Ismay and Mr George Abell [1] should fly to London with the first draft, and ' hammer it out clause by clause with the Government.'

During Lord Ismay's absence, Jinnah and Gandhi met, by accident, for the first time in three years. They both had appointments with the Viceroy and by ' a freak of chance the interviews overlapped.' Lord Mountbatten used the brief encounter well : he brought them together in amiable conversation which ended with the two leaders deciding to meet again, privately, and talk over their problems. This last conference between the old warriors, at Jinnah's bungalow in Delhi, was more picturesque than useful : neither of them would budge from his convictions and the hour passed with futile discussion, warmed by mutual cordiality.

The excitement and solemnity of these days and events is intensified by observing the time passed, and the distances travelled, by these last officials of the British *Raj*. Aircraft flew back and forth between Delhi and London, covering in little more than a day the journey Clive had made in many months. Within 145 days, the Viceroy and his staff succeeded in relinquishing the continent their forbears had held, and nurtured, for 200 years.

Lord Ismay had left Delhi on May 2 : two days later, he arrived in London, where he remained until the end of the month. During the first week of his visit, the Plan was revised and approved by the British Government ; and on May 10, Mr Campbell-Johnson ' put out the momentous communique ' announcing that the Viceroy had invited the League, Congress, and Sikh leaders, and the representatives of the Indian States, to meet him on May 17, when he ' would present to them the Plan ' which His Majesty's Government had ' now made for the transfer of power to Indian hands.'

The Viceroy sent Sir Eric Miéville to Mr Jinnah with a copy of the

[1] Private Secretary to the Viceroy. Later Sir George Abell.

Plan: he also gave a copy to Pandit Nehru, who was his guest at the time. This led to an impasse: Nehru 'vehemently' refused to accept some of the terms, and the 'momentous communique' had to be withdrawn. Lord Mountbatten then sent a telegram to Lord Ismay, announcing that more changes would be necessary in the Plan. This alarming pattern of negotiation, involving Whitehall and New Delhi, aircraft and telegraph, ended with a summons to the Viceroy, 'courteous but firm,' that he should return to London 'for consultation.'

Lord Mountbatten arrived in England on May 19: twelve days later, on Saturday, May 31, he returned to New Delhi, with Lord Ismay, carrying the final, irrevocable Plan, approved by the British Cabinet. There were to be no more conferences, no more acrid exchanges, or flights of delegates to and fro: the Viceroy summoned the leaders to meet him on Monday morning, when he would announce the absolute decision that India was to be divided. Mohammed Ali Jinnah would have most of the prize he had fought for; and Pakistan and Hindustan would go their separate ways, with full Dominion status, and the right to secede from the Commonwealth if they chose. The day for the final cleavage was to be only three months away—August 15, 1947—almost a year earlier than Mr Attlee had planned when he entrusted the last Viceroy with his task. From this date also, the princely Indian States would no longer owe allegiance to the British Crown; they would be free to keep their independence, or to accede to either of the new dominions, as they chose.

Jinnah had to pay for his victory: within the greater scheme of Partition was to be the lesser slicing he had always feared: the provinces of Bengal and the Punjab were also to be divided. The right of the Muslim-majority areas to accept, or reject, federation with the new state of Pakistan, was to be decided by the free will of the people—voting, in the case of West Punjab, East Bengal, and Sind, through their elected representatives in the Provincial Assemblies; in Baluchistan, through the Shahi Jirga—the council of chiefs; and in the North-West Frontier Province, and Sylhet—the Muslim-majority area of Assam—by the general vote of the people themselves, through their adult male population.

The meeting on June 2 lasted two hours. Mr Campbell-Johnson

described [1] the mood of the leaders after they had read their copies of 'the Plan.' Pandit Nehru said that 'while there could never be complete approval' by Congress, 'on balance they accepted it.' The Quaid was reluctant to commit himself: he said that he would need to go to the Working Committee of the Muslim League, and to 'the people,' for a final decision—not with any intent of 'wrecking the Plan,' but 'with the sincerest desire to persuade them to accept it.' He assured the Viceroy that he would do his 'best.'

Lord Mountbatten once more 'tried to hustle the East,' and succeeded. He asked that the reactions of Congress, the League, and the Sikhs, should be declared to him by midnight; and by midnight the leaders answered him. Jinnah came in person, but the way was not easy. Mr Campbell-Johnson recorded [2] that 'No amount of pressure' from the Viceroy could make the Quaid agree to 'firm acceptance' without the consent of the League. 'Nothing Mountbatten could say would move him.' With his peculiar care—reminiscent of the early days of argument before the judges in the Bombay law courts —Jinnah insisted that he was 'not constitutionally authorized to make a decision without the concurrence of the full Muslim League Council.'

Lord Mountbatten then said, "If that is your attitude, then the leaders of the Congress Party and Sikhs will refuse final acceptance at the meeting in the morning: chaos will follow, and you will lose your Pakistan, probably for good."

The Quaid shrugged his shoulders and answered, "What must be, must be."

The Viceroy made his last appeal: "Mr Jinnah! I do not intend to let you wreck all the work that has gone into this settlement. Since you will not accept for the Muslim League, I will speak for them myself. I will take the risk of saying that I am satisfied with the assurances you have given me, and if your Council fails to ratify the agreement, you can put the blame on me."

Lord Mountbatten made one condition: he asked that when, at the next morning's session, he would say, "Mr Jinnah has given me assurance which I have accepted and which satisfy me," the Quaid should 'in no circumstances contradict;' and that, when the Viceroy looked towards him, he should nod his head 'in acquiescence.'

[1,2] *Mission with Mountbatten*, pp. 99–103.

Quaid-i-Azam agreed, and Lord Mountbatten asked his last question. Did Jinnah consider that the Viceroy would be justified in advising Mr Attlee to 'go ahead and make his announcement' in the British Parliament?

Jinnah answered, "Yes."

The meeting next morning began with some bitter remarks from the leaders, before the discussion 'moved into calmer water.' Quaid-i-Azam revealed all the history of his mind in two episodes, during this last talk at the oval table over which the grim decisions had been made. Mr Campbell-Johnson recalls [1] the moment when Lord Mountbatten presented the leaders with a formidable document entitled, *The Administrative Consequences of Partition*. He suggested that they should consider it first, before it was submitted to a 'Cabinet meeting'—a slip of the tongue, as the Viceroy had meant to say 'Interim Government.' Jinnah remonstrated, thinking that Mountbatten was referring to the British Cabinet. When the error was explained, Jinnah—so meticulous in the use of words—said, "A spade should be called a spade," and remarked that *his* mind always 'worked on constitutional lines.'

The second episode was towards the end, when the Quaid spoke of his policy for Pakistan. The vigour of his aspirations, and his passion for justice—above racial fears and the disease of creeds—were disclosed as he 'declared stoutly' that, in Pakistan, 'it would be his intention . . . to observe no communal differences.' All who lived in the State he created would be, he said, 'fully fledged citizens.' The old 'ambassador of Hindu-Muslim unity' had died hard in the advocate for Muslim freedom.

* * *

On the evening of the same day, June 3, following a gramophone recording of a Chopin polonaise, the Viceroy announced the Plan in slow, deliberate phrases, on All-India Radio. Then Pandit Nehru spoke, in both English and Hindi. He said, "We are little men serving great causes, but because the cause is great, something of that greatness falls on us also." Then Quaid-i-Azam spoke, of the 'momentous decisions,' the 'grave issues,' and the 'complex political problem.' His speech was in English, and it had to be translated

[1] *Mission with Mountbatten*, pp. 104–5.

into Urdu, so that Muslims all over India could know that he had won them their nation. Jinnah besought his listeners to 'galvanize and concentrate' all their energies 'to see that the transfer of power' was made 'in a peaceful and orderly manner.' He said also, "The world has no parallel for the most onerous and difficult task which we have to perform." Then he paid Lord Mountbatten a tribute, no doubt sincere but also mixed with diplomatic hope for the days to come: he said,

> I must say that I feel that the Viceroy has battled against various forces very bravely, and the impression that he has left on my mind is that he was actuated by a high sense of fairness and impartiality; and it is up to us now to make his task less difficult and help him as far as lies in our power. . . .

At the end of the speech, carefully written, and rehearsed, Jinnah was suddenly spontaneous: he raised his voice and said, "Pakistan Zindabad!", which was not in the script.

On June 10 and 13, the Plan was ratified, respectively, by the Muslim League and Congress. By July 20, the 'free will of the people' was known: the Muslims in British India—including the proud, sturdy Pathans of the north-west, where the Congress party had been influential for so long—had overwhelmingly endorsed the plan for Pakistan.

The map of India was to be changed: the massive red pear, that had been an ornament in English atlases for almost a century, was now to be sliced, but not merely in two. A country, half the size of the United States, but with two and a half times its population, was to be divided so that Hindu India would form a gigantic wedge— one thousand miles wide—between East and West Pakistan. It was as if George Washington had united California and Massachusetts into one state, with an alien nation spread between. The two Muslim territories, speaking different languages, one facing the east, the other the west—to be permitted no land communication—were the Pakistan that Jinnah had won. The only bonds between the two great territories were a fierce wish to be rid of Hindu domination, and their belief in Islam.

The frontiers for this division were defined by a Boundary Commission under Sir Cyril (now Lord) Radcliffe—a choice to which

1947: PARTITION

Quaid-i-Azam agreed. Sir Cyril Radcliffe's task was prodigious: wherever he drew his timid lines on the map, he was sure to offend.

The Quaid was shocked by the Award: he spoke of the 'grave injustice' to Pakistan, but even over such a fearful dispute as this he was 'strictly constitutional.' He had accepted Sir Cyril Radcliffe as Chairman of the Boundary Commission; therefore he accepted his verdict, as an advocate before his judge. When Jinnah's associates urged him to protest, he answered, "No, we agreed to arbitration— we must abide by that arbitration."

The army, the navy, and the air force, and the assets of British India, were also to be divided. Older British officers, who had served in India for the better part of their lives—proud of their Muslim, Sikh and Hindu troops, as a general might be proud of a regiment drawn, into one tradition, from England, Scotland and Wales—had to submit to their soldiers being distributed according to their religion.

Lord Ismay protested against this breaking up of the forces on communal lines: he said to Quaid-i-Azam, "You have probably the finest army in the world, with tremendous prestige in the battlefield. It will be tragic if you do not keep them as now, with their wonderful regimental tradition." He reminded the Quaid, "An army is not just a collection of men with rifles and swords: it is a living entity, with one heart, one soul, one brain, and one set of organs. If you perform a surgical operation, you will kill it."

Jinnah answered, "You do not understand the psychology of these people—these *opposed* people."

So the soldiers were shared out, with their guns and their ammunition, and they became enemies. The aircraft, and the ships of the Royal Indian Navy, were dealt out, like cards in a game: those ships that arrived in the port of Karachi had not, among them, a barrel of fuel or oil left: they had to lie and wait, defenceless, beside the docks.

Such trivial objects as desks and typewriters had also to be distributed; and in this game of 'one for you and two for me' the Muslims were at a disadvantage. The little officials, the managers and clerks in India, had been mostly Hindus, who have an aptitude for busyness and petty authority. The Muslims lacked these talents, and when they ultimately unpacked their share of the sad trophies of freedom, in the cities and towns of the new Pakistan, they found that they had been given little out of which to create the offices of government. More serious than the ships, the aircraft, or the typewriters, was the equipment of hospitals, which had also to be shared. In Karachi, the few harassed doctors found that vital parts of surgical apparatus had been removed. With more zeal than skill or experience, the technicians had to prepare the hospitals for the throngs of maimed and dying refugees who poured into the capital.

Quaid-i-Azam had mentioned the 'onerous and difficult task' to be performed: he had also appealed for 'peace and order'—words that were as ineffectual as feathers in a storm. Fourteen million people were to move across the new frontiers, one way or the other, before Jinnah died, thirteen months after Partition. The first of these millions began to pack their dusty treasures into bundles within an hour of the Viceroy's broadcast. Fear, like some terrible, unnatural monsoon, lay dark and heavy over all India. In late June, and July, the fear begat slaughter. An Englishman standing at a window in a certain city saw a hefty dockhand, armed with his big steel cargo hook. The man realized his strength: he rent the clothes and ripped the body of a woman who happened to be standing near by. Then he repeated the horror on five others as he walked up the street.

Sir Francis Tuker's book, *While Memory Serves*, describes some of the terrors and illustrates them with photographs that are appalling. The multitudes moving east met the multitudes moving west: they were frenzied, bewildered, and without pity; and most of the men were armed.

The British were quitting India at last. Those that remained did what they could to hold back the bloody stampede, but they had become futile before such a halocaust. They were aliens, without authority, in a chaotic land: all they could do was to pack and return to the West.

The killing was horrible to Mohammed Ali Jinnah, who had always been repelled by frenzy and cruelty. He was still in his house in Delhi when the reports of slaughter were brought to him; but he was helpless exhausted by the long struggle of words, already emaciated by his stealthy disease, and unable to lessen the agony his people must pass through to achieve the land he had promised them. Perhaps he had envisaged the strange darkness that was the inevitable price of what he had set out to create : four years earlier, at the Delhi session of the Muslim League, he had said of Pakistan,

> It may come in my lifetime, or not. You will remember these words of mine : I say this with no ill-will or offence. Some nations have killed millions of each other, and yet an enemy of today is a friend of tomorrow. That is history.

PART EIGHT

FLIGHT INTO KARACHI

ON August 7, 1947, Mohammed Ali Jinnah flew from Delhi to Karachi, to become the first Governor-General of Pakistan. There had been one last conflict of the mind, with Lord Mountbatten, after Congress had asked him to remain as Governor-General of the new India. Some of the Viceroy's staff expected that the Pakistanis would invite him to be their Governor-General also, but there was no gesture from the Muslim League. When Lord Ismay pressed Liaquat Ali Khan for a decision, he answered, " There is none, yet." A few days later, Quaid-i-Azam announced that his followers insisted on his being their first Governor-General. The decision was mentioned at a press conference between the Viceroy and the journalists: among them was Mr Ian Stephens, who has recorded that certain ' items ' in Lord Mountbatten's ' conduct ' were ' disquieting.' He wrote,[1] ' His weak point, some said, was his vanity . . . when Mr Jinnah's decision to become Pakistan's first Governor-General was disclosed, his pride had seemed hurt, though we thought needlessly : for how could anyone, however able, function effectively as Governor-General of both the new Dominions ? '

Members of Lord Mountbatten's staff thought differently. They ' assumed ' that Jinnah ' would be bound to prefer the status and powers of Prime Minister.' [2] They did not know of his increasing malady—a possible and valid reason for his not wishing to bear the formidable tasks which he delegated to the younger and stronger Liaquat Ali Khan.

* * *

Quaid-i-Azam made the flight to his new capital—the town where he had been born, seventy years before—in the Viceroy's silver Dakota. With him was his sister, also Lieutenant S. M. Ahsan, the naval A.D.C., and Flight-Lieutenant Ata Rabbani, the air A.D.C. For Flight-Lieutenant Rabbani this was the fulfilment of a dream. A few days before, while travelling in a train towards Delhi, he had

[1] *Horned Moon*, pp. 112–13.   [2] *Mission with Mountbatten*, p. 127.

read in a newspaper of the arrangements for Jinnah's flight into Karachi. He leaned back, thinking what great fortune it would be if he were chosen to fly his leader on this great day. When he arrived in Delhi, he was summoned by Liaquat Ali Khan, who said, " How would you like to be A.D.C. to the Quaid ? " Flight-Lieutenant Rabbani answered that he would ' love to.' Liaquat Ali Khan said, " Well, you had better go in and see the old man. He wants a chat with you." After a brief talk, Quaid-i-Azam said, " All right. Tell Liaquat that I approve of his choice."

Mr Jinnah had stored away his perfect English clothes : he wore, instead, a new white *sherwani*. He walked towards the aircraft, with his sister, and their little court. Flight-Lieutenant Rabbani carried a cane basket, full of documents : a servant carried a bundle of newspapers, to be read during the journey. As he stepped into the aircraft, Quaid-i-Azam looked back towards the city in which he had fought for, and won, Pakistan : he said, " I suppose this is the last time I'll be looking at Delhi." As the aircraft taxied out he said, " That's the end of that."

The journey lasted four hours. After eating a basket luncheon, Jinnah turned to his newspapers. The new As.D.C. had not seen this ritual before, and they both remarked on the precise way in which their master lifted the papers from the pile on the left, read them, folded them again, and built up a pile on his right. If any emotions were awakened by what he read—the long accounts of his own achievement—the emotions did not show. He spoke only once, when he leaned over to Flight-Lieutenant Rabbani, offered him some newspapers, and said, " Would you like to read these ? " From then, he was silent.

The Dakota came near Karachi : the Quaid-i-Azam looked down and saw thousands of people, in white clothes—a snowfield of the Muslims he had freed—on the edge of the desert. Refugees were pouring into the city along all the roads, their noisy little carts piled high with the possession they had salvaged before they fled. They washed their white shirts in any little pool they could find : they dried them in the sun, and then joined the multitude, to watch the Dakota circling over the aerodrome. One of the As.D.C. said afterwards, " When the Quaid looked down and saw all those people waiting for him, he suddenly became buoyant and quite young."

The aircraft landed and Mr Jinnah was the first to step out, followed by his sister. The people cried, " Pakistan Zindabad ! Pakistan Zindabad ! " They pressed forward, close, hot and frenzied, extending their hands so that they might be as near as possible to their deliverer.

Quaid-i-Azam was resolute and solitary. He handed a despatch-case of papers to the naval A.D.C., saying, " Now, I want you to be sure to look after these." Then he shook hands with leaders of the Muslim League who were near him. Many of them wept as he passed by.

The white sea of people spread between the aerodrome and Karachi, and, as the Quaid drove towards the city, a way was cleared for him. The cries of " Pakistan Zindabad ! " rose like a screeching wind from the close-packed throng. Only once was there a lull, when the car came to a stretch of road where the men outside the houses were grave and silent. Mr Jinnah asked the reason and was told, " This is no doubt a Hindu section, and, after all, they have very little to be jubilant about."

Among the thousands who cheered the Quaid were old Fatima Bai, who had scolded him as a boy, for reading his books so late into the night, and Nanji Jafar, with whom he had played marbles in the street. Mohammed Ali Jinnah had kept his promise : he had stood up from the dust, so that his clothes were unspoiled and his hands clean for the tasks that fell to them. These two people, whose horizon had never spread beyond the sand dunes of Sind, were among those whom he had freed : but they were lost in the impersonal white multitude, and they had to watch his advent from afar.

Quaid-i-Azam arrived at Government House, and as he walked up the steps he made a statement that was remarkable : he said to Lieutenant Ahsan, " Do you know, I never expected to see Pakistan in my lifetime. We have to be very grateful to God for what we have achieved."

The thousands of excited Muslims moved in from the airport : all day, and late into the night, they covered the land about Government House. But the Quaid seemed unaware of what their adoration meant ; unaware of the emotions that his arrival had stirred. With an A.D.C. beside him, he climbed the staircase and examined the house which had recently been the home of the Governor of Sind.

He walked from room to room, saying, "This wing will be occupied only by myself and Miss Jinnah. These two rooms will be only for very important people : I do not wish to have governors of provinces or ministers in these rooms—only very important people, like the Shah of Persia, or the King of England."

As the glory of the day began to fade, Jinnah became wholly practical. He said to one of his staff, "I want a radio installed immediately, so that I may hear the news." The aide, who was new and did not know his master very well, said, "But you are tired, sir. Why not leave it until the morning?" Quaid-i-Azam answered quickly, "Don't try any of those delaying tactics with me."

In the days that followed, there was much to do : a government had to be built, with all the paraphernalia of bureaucracy, in rooms where there were few desks or chairs, paper or pencils. But these first men were zealots : the offices were furnished, telephone wires were strung, typewriters began their insistent clatter, and the Pakistanis created their own little Whitehall, almost overnight. Error and folly were inevitable, but those Europeans who knew the character of India, and who remained to help, saw order emerging from chaos, and they were amazed. A Scottish businessman was beside a railway line two miles from Karachi when a locomotive was derailed, while shunting, in the dark. A breakdown train arrived within half an hour. The workers hurried to their task : they chanted " Pakistan Zindabad ! Pakistan Zindabad ! " and laboured until they got the locomotive back on the rails. The Scotsman said, "I have been in the sub-continent twenty-one years and have never seen such a sight before. My faith in Pakistan dates from that hour."

Mohammed Ali Jinnah was the focus of this new nation, forming about the new capital. He was the inspirator of all, yet he remained a private, aloof master, seeking no warm contact with the masses of his followers. He spent most of the time within Government House, weary, ill, yet undaunted. While the government of the biggest Muslim state in the world was being built up about him, he walked through the rooms of his new, immense home, examining every detail. He went to the library and saw that the shelves were empty. "Where are the books?" he asked.

"The Governor of Sind took them with him," he was told.

"They belong here," he answered. "Go and bring them back."

"YOU ARE FREE"

He then examined the inventory of the house and found that a croquet set was missing. He was told that the military secretary to the Governor of the Punjab had taken the mallets and hoops to Lahore. Jinnah remembered : when he went to Lahore some weeks later, he ordered that the mallets and hoops should be returned.

While Quaid-i-Azam was caught up in this exasperating care of detail, he was also writing the greatest speech of his life. He would leave these fault-finding expeditions to return to his desk, where he worked, for many hours, on the Presidential Address he was to give to the Constituent Assembly of Pakistan, on August 11. On that day he said to his people :

> You are free ; you are free to go to your temples, you are free to go to your mosques or to any other place of worship in this State of Pakistan. You may belong to any religion or caste or creed—that has nothing to do with the fundamental principle that we are all citizens and equal citizens of one State. . . . Now, I think we should keep that in front of us as our ideal, and you will find that in course of time, Hindus would cease to be Hindus, and Muslims would cease to be Muslims, not in the religious sense, because that is the personal faith of each individual, but in the political sense as citizens of the State.

The words were Jinnah's : the thought and belief were an inheritance from the Prophet who had said, thirteen centuries before, " All men are equal in the eyes of God. And your lives and your properties are all sacred : in no case should you attack each other's life and property. Today I trample under my feet all distinctions of caste, colour and nationality."

Quaid-i-Azam's appeal for tolerance was made in English to seventy million people, of whom merely ten per cent were literate, even in their own language. But it proved his broad humanity, and that he had not forgotten the group of Hindus beside the road, who had been so silent as he drove past, into his capital.

The Quaid's argument was neither comprehended, nor needed : the throngs of refugees—Hindu, Sikh, and Muslim—still met in terrible clashes of cruelty that neither the Government of India, nor of Pakistan, could subdue. In Delhi, Lord Ismay saw Pandit Nehru go out among the killers, with his bare hands, trying to quell them. Nehru was equally appalled by the wilful butchery and, like the Quaid, he had to wait until these mass passions exhausted themselves and gave reason a chance.

The plea for forbearance was repeated when Mr Jinnah was inaugurated as Governor-General, in the presence of the Viceroy, on August 14—the eve of Independence. Over them flew the new flag that had been chosen by the Quaid and Liaquat Ali Khan for Pakistan: it was three-quarters green, for the Muslim majority, and one-quarter white, for the minorities in their midst. Liaquat Ali Khan reminded his listeners that it was not 'the flag of any one political party or community.' He said, " As I visualize it, the State of Pakistan will be a State where there will be no special privileges, no special rights for any one particular community or individual. It will be a State where every citizen will have equal privileges and they will share equally all the obligations that lie on the citizens of Pakistan."

* * *

On August 15, the members of the Pakistan Cabinet were sworn in. When they were assembled at Government House, and ready, Flight-Lieutenant Rabbani went up to escort Quaid-i-Azam to them. The A.D.C. has described the episode. " The Quaid was standing there, in his room, more immaculate than ever, it seemed. All he said was ' Shall we move?' He walked down the stairs, and when we came to the first floor, he paused. The ceremony was to be in the open, and the Quaid went on to the balcony, where he could not be seen, to look at the members of the Cabinet, and the crowds beyond. He smiled. It was the first time I had ever seen a look of happiness on his face. I said to him, ' Sir, it is becoming cloudy: it might rain.' He answered, ' No, I know these clouds well. Karachi clouds have no water in them.' We continued downstairs and the Quaid went through the ceremony, without showing any emotion. When it was all over I escorted him back to his room. As I left him, he smiled again, but only to himself."

* * *

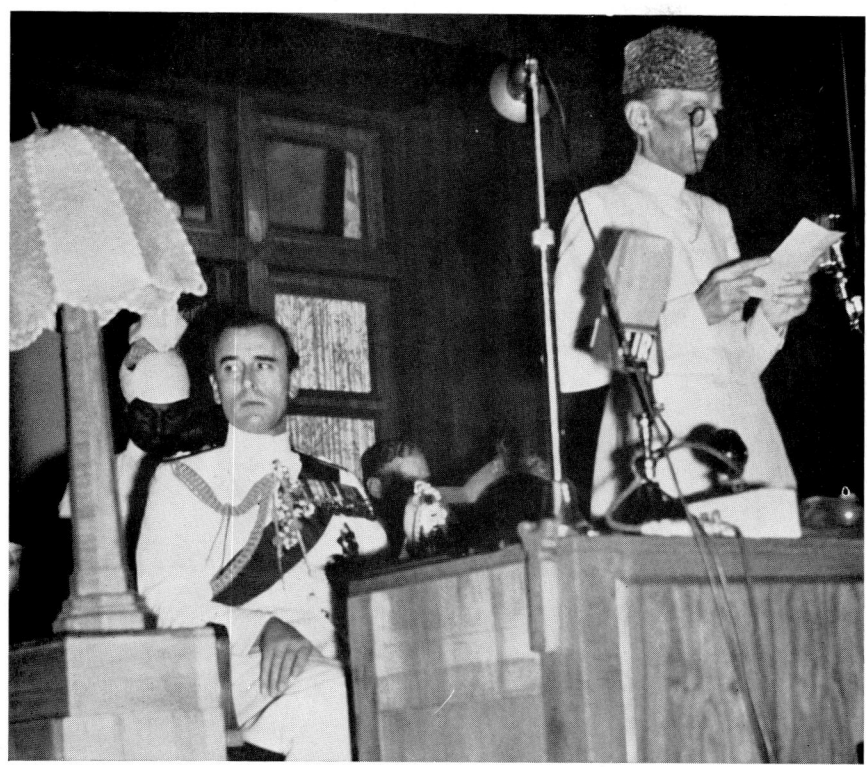
LORD MOUNTBATTEN LISTENING TO MR JINNAH'S INAUGURAL SPEECH AS THE FIRST GOVERNOR-GENERAL OF PAKISTAN, AUGUST 14, 1947

Partition he had hoped to use British officials in making his Muslim State; he even knew which ones he wished to retain, and for how long. He said to General Sir Douglas Gracey, "Ten years is the limit I have fixed for asking the British officers to stay." This peremptory decision involved the private inclinations of Britons who were already tired with the long wrangle of Indian affairs, and anticipating the courtesies of a small house in an English shire. But, when they were asked, they stayed. Quaid-i-Azam named them: he said to Lord Ismay, "I want Sir Archibald Rowlands [1] to be my financial adviser; I want Sir George Cunningham [2] to be Governor of the North-West Frontier; I want Sir Francis Mudie [3] to be Governor of West Punjab; I want . . ." Mr. Jinnah knew exactly what he required from each of these men, whose love of India might interest some historian of the future, seeking for the quiet theme of the humanities, moving through the clamour of political history. Sir George Cunningham had already retired, to become Rector of St Andrews University: when the request arrived, for him to return and begin again, he answered, "I'll come."

Two days after Partition, the Quaid proved that this devotion of the British was not to be used without respect and appreciation, as far as he was concerned. August 17 was a Sunday, and the Anglican Archdeacon had arranged for a special service of prayer and thanksgiving, in Holy Trinity Church, the Anglican Cathedral in Karachi.

[1] Sir Archibald Rowlands, G.C.B., M.B.E., the last British Finance Minister in India.
[2] Sir George Cunningham, G.C.I.E., K.C.S.I., O.B.E., had been Governor of the North-West Frontier Province from 1937 to 1946.
[3] Sir Francis Mudie, K.C.S.I., K.C.I.E., O.B.E., Governor of Sind from 1946 until Partition.

The Archdeacon had also composed a special prayer, in which the Quaid was mentioned. When Jinnah heard of this, he asked that he might be allowed to attend the service, in State.

In recording this solemn act, Mr Wilfred Russell wrote,[1] 'Mr Jinnah, who knew only too well the orthodox fervour of many Muslims, might well have been taking a political risk in making this graceful and moving gesture to the Christian community of Karachi.'

* * *

Unlike the creators of other nations, such as Washington, Cavour and Bismarck, Mohammed Ali Jinnah had achieved his aim without the support of an army. He never seemed, before Partition, to consider the part soldiery might play in forming an independent state. General Sir Frank Messervy, the first Commander-in-Chief of the Pakistan army, has said :[2] "Jinnah was not really interested in the army : he had no ideas on the subject, and said to me, 'I have no military experience : I leave that entirely to you and Liaquat.'"

There was a nice episode, revealing Jinnah's attitude to military authority, when he attended a march past, in Dacca, in March 1948. When he stood up to take the salute he was some three feet out of position. The Commander-in-Chief whispered, "You must stand *here*, sir."

"Why?" asked Quaid-i-Azam.

"Because this is a military occasion."

"Very well," replied Jinnah, and moved up.

Quaid-i-Azam showed no more detailed interest in the formation of the air force than of the army : to him, aircraft were merely a means of travelling quickly from one place to another. But, for some reason, the establishment of the Pakistan navy interested him. One naval officer explained this by recalling that Jinnah had been concerned with ships and docks thirty years before, when he had been lawyer to a seamen's and firemen's union in Bombay. Perhaps he realized that, for as long as the Hindus remained hostile, sea communication between East and West Pakistan was vital if his nation was to survive. This is a more reasonable explanation of the lively interest he took in the task that fell to Rear-[later Vice-] Admiral J. W. Jefford, who took over Pakistan's navy on August 13. He

[1] *Indian Summer*, p. 127. [2] To the author.

began with one frigate, two minesweepers and some coastal craft lying alongside the docks in Karachi, one frigate at sea, and two more frigates and four minesweepers still held in Bombay for refitting. There were two shore bases in Karachi, but no administrative or repair facilities, stores or ammunition. There were only two Pakistani officers who had served in the navy for more than eight years. A headquarters staff was created and a base built, with naval and ordnance stores. East Pakistan—one thousand miles away—had no naval station. The Hindus would permit no land communication between the two Pakistans, so the Admiral flew a complete wireless station and crew to Chittagong, where a base was ultimately built. This was the spirit in which this robust, imaginative sailor set about creating a navy out of nothing.

The Admiral remained in Pakistan five years, during which he achieved not only the establishment of a young naval power, but also the genesis of a tradition. Before he departed, for England, the ratings of the Pakistan Navy drew lots, so that one thousand of them could entertain him to dinner in a cinema in Karachi. Such a man was likely to enjoy the trust of Quaid-i-Azam.

Admiral Jefford has written of Mohammed Ali Jinnah : [1] 'He was a very great man : by the time that he got Pakistan for the Muslims he was a demi-god to the masses ; yet he was no demagogue, and he lacked the man-to-man approach of Liaquat Ali Khan. . . . The Quaid never courted popularity in any way. By nature he was cold and reserved, but occasionally there would be an unexpected flicker of humanity. And he hated sycophants. There was an instance of this after the Inaugural Ceremony on August 14, 1947. The Viceroy had taken off for Delhi and the Quaid was in Government House, with some of his Pakistani friends. Lord Mountbatten had been staying with the Quaid, so both the Union Jack and the Governor-General's flag were flying, side by side. Thinking to please Jinnah, one of his followers suggested that as the Viceroy was no longer on Pakistani soil, the Union Jack might be hauled down. The Quaid fixed him with his coldest and glassiest stare and said, " The correct time for hauling down flags is sunset : to do so before would be an insult to the King, who has just made me Governor-General, and who has signed the Message that created Pakistan. " '

[1] In a memorandum to the author.

The Admiral was encouraged because he knew that the Quaid always 'had a soft spot for the Navy,' and because his was the first service 'officially inspected by the Governor-General.' There was a time when Admiral Jefford was worried whether the Finance Ministry would produce funds for the two destroyers he thought essential to the service. The Quaid, usually so attached to his beloved 'constitutional methods,' answered this doubt by drawing the Admiral aside one day after lunch and saying, " Go right ahead and make the necessary plans : I shall see that you get your destroyers."

Only once was there any grave difference between the Quaid and the Admiral : it admitted no anger and ended, most remarkably, in a change to King's Regulations and Admiralty Instructions.

Late in 1947, Admiral Sir Arthur Palliser, C.-in-C. East Indies Station, announced that he would pay his formal call on Quaid-i-Azam and the new State of Pakistan. It was expected that Mr Jinnah would respect the regulation and tradition, of returning the call to the Admiral's flagship. The Quaid approved all the plans but this : he would not return the call in person but would send his Military Secretary. The Admiralty were informed, and there was a hubbub among their Lordships in Whitehall. Admiral Jefford then asked to see the Governor-General, ' as his Naval Advisor,' to ' explain the Naval point of view.' Here was a legal argument after the Quaid's own heart : he answered, " Tell the Naval C.-in-C. that he is NOT *my* Naval Advisor but that of the Government of Pakistan, but that I would be pleased to see him, as Admiral Jefford, to clarify the Naval point of view."

Admiral Jefford arrived at Government House ' fully prepared,' as he has written, ' for a stormy session ending with " Off with his head." '

But the Quaid was in ' a cheerful mood ' and he met the Admiral at the door—a gesture that ' shook all the other characters to the core.' As they walked into the sitting-room, Mr Jinnah said, " What about a whisky and soda ? "

This courtesy over, Admiral Jefford quoted King's Regulations and explained the traditional procedure of Governors-General when Naval Commanders-in-Chief came into port, to pay formal calls.

The Quaid answered, " Now look here, Jefford : I am in a very different position from, say, the Governor of a West Indian colony in the eighteenth century, with Nelson or someone like that calling on him. Here I am, in 1947, Governor-General of a sovereign, self-governing state, which has just been given its freedom by the British." Mr Jinnah explained that his people knew nothing of 'protocol or official calling,' and that they might misunderstand, or condemn, his action if, as Head of the State, he went to Admiral Palliser in person. But he asked that a 'purely Naval message' be sent inviting the Admiral to bring his wife and family to stay at Government House, and saying how pleased he would be to attend a social function on board the flagship.

The Governor-General and Admiral Palliser met with mutual good grace and pleasure, but the effect of the episode on Whitehall was startling, and permanent. Admiral Jefford was later able to inform the Quaid that, because of his protest, Governors-General would no longer return Admirals' calls in person ; that King's Regulations and Admiralty Instructions—' inviolate as the New Testament to a dyed-in-the-wool Naval officer '—had been changed accordingly.

* * *

Until Quaid-i-Azam died, the Military Secretaries to the Governor-General were both British officers. The first of these, Colonel E. St J. Birnie, of the Guides Cavalry (Frontier Force), had already proved himself in two remarkable adventures. In 1927, while big game hunting in the Mandla Forest, he had been bitten in the arm by a tiger. This first taste gave the tiger no pleasure : he wrenched the Colonel's rifle from his hands and walked off with it, into the jungle. The Colonel had also been a member of the 1933 Mount Everest Expedition and had endured eight days and nights at 25,700 feet. He was therefore a man of unusual stamina, and any one's match in a test of will or endurance.

On July 21, 1947, Colonel Birnie wrote, in his diary, ' This morning I was told that I was to go at once to see Liaquat Ali Khan, as I was being considered as military secretary to Mr Jinnah. This surprised me a good deal : I presumed that he would select a Pakistani. My interview with Liaquat Ali Khan went well and I like him very much.' Next day, he saw Mr Jinnah in Delhi : his appointment was confirmed, and he was asked to fly immediately to Karachi and prepare Government House for the Quaid's arrival.

On July 23, the Colonel recorded his 'first impression of Jinnah' as 'most favourable'. 'He spoke so sincerely and nicely of the British that I knew I could not refuse to do my best for him.' Five weeks later, in Karachi, he wrote, 'At dinner tonight, Jinnah spoke most feelingly to us of all his past, and his sincerity and honesty have completely captivated everyone in the house.'

Colonel Birnie's diary covers the important first months of the history of Pakistan. On August 29, he wrote:

> Atrocities on both sides have been terrible in the last fortnight; the greatest danger has existed in the fact that so many people on both sides have panicked and made things worse. There are thousands of refugees of both communities in camps, both in India and Pakistan, whose homes have been burnt to the ground and who have lost everything they possess. It is this complete distrust of each other that is the most serious aspect of the whole situation.
>
> Three brigades of British troops would be sufficient to hold the balance and keep the peace, but, unfortunately, this is no longer possible. . . .
>
> Attacks on trains have increased, chiefly organized by the Sikhs. Harrington Hawes . . . had a very narrow escape when his train was derailed. After making their way, on foot, to the nearest railway station, the train was looted by 200 Sikhs who had previously killed the entire staff of the station. He managed to get most of the passengers on to the roof of the station where, 24 hours later, they were rescued by a relief train. . . .
>
> I never go unarmed now, in the Quaid's company. Naturally, a certain group of terrorists have sent in their threats that they will get him sooner or later.

The perils and anxieties continued: during a 'top level party' given by Quaid-i-Azam on September 7, where some fifty people came to meet the Sheikh of Kuwait, there was a demonstration at the gates of Government House. Colonel Birnie had to leave the party, 'a pleasant affair, held near the swimming pool,' to quell some three hundred 'employees of the secretariat' who demanded to see the Quaid. The Colonel wrote:

> I . . . tried to persuade them to appoint one or two leaders who would come forward and state their case. I soon realized

that they had no leaders and were merely all upset at the rumours of massacres of their families in East Punjab. . . . One could not sufficiently sympathize with them, and I had already instructed the police to handle them with the utmost patience.

They declared they would not leave until the Quaid came and spoke to them. . . . Eventually he came out on to the back upstairs verandah of his rooms, and addressed them, briefly, saying that everything possible was being done to help in getting their families out. He then instructed them to keep discipline and leave the grounds.

Immediately, there were cries of ' Quaid-i-Azam Zindabad.' The crowds then marched out without any fuss. Jinnah undoubtedly has great authority over these people and one wonders who can possibly, eventually, take his place.

The Quaid would not confess his weariness, even to himself: late each night, he worked at his desk, trying, with the quiet appeal of the written word, to cool the passions of the refugees. The reports that came in each day were terrible. Colonel Birnie wrote, also on September 7, of ' a very bad week ' in Delhi. Sikhs, ' in organized bands,' had ' broken into Muslim shops and looted them ' : they ' held up cars and murdered any Muslims they could lay their hands on.' In Delhi alone, ' somewhere between 1500 and 2000 Muslims ' had been killed. The Colonel continued, in his diary :

> To add to our troubles in forming a new Dominion, we have now to organize mass distribution of food and medicines to thousands of destitute people and to move literally hundreds of thousands out of India into Pakistan, where, incidentally, there are no houses for them. . . .
> These countless thousands must now be wondering whether life under British rule, under which they had complete security, was not better than their now desperate plight.

* * *

This last year of Mohammed Ali Jinnah's life was saddened by his despair over the fate of Kashmir. Lord Mountbatten had advised the rulers of the five hundred and sixty-five Indian States to accede to one or other of the new Dominions, before the transfer of power. Their choice, of Pakistan or Hindustan, had been determined by expediency—by their geographical position in relation to the new frontiers, or by the predominance of Hindus or Muslims in their population. All but the rulers of Junagadh, Hyderabad and Kashmir had agreed. The fortunes of beautiful Kashmir—the source of three of the great rivers that succour West Pakistan—were governed by different factors : the chief and most alarming was that this predominantly Muslim State was ruled by a Hindu Maharaja, an insensitive despot, both rich and powerful.

There was also, in Kashmir, a ruling class of Hindus—Kashmiri Brahmins—whose loyalties drew them towards Hindustan. Many of them had become important leaders in Indian politics, and their voices were powerful in the councils of Delhi. Chief of them was Pandit Nehru, whose emotions over his native land were described when he said to a British army officer," In the same way that Calais was written on Mary's heart, Kashmir is written on mine."

Thus, at the time of Partition, Kashmir was herself tragically divided. A multitude of middle-class and poor Muslims—who formed eighty per cent of Kashmir's population—and who saw their only salvation in joining Pakistan—were dominated by a powerful Hindu minority, and ruled by a Hindu who wanted to accede to India, but who was naturally alarmed by the dangerous strength of his own people, and afraid to declare his mind.

This confusion of loyalties led to the first considerable dilemma in the affairs of divided India. Within fifteen days of Partition, Lord Mountbatten had become so alarmed at the prospect of conflict in Kashmir that he asked Lord Ismay ' to do his best to get the Maharaja to make up his vacillating mind ', and induce him to ' accede without further delay to whichever Dominion he and his people desire. . . .' [1]

The Maharaja would not decide, and while he boggled and intrigued for his own profit, his people acted for him. At the end of August his Muslim subjects in Poonch—part of western Kashmir that bordered on Pakistan—revolted and formed their own Azad [Free] Kashmir Government. The Maharaja then ordered his troops to expel thousands of Muslims from the district of Jammu. On October 24, news reached Quaid-i-Azam in Karachi that five thousand guerrilla tribesmen from the North-West Frontier had crossed into Kashmir to help their fellow Muslims. Two days later, the Maharaja declared his

[1] *Mission with Mountbatten*, p. 177.

mind: he acceded to India and asked for the support of Indian troops. The terrible, long tragedy had begun, and on that day, October 26, Mr Jinnah flew to Lahore, to be nearer, and able to watch the fate of the Muslims in Kashmir.

Colonel Birnie wrote in his diary:

> The Quaid and Miss Jinnah left for Lahore on Sunday. . . . Quaid's visit is in connection with the troubles in Kashmir, which are becoming very serious. Mountbatten is to join him in Lahore to discuss the problem. The whole situation is really shocking: the root of the matter is that neither community has the slightest confidence in the other; they both thoroughly distrust each other.
>
> Jinnah has many high principles, and many of his apparent indecisions are due to the fact that he is in doubt as to what line is the correct one to follow. He refuses to decide until he has sifted the question from every point of view. His principles, although broadcast to all and sundry, have little apparent effect on his people. . . . We must not forget that some of them, in fact, millions, have lost everything they possessed and are desperate, and so easily led to senseless revenge.

Two phrases from this entry in Colonel Birnie's diary apply grimly to the tasks that the Quaid had to face when he arrived in Lahore. The Colonel wrote of Jinnah's refusal ' to decide ' until he had ' sifted the question from every point of view,' and of ' senseless revenge.' As Governor-General, he had to sift a question of dreadful magnitude, immediately. Indian troops were being flown into Kashmir and the land was horrible with ' senseless revenge.' The Quaid wished to send in his half-formed army, to protect the Muslims. Field-Marshal Sir Claude Auchinleck [1] flew to Lahore at an hour's notice and reasoned with the Quaid: he explained that the presence of Indian troops in Kashmir was justified, since the Maharaja had acceded: any action by the Pakistan army would force him to withdraw all British officers, including the Commanders-in-Chief of both India and Pakistan. The desperate move was abandoned.

[1] Commander-in-Chief in India before Partition: at the time of the episode described above, he was Supreme Commander administering partition of the Indian Army.

Soon after this crisis,[1] the Quaid—melancholy and ill—was obliged to stay in bed. Colonel Birnie wrote:

> Quaid-i-Azam is still in Lahore and is being kept there as he still runs a low temperature and it is not wise for him to make the air journey. Everything is, as a consequence, at a standstill. Any file sent by me to the Private Secretary is either not shown him at all (presumably on the doctor's advice) or else comes back with the remark that he cannot attend to it until he returns here, and, as that date is indefinite, nobody knows what to do. Even the Ministers are devastated as they can get no decisions on anything.

★   ★   ★

During these weeks of illness in Lahore, the Quaid was the guest of the Governor of the West Punjab, Sir Francis Mudie, who had known him, through many hazards and arguments, since 1936. It is perhaps touching that Jinnah should have endured these terrible crises, as Governor-General of free Pakistan, while he was the guest of an Englishman—one who had stayed, and who wrote,[2] ' Jinnah impressed me more, I think, than anyone else I have ever met, and I was very fond of him. . . . It is difficult to say why. . . . He was cold—at least, that was the impression he gave—but I never found him harsh. He was, of course, hard. He never, if he could help it, compromised. . . . Officially, until the end, when he was obviously very ill, I found him open to reason, or at least to argument. . . . I got to know that I could trust him absolutely. He was thoroughly loyal to those who had supported him in the past.

'In judging Jinnah, we must remember what he was up against. He had against him not only the wealth and brains of the Hindus, but also nearly the whole of British officialdom, and most of the Home politicians, who made the great mistake of refusing to take Pakistan seriously. Never was his position really examined.'

Sir Francis Mudie has recalled, 'He was in bed in my home in

---

[1] In April 1948, when the increasing strength of Indian forces in Kashmir threatened to overwhelm the Azad Kashmir Government, Pakistan eventually sent regular troops to help them. The fate of the troubled State lies outside the scope of Jinnah's story: four months after his death a cease-fire line, between the Indian and Pakistan forces, was fixed by the Kashmir Commission appointed by the United Nations Security Council.

[2] In letters to the author.

Lahore for three weeks . . . and never, even by a sign, indicated that he would not shortly be all right again.'

On December 1, Quaid-i-Azam returned to Karachi from Lahore. Colonel Birnie wrote in his diary, ' I was quite definitely shocked to see him. He left here five weeks ago, looking 60 years of age. Now he looks well over 80. . . . I drove from the airport with him and Miss Jinnah and felt most sorry for him. He openly said that his fever was due to mental strain and that he prayed for a chance of getting away, anywhere, where nobody could worry him, for at least a fortnight.'

Two days later, the Governor-General seemed ' stronger.' Colonel Birnie had arranged a ceremony—' the Bodyguard posted and all the Staff in Full Dress white, and civilians in morning coats '—to receive the Envoy Extraordinary and Special Representative of the King of Afghanistan.' The Quaid ' went through the ceremony well.'

As Christmas Day came near—Jinnah's last birthday—he enjoyed a refreshment of spirit. No occasion showed this more pleasantly than the night when he dined with the officers of the Royal Scots, before they sailed for home. It was a grand dinner, with silver trophies on the tables, pipers, and wines most carefully chosen. At the end, the Princess Royal was toasted, as Colonel-in-Chief of the Regiment ; then the King. It is an old rule with the Royal Scots that no further toasts are proposed at dinner, but, on this occasion, the commanding officer rose and said, looking at Quaid-i-Azam, " Your Excellency, it is such an honour to have you with us that I am going to break tradition. We consider ourselves good fighters : we consider you to be a good fighter also." The Quaid stood up, and said, " Gentlemen, may I further break the tradition of your regiment and reply ? I shall never forget the British who have stayed in Pakistan to help us begin our work : this I shall never forget."

On the way home in the car, Jinnah opened his heart to Colonel Birnie, and spoke of his debt to his sister for her long years of devotion to him, and for the way in which she had helped to lead the women of Pakistan towards emancipation. He spoke also of his admiration for the British : he said, " Yes, that is the thing you have got—that is it—traditions are the strength of your country."

★   ★   ★

There had been only one continuous disagreement between the Quaid and his Military Secretary : the Colonel could not induce Mr Jinnah to sanction arrangements for his own protection, which seemed necessary with so many wild assassins at large. He had asked for authority to build a high wall that would shut off the part of Government House in which the Quaid lived. When the plan was first proposed, Jinnah had answered, "It is very nice of you to take precautions, but I am not the sort of Governor-General you have been used to. I am one of the people. No harm will come to me."

Colonel Birnie had protested, "But a Hindu might shoot you," and Mr Jinnah had repeated, "No, I am here with my people. No harm will come to me." He had added the characteristic remark, "Anyhow, it is a waste of money."

The Colonel's term as Military Secretary was almost ended and the Quaid had asked him 'to start looking for a suitable substitute.' Colonel Birnie wrote, 'I gather he again wants an Englishman.' But, it seemed, he would have to depart having lost this one battle, over the protecting wall. Then, events suddenly helped him to final victory. On January 30, 1948—soon before Colonel Birnie sailed for England—Mahatma Gandhi was assassinated, in New Delhi.

Quad-i-Azam was staying at his little beach house, a few miles from Karachi, when the news reached him. He drove back to Government House, and, while walking up the stairs with Colonel Birnie, he said, "About that wall—you can start building it immediately."

* * *

IN THE GARDEN

> *Behold him in the evening tide of life* . . .
> *By unperceiv'd degrees he wears away;*
> *Yet, like the Sun, seems larger at his setting* . . .
>   *The Grave*, ROBERT BLAIR.

JAMSHED NUSSERWANJEE, the old Parsee friend [1] who was so fond of Mohammed Ali Jinnah, sought him one day in the garden of Government House and found him dozing on a seat. The Quaid looked up and said, "I am so tired, Jamshed, so tired."

[1] See pp. 94–5.

THE TIRED LEADER

This was early in February 1948, six months after Jinnah had flown in to claim his realm.

He had always been too busy to sit out of doors and doze like this. When he owned his first garden, on Malabar Hill in Bombay, in the early days of his political career, he would hurry along the paths in the morning, complaining if the flowers were mixed. "Like a jungle," he would say. He liked phlox and petunias in nice straight lines, but he never paused to pick a flower, and seldom sat in idleness to enjoy the view.

The Quaid's habits changed during this last year of his life : he would sometimes sit in the garden of Government House and permit what was a novelty to him—moments of contemplation in the shade, followed by a short nap. Sometimes, while walking through the garden, he would bend down and pick a carnation for his coat.

One morning, also in February, Mr Ian Stephens went to see the Quaid. He wrote [1] afterwards, '. . . at that time, though no one realized it, the creator of Pakistan was dying, his lungs riddled with the unsuspected tuberculosis which a few months later killed him.' The Quaid had kept his secret—the warning of the Bombay doctors, three and a half years before.

Mr Stephens wrote, ' Mr Jinnah looked better than when I had seen him shortly before Partition, and I said so. During an unexpectedly long interview, 70 minutes, which baffled his secretaries, he ranged widely over the course of Indo-Pakistani affairs during the previous seven months—a dramatic, fascinating story, as told by such a man.' At the end, the Quaid said, " Yes, Mr Stephens, thank you, I feel better ; I am better. They say I have been ill. I have not. I know. I get tired."

The ' thin, handsome lips moved with the restrained, characteristic smile ' as Quaid-i-Azam went on, " It is natural that I should. I am not young, I have responsibilities. . . . So, when I get tired, Mr Stephens, I rest. It is simple. I tell my doctors to go away. I know what to do. I will not have them fussing ; they might annoy me. No, I was not ill at all."

*   *   *

Each man is a hundred men within himself, so that he presents a

[1] *Horned Moon*, p. 50.

different facet to almost every being he meets. The many who had known Jinnah disagreed as to his hardness of heart, his solitariness, and his charm, but, from the beginning to the end, no one ever doubted his integrity. Sir Stafford Cripps, who first knew him in the early 1930's, regarded him as 'a man of the highest probity and honour; difficult to negotiate with, for the very reason that he was so determined in his purpose.' Field-Marshal Sir Claude Auchinleck said of Jinnah, "I admired him; his tenacity and tremendous personality—his inexorable determination." Lord Wavell, with whom Mr Jinnah had failed in friendship, sighed when he was asked for his opinion, and said, "He was a very difficult man to deal with."

Those who worked near the Quaid—the younger Pakistanis who served him after Partition—were devoted, but intimidated. One of his secretaries has said, "Even Jinnah's warmth was calculated." Another has said, "Quaid-i-Azam was very old and tired when I went to him. All my feelings were subdued into awe of him. But there were many endearing qualities. Sometimes he would be sharp-tempered and would wave me away when I spoke to him. After a few minutes he would ring and I would go into him. Then came kindness, and his apology. 'I am old and weak and sometimes I am impatient: I hope you will forgive my bad manners.'"

But this gentleness was seldom revealed. A member of Lord Mountbatten's staff is reported to have described the Quaid as 'the rudest man east of Suez.' When this story was told to Mrs Neville Wadia, the Quaid's daughter, she answered, "My father was arrogant, but never rude. If you examine each incident in which he is accused of rudeness, you will find that the other person was clumsily rude first."

It was true that Quaid-i-Azam had always been quick with reproof. There is a story of Mr Ramsay MacDonald saying to him, "Mr Jinnah, you know that we are hoping to grant self-government to India, and I shall need men to be Governors of Provinces;" and, Jinnah's answer, "Mr MacDonald, are you trying to bribe me?" And he could reprimand those who admired him most. Once, in London, when Mr Jinnah was about to take off by air, for Bombay, an old, devout Muslim appeared on the aerodrome with the one wish that he might shake the Quaid's hand. He had hurried all the way from the east end of London in a taxi-cab, which had cost him several pounds. Someone led the disciple to Jinnah and told him the story of the cab. The Quaid shook the old man's hand, but he said, in a scolding voice, " Oh, you Muslims are so extravagant."

The Quaid rejected all adulation when it was emotional. He went, one day, to a small town where he was welcomed by a big procession of peasants. They cried out, " Maulana Mohammed Ali Jinnah Zindabad ! " *Maulana* is a religious title, and this the Quaid resented. He halted the procession, pointed his finger at the crowd, and said, " Stop calling me Maulana. I am not your religious leader. I am your political leader. Call me Mr Jinnah, or Mohammed Ali Jinnah. No more of that *Maulana*. Do you understand me ? "

The people were amazed : they had thought to honour him. They became silent, and he drove on.

Women stirred qualities in the Quaid that give a different and gentler view. There is a happy story told of a young girl who was introduced to him, some time before Partition. She confessed to an older woman, later, that she had fallen in love with Mr Jinnah's hands —the hands he cared for and used so effectively. The woman repeated the story to the Quaid, and he was amused. Next day, when he went to the races, he found that he was sitting next to his young admirer, so he said to her, mischievously, " Now, young lady, don't keep looking at my hands."

Older women liked his distinguished looks, and the courtly manner he could affect, in drawing-rooms. Lady Wavell said of him, " Mr Jinnah was one of the handsomest men I have ever seen ; he combined the clear-cut, almost Grecian, features of the West, with Oriental grace and movement." Begum Liaquat Ali Khan has said, " The first time I saw Jinnah he captured my heart. He gave the impression of being haughty and conceited, but once you came to know him he was deeply human."

Perhaps Mrs Naidu's estimate of Jinnah, made when he was still in his thirties, remains the wisest of all. She wrote :

> A casual pen might surely find it easier to describe his limitations than to define his virtues. His are none of the versatile talents that make so many of his contemporaries justly famed beyond the accepted circle of their daily labours. Not his the gracious gifts of mellow scholarship, or rich adventure or radiant conversation ; not his the burning passion of philanthropy or

religious reform. Indeed, by his sequestered tastes and temperament, Mohomed Ali Jinnah is essentially a solitary man with a large political following but few intimate friendships; and outside the twin spheres of law and politics he has few resources and few accomplishments.

But the true criterion of his greatness lies not in the range and variety of his knowledge and experience, but in the faultless perception and flawless refinement of his subtle mind and spirit; not in a diversity of aims and the challenge of a towering personality, but rather in a lofty singleness and sincerity of purpose and the lasting charm of a character animated by a brave conception of duty and an austere and lovely code of private honour and public integrity.

* * *

Of what did Mohammed Ali Jinnah think as he dozed in the garden? Mrs Naidu had written of his 'singleness and sincerity of purpose,' and of his 'lovely code of private honour and public integrity.' But she had also regretted his lack of ' the gracious gifts of mellow scholarship.' It was true that he never seemed to see himself in relation to history: even when he was at the age when most old men enjoy their memories, he spared little time for such pleasures. He never even returned to the house in Newnham Road, where he had been born, seventy-one years before. It would have been a proud sensation for any man, to walk from the splendours of Government House—the symbol of achievement—back to his humble birthplace; to look up at the two first floor rooms and say, " There I began, and I have made a nation." But, for Jinnah, yesterday was done with and a dead thing.

* * *

ZIARAT, AND THE LAST TASK

DURING February and March of 1948, Quaid-i-Azam still worked long hours at his desk. His secretary at this time has said, " His seriousness was contagious: there was no lightness or humour in our work. When Bills arrived for him to sign, he would go through them sentence by sentence. 'Clumsy and badly worded,' he would complain. I had to prepare myself beforehand for a cross-examination on the Bill, as if I had been the Minister who drafted it. He would say, 'Split it up into more clauses!' 'This should go back and be re-written!' When I pleaded, 'You will be holding up a useful piece of legislation,' he would relent. But his vigilance did not weaken. 'They can't hustle me,' he would say. 'I won't do it.'"

In these last months, the Quaid had to deal with a bigger world than ever before: on December 30, the quarrel over Kashmir had been taken to the Security Council of the United Nations, where it still awaits solution. The problem dismissed so casually by Pandit Nehru in 1942, when he said that, 'except for a small handful of persons,' there was 'no difference between Hindu and Muslim,' was no longer a dilemma in Westminster: it was a tragedy for all the nations to decide, and beyond Mr Jinnah's control.

In March, the Quaid made one more gallant effort in drawing his people together: he flew the thousand miles to East Pakistan, and endured a programme of receptions, reviews and speeches, during several days. His appeal to the students in Dacca showed that power had not changed his mind: he said,

> My young friends, students who are present here, let me tell you as one who has always had love and affection for you, as one who has served you for ten years faithfully and loyally; let me give you this word of warning. You will be making the greatest mistake if you allow yourself to be exploited by one political party or the other.

From April 15, for seven days, Mr Jinnah was on the North-West Frontier, where there were more receptions, reviews and speeches: when he returned to Karachi he was too ill to work at his desk for very long. His secretary has said, "The Quaid spent most of the day upstairs, in his own room. But his passion for newspapers did not abate: even the teleprinter tape had to be rolled up and taken to him. He would lie on the sofa, running the yards of news through his fingers."

Sir Francis Mudie, one of Mr Jinnah's last guests in Karachi, has recalled, "I stayed with him for a few days late in May. He was very ill and spent most of the time in bed. We had a rather violent difference of opinion over the Punjab Ministry—yet, within two hours, he got up and said goodbye to me at three in the afternoon, and could not have been nicer."

* * *

In May, the Quaid had appointed a new naval A.D.C. to his staff—Lieutenant Mazhar Ahmed, who was to serve him until he died. In June, Mr Jinnah moved, with his little court, to a bungalow at Ziarat, seventy miles or so from Quetta.

Lieutenant Ahmed has described the bungalow, 'high in the rocky hills, with a tennis court, fruit trees, and a garden that smelled of juniper and wild lavender.' He has said, " We raised the Governor-General's dark blue flag over the quiet house and hoped that the Quaid would rest. But it was not in his nature. The black despatch-boxes arrived each day from Karachi, with M.A.J. stamped on them, in gold. They were full of work to be done. My clearest memory of him is of his slim hands, busy with papers.

"I think that I was always intimidated by him: he could be so formal. But, sometimes, he would relax and tell us stories: usually they were planned for our good. He would raise his long finger, shake it at us, and begin, 'I tell you . . .'

"I remember one story, of his visit to the Jakko Hills in Simla, where he went for a walk with some peanuts in his pockets. He threw them to the monkeys that dwell there, and was surprised to see that none of them moved—there was no mad rush for the nuts. Then a big, fat old monkey climbed down from a tree and went towards the peanuts. All the chattering of the monkeys ceased: they made way for their leader, and would not eat until he had eaten. When Mr Jinnah had finished this story, he said, 'You see, even monkeys have discipline.'

"We could not look at his thin body without being sad for him. One morning he said that he must have some woollen vests, as the days were cold. I pointed out to him that they must be women's size, and he smiled. I bought them from a shop in Quetta, and, after the first wash, there were holes in them. I said I would have them changed, but there were no more, so the shop-keeper had the vests darned. Quaid-i-Azam was not satisfied with this and thought that the price should be reduced. I brought him back five rupees from the shop-keeper, and he said, ' Good boy. You must learn the value of money.' "

* * *

In one of the main streets of Karachi, near the Governor-General's house, the masons had recently finished a realistic monument to Mr Jinnah's faith in Pakistan—the big, imposing State Bank; the nation's bank, with its own currency as a sign of its economic freedom.

Nobody could discourage the Quaid from opening the bank himself. When his speech was written, his naval A.D.C. suggested that it might be sent to Karachi for the Prime Minister to read, in his stead. The Quaid did not answer: he waved his hand in dismissal, and the A.D.C. left the room. Two days later, the Governor-General flew from Quetta to the Capital, to perform his last task.

In the archives of the Karachi broadcasting station there is a gramophone record of the speech that the Quaid made, on July 1. The voice is thin and harsh with age, but the inflections, the pauses, and the careful prolonging o words of particular importance, prove that his experience as an actor, fifty years before, had not been forgotten. His timing of the first sentence was splendid: the words were simple enough, but he gave them unusual distinction. He said, " Mr Governor, Directors of the State Bank, Ladies and Gentlemen, the opening of the State Bank of Pakistan symbolizes the sovereignty of our State in the financial sphere, and I am very glad to be here today to perform the opening ceremony."

Towards the end, the Quaid made his last comment on the confusion of the world. He said:

> The economic system of the West has created almost insoluble problems for humanity, and to many of us it appears that only a miracle can save it from the disaster that is now facing the world. It has failed to do justice between man and man and to eradicate friction from the international field. On the contrary, it was largely responsible for the two world wars in the last half-century. The Western world, in spite of its advantages, of mechanization and industrial efficiency, is today in a worse mess than ever before in history. The adoption of Western economic theory and practice will not help us in achieving our goal of

creating a happy and contented people. We must work our destiny in our own way, and present to the world an economic system based on the true Islamic concept of equality of mankind and social justice. We will thereby be fulfilling our mission as Muslims and giving to humanity the message of peace which alone can save it and secure the welfare, happiness and prosperity of mankind.

Every possible splendour had been summoned for this day. The Quaid drove to the State Bank in one of the old Viceregal coaches, from Delhi, with Miss Jinnah beside him. Six horses drew the coach, and the escort wore the startling red uniforms of the bodyguard that had accompanied the Viceroys, in the grand old days before Partition. For the first, and the last time, the people of Karachi saw their deliverer driving among them, with all the panoply of a ruler. There had been one amusing incident before the procession left the Governor-General's House : the Quaid had leaned over to his Military Secretary, who had arranged all these splendours, and said, " Colonel Knowles,[1] I hope these horses have been exercised sufficiently."

Lieutenant Mazhar Ahmed has described the last episodes of the day. " Quaid-i-Azam was very weak and tired as he stepped into the coach. The thousands of people pressed towards him, as if they wished to touch him, but the outriders made this impossible ; so the near ones extended their hands towards the coach—as if this would complete their ecstasy. When we arrived back at Government House, we climbed the stairs together and turned right, towards Mr Jinnah's room. After a few paces he dismissed me. At the top of the stairs I turned and saw him staggering towards his door. I knew then how ill he was, but I did not dare go back to help him : it would have been an intrusion he would never allow."

*   *   *

[1] Colonel Geoffrey Knowles had succeeded Colonel Birnie as Military Secretary to the Governor-General in February 1948.

THE LAST DAYS[1]

IT must have been written many times, that a man reveals all his life in the way he dies. This was true of Mohammed Ali Jinnah. Although his slim body—which came to weigh only seventy pounds—moved so vitally, and his eyes kept their fire, those who were near him saw that his will, not his physical strength, was deciding when he should die.

Miss Jinnah has recalled, "For several years before his death there was a constant tug-of-war between his physicians and the Quaid-i-Azam. They warned him to take long intervals of rest and short hours of hard work, but he did exactly the opposite, knowing full well the risk he was running. Often his doctors complained to me that he ignored their advice." Whenever Miss Jinnah said to her brother, "You must see a doctor," he would answer, "No. I've got too much to do. I can't waste my time."

Back in the bungalow at Ziarat, twenty-three days after the opening of the State Bank, the Quaid had to yield, with more stubbornness than grace, to the constant care of a doctor. Lieutenant-Colonel Ilahi Bakhsh, a graduate of Guy's Hospital, London, who had also played cricket for Leicestershire, was chosen for the task.

He first saw the Quaid at eight o'clock on the morning of July 24 and found him 'shockingly weak and thin,' with an 'ashen grey complexion.'

"There is nothing wrong with me," Mr Jinnah protested. "I have stomach trouble and exhaustion, due to over-work and worry. For forty years I have worked for fourteen hours a day, never knowing what disease was."

He went on, with the insistence of an advocate pleading a case in which he did not believe, rather than with the despair of a sick man. "For the last few years I have had annual attacks of fever and cough. My doctors in Bombay regarded these attacks as bronchitis . . . for the last year or two, however, they have increased, both in frequency and severity, and they are much more exhausting."

---

[1] This description of the closing weeks of the Quaid's life is based on the reports of, and interviews with, Lieut.-Colonel Ilahi Bakhsh, the doctor who attended him, Sister Phyllis Dunham, his nurse, Colonel Geoffrey Knowles, his Military Secretary, and Lieutenant Mazhar Ahmed, his naval A.D.C

Dr Bakhsh did not interrupt: he noticed that, while Mr Jinnah talked, he lost breath after each sentence, and that he moistened his lips, nervously.

Quaid-i-Azam continued, " About three weeks ago I caught a chill and developed fever and a cough, for which the civil surgeon at Quetta prescribed penicillin lozenges. I have been taking them ever since; my cold is better, the fever is less, but I feel very weak. I don't think that there is anything organically wrong with me. The phlegm which I bring up is probably coming from my stomach, and if my stomach can be put right I will recover soon."

Dr Bakhsh did not accept this cheerful diagnosis: other doctors were summoned and tests were made. They confirmed what Dr Bakhsh suspected, and Jinnah knew, that he was dying of a disease of the lungs.

After he had told the Quaid the ' grave news ', the doctor wrote in his diary, ' I watched him intently. He remained quite calm, then said, " Have you told Miss Jinnah ? " When I answered, " Yes," he said, " No, you shouldn't have done it. After all, she is a woman. However, it does not matter. What is done is done. Now tell me about it. How long will the treatment take ? I should like to know everything, and you must not hesitate to tell me the whole truth. " '

The doctor told the ' whole truth,' but the Quaid remained stubborn. At first he refused to engage a nurse: he wished only his sister to care for him. A ' lady compounder ' was brought in to help: her first simple task was to take his pulse and his temperature.

When the Quaid asked the ' lady compounder ' what his temperature was, she refused to tell him without the doctor's permission. This glimpse of ' constitutional methods,' in a sphere different from his own, delighted him.

Then came an argument over the simple matter of the Quaid's pyjamas. Dr Bakhsh said to him, " Sir, the silk pyjamas you have been wearing are too thin for you. There is danger of your catching cold."

Mr Jinnah answered. " I have only got silk ones, but I intend to have some made of handloom cloth."

The doctor protested, " Sir, cotton will not do; you must have woollen ones . . . without your permission I have ordered thirty yards of Viyella cloth from Karachi."

The Quaid had only one, old, familiar argument left : he said, " Listen doctor, take my advice. Whenever you spend money on anything, think twice whether it is necessary—in fact, essential or not."

Guy's, and county cricket, had given Dr Bakhsh a will of his own : he said, " Sir, in your case, whenever I make a decision, I think many times before I put it to you. I have come to the conclusion that woollen pyjamas are absolutely essential for you."

The Quaid smiled and answered, " All right, I give in."

* * *

The bungalow at Ziarat, ' high in the rocky hills,' was remote from the Capital, where the Prime Minister, and the government, waited hour by hour for news of the Quaid. Three days after Dr Bakhsh had declared his ' grave news,' Liaquat Ali Khan arrived at Ziarat and spent half an hour with the Governor-General.

Afterwards, he went to Dr Bakhsh and asked for his diagnosis. The doctor believed that, as he had been summoned by Miss Jinnah, not by the State, he was justified in refusing an answer. He said, " I have not made it yet."

Liaquat Ali Khan then asked, " What do you suspect ? "

Dr Bakhsh answered, " I have ten diseases in my mind. I must be certain."

Mr Mahommed Ali, Secretary to the Cabinet, was with Liaquat Ali Khan : he said, " It is your duty to tell the Prime Minister exactly what is wrong with Quaid-i-Azam—we in the Government must be ready for any consequences."

Dr Bakhsh agreed, but added that he ' would not disclose anything ' without the permission of his patient.

Next morning, the Quaid said to him, " What did the Prime Minister ask you about me ? "

The doctor answered that he had ' told him nothing,' and Quaid-i-Azam said, " Congratulations. I, as head of the State, will tell the nation about the nature and gravity of my illness when I think it proper."

On July 29, X-ray photographs proved the damage to the Quaid's lungs to be more terrible than was supposed. On the same day, the Nursing Superintendent of the Civil Hospital in Quetta—an Englishwoman, Sister Phyllis Dunham—arrived to nurse him.

Their relationship opened with challenge : when Sister Dunham began to adjust the Quaid's pillows, he said, "Leave me alone; don't touch me."

The Sister answered, "All right : if you don't wish to be helped, I won't help you. The doctor has ordered . . ."

Mr Jinnah interrupted, "I don't take orders. I give orders."

Sister Dunham withdrew the word 'ordered' and said, "The doctor has *requested* . . ."

When he refused his medicine, the Sister tried to humour him. "Come on, sir. You'll soon get into my ways, and I'll get into yours."

The Quaid grumbled, "I have no special ways : it is just common sense."

Sister Dunham decided, after four days, that her patient was 'too difficult,' and she suggested to Dr Bakhsh that a male nurse would be better in her place.

When the doctor told the Quaid, he answered, "No, I won't have a male nurse. She *must* stay. I like her."

Next time Sister Dunham came into the room, she was carrying a brush and comb. The patient smiled, fell back on his pillow as she brushed his hair, and said, "Ah, you are trying to cover up my bald patch."

* * *

On August 9, the doctors decided that the Quaid must be moved from the perilous heights of Ziarat, to Quetta. On the 12th, Lieut. Ahmed 'sat up all night' to make arrangements for the journey next day. When the Quaid was told that all was ready, he said, "But I will not move until I am dressed : I will not travel in my pyjamas."

A new coat was brought—one that he had ordered in Karachi and never worn before. Then his pump shoes : then his monocle, on its grey silk cord—in memory of the pride that had thrilled him, when he was a student trudging to his lodgings in Kensington, fifty years before. A fresh, snowy handkerchief was brought and unfolded : he held it between his fingers. Then, Mazhar Ahmed, with the help of the military A.D.C. and two Pathan servants, carried the Quaid's frail body on a stretcher, down the stairs.

Lieutenant Ahmed has said, "When I lifted Quaid-i-Azam into the car, I had to hold him so close that his cheek was next to mine, and

I could hear his soft breathing. I placed him on a mattress, but not quite where he would be comfortable. I was still holding him when he said, 'Mazhar, you are out of breath. And I am out of breath. Let us pause.' So I waited a moment, and then I moved him again. I asked him, 'Are you comfortable?' He smiled, so sweetly, and then asked, 'Where is my handkerchief?' I found it for him: then the others all got into their cars and the journey began.

"When we arrived at the Residency at Quetta, I carried Quaid-i-Azam up to his bed. He smiled as I tucked him in, but he did not speak."

* * *

On August 16, Dr Bakhsh was able to tell his patient that there was a forty per cent improvement in the condition of his lung. "How long will it take to be a hundred per cent?" asked Mr Jinnah. Two days later, he was able to begin work again, on government papers, for an hour a day; and when Mr Mahommed Ali arrived again from Karachi, he thought the Quaid 'mentally more alert and altogether more like his old self.'

A few days later, Quaid-i-Azam got up and walked a little, in his room: he ate spaghetti, peaches and grapes, and talked of his wish to return to Karachi. "Don't take me there on crutches," he said. "I want to go when I can walk . . . I would dislike being carried on a stretcher from the car to my room."

This was the last sign of his valour. On August 29, he said to Dr Bakhsh, "You know, when you first came to Ziarat, I wanted to live. Now, however, it does not matter whether I live or die."

Dr Bakhsh wrote in his diary afterwards, 'I noticed tears in his eyes. . . . I could not account for his dejection. . . . The explanation he offered was that he had completed his job, but I found this enigmatic and evasive. Was his job incomplete five weeks before? Had he done something in the meantime which had given him a sense of fulfilment? I could not help feeling that something had happened to undermine his will to live.'

On the evening of September 5, the Quaid developed pneumonia: for three days he suffered increasing temperature, and restless spells during which he muttered what was in his dying mind. Almost the last rambling words were about Kashmir: he suddenly raised his voice in anger and said, " The Kashmir Commission have an appointment with me today. Why haven't they turned up ? Where are they ? "

On September 10, Dr Bakhsh had to tell Miss Jinnah that there was little hope of her brother living for more than a few days. Next morning, three aircraft were landed near by, including the Quaid's beautiful Viking, to which he was carried on a stretcher. The British pilot and crew lined up and gave him a smart salute, and, slowly, Jinnah raised his hand and saluted them in return. Within a few minutes the aircraft was flying at 7,000 feet, over the rugged Quetta hills.

At 4.15 that afternoon—September 11—the aircraft landed at Mauripur, where the thousands of Pakistanis had waited to welcome the Quaid on the great day of his flight into Karachi, thirteen months before. There was but a small group of people to meet him now : the arrival had been kept as private and secret as possible, and even the Prime Minister had been telephoned from Quetta and asked not to come to the aerodrome.

Near the aircraft stood Colonel Geoffrey Knowles. He watched the stretcher being carried out of the aircraft and, as it was turned towards the blazing sun, he saw the Quaid's hand move from the covers, rising slowly to shield his eyes.

The stretcher was placed within an army ambulance : Miss Jinnah and Sister Dunham climbed in and the journey into Karachi began. Soon after the little procession had passed by a crowded refugee slum, outside the city, the ambulance broke down. For over an hour, the driver fiddled hopelessly with the engine, until another ambulance was brought from Karachi.

Sister Dunham has described the terrible hour of waiting. " We were still near enough to the refugee camp, and the mud, to be pestered by hundreds of flies. I found a piece of cardboard and fanned Mr Jinnah's face, to keep the flies away. I was alone with him for a few minutes and he made a gesture I shall never forget. He moved his arm free of the sheet, and placed his hand on my arm. He did not speak, but there was such a look of gratitude in his eyes. It was all the reward I needed, for anything I had done. His soul was in his eyes at that moment."

The last lap of the journey began : there was no flag on the ambulance, so it moved through the city unnoticed by the crowds who had come out to enjoy the first cool breeze of evening. At ten minutes past six o'clock the ambulance arrived at Government House, and the Quaid was carried up to his room. The doctors and Sister Dunham tried to stimulate him with a heart tonic, but he was so weak that the potion dribbled from the corners of his mouth.

* * *

The bells of the Anglican Cathedral sounded seven o'clock : a few minutes later the Muslim *muazzins* began to climb to the minarets above the mosques, to call the people to their sunset prayers :

> God is the Greatest—God is the Greatest . . .
> I bear witness that nothing deserves to be worshipped but God . . .
> I bear witness that Muhammad is the Messenger of God . . .
> Come to Prayer
> Come to Prayer . . .
> God is the Greatest
> God is the Greatest
> Nothing deserves to be worshipped but God.

The doctors raised the end of Quaid-i-Azam's bed, to hasten the flow of blood to his heart. Then they tried to inject a drug into his veins, but the veins had collapsed. At 9.50, Dr Bakhsh leaned over and whispered, " Sir, we have given you an injection to strengthen you, and it will soon have its effect. God willing, you are going to live."

Quaid-i-Azam moved his head and spoke for the last time : he said faintly, " No, I am not." Thirty minutes later he died.

* * *

Through the night, the news passed along the bazaars to the edges of the city, in a mingling of shouts and whispers. The multitude closed in about the tall dark walls of Government House. The evening breeze had faded and the night was heavy and cruelly hot : the sea of white garments spread far into the darkness, and the excited hundreds that were nearest the wall touched it with their fingers and mumbled their prayers.

Slowly, weaving his way among the people, came a man carrying a shroud and a little bottle. The shroud had been soaked in the holy water of ZemZem—the spring that Ismail had released from the desert: the bottle contained the remains of some attar that had been sprinkled on the tomb of the Prophet at Medina, when the man went there as a pilgrim.

Quaid-i-Azam was wrapped in the shroud, and the attar was sprinkled on him, before he was buried in the heart of the city—in the dust from which he had stood up, in valiant pride, when he was a boy.

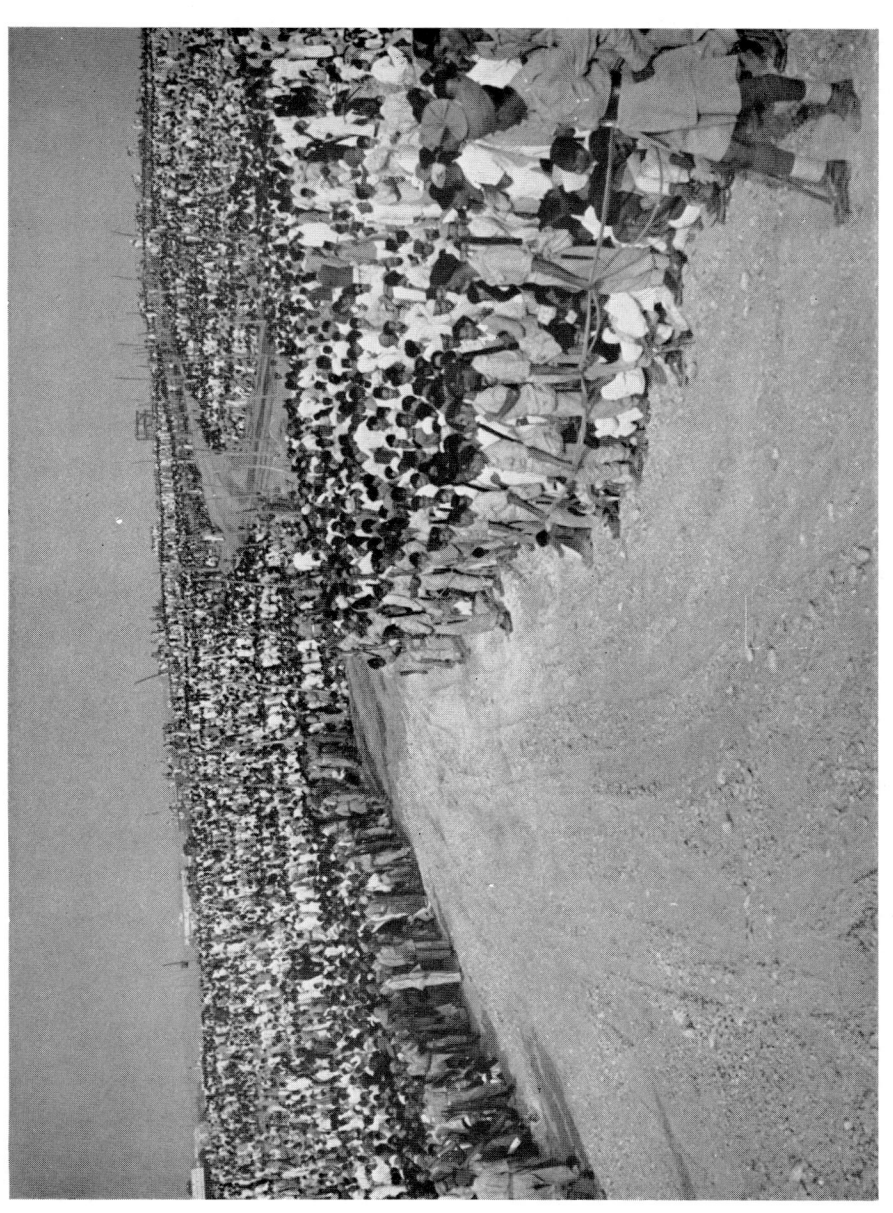

KARACHI : THE DAY OF MOHAMMED ALI JINNAH'S BURIAL

BIBLIOGRAPHY AND INDEX

BIBLIOGRAPHY

Of the many books consulted, the following have been the greatest help to the author:

Mohomed Ali Jinnah, An Ambassador of Unity, His Speeches and Writings, 1912–1917, with a biographical appreciation by Sarojini Naidu (Ganesh, Madras).
Immortal Years, Sir Evelyn Wrench (Hutchinson, 1945).
Dadabhai Naoroji: The Grand Old Man of India, R. P. Masani (George Allen & Unwin, 1939).
Mohammed Ali Jinnah (A Political Study), M. H. Saiyid (Muhammad Ashraf, Lahore, 1945).
History of the Indian National Congress, P. Sitaramayya (Bombay, 1947).
Lahore: Its History, Architectural Remains and Antiquities, Syad Muhammad Latif (Lahore, 1892).
The Making of Pakistan, Richard Symonds (Faber, 1950).
Makers of Pakistan and Modern Muslim India, A. H. Albiruni (Muhammad Ashraf, Lahore, 1950).
India in Transition, H.H. the Aga Khan (Bennett, Coleman & Co., 1918).
The British Impact on India, Sir Percival Griffiths (Macdonald, 1952).
Speeches of the Earl of Minto, 1905–1910.
King George V. His Life and Reign, Harold Nicolson (Constable, 1952).
An Indian Diary, Edwin S. Montagu. Edited by Venetia Montagu (Heinemann, 1930).
Gandhiji, Through My Diary Leaves, Kanji Dwarkadas (Bombay, 1950).
Letters of Iqbal to Jinnah (Muhammad Ashraf, Lahore).
Muslim India, Mohammed Noman (Kitabistan, Allahabad, 1942).
Recollections and Reflections, Sir Chimanlal Setalvad (Padma Publications, Bombay, 1946).
Grey Wolf, H. C. Armstrong (Arthur Barker, 1932).
An Australian in India, Rt. Hon. R. G. Casey (Hollis & Carter, 1947).
The Second World War, Vol. IV, Winston S. Churchill (Cassell).
Jinnah Faces an Assassin, 'A Barrister-at-Law' (Thacker, Bombay, 1943).
Verdict on India, Beverley Nichols (Jonathan Cape, 1944).
Jinnah-Gandhi Talks (Central Office, All-India Muslim League, 1944).
And So to Pakistan, Altaf Husain (Government of Pakistan, 1954).
While Memory Serves, Lieut.-General Sir Francis Tuker (Cassell, 1950).
Horned Moon, Ian Stephens (Chatto & Windus, 1953).
Mission with Mountbatten, Alan Campbell-Johnson (Robert Hale, 1951).
Indian Summer, Wilfred Russell (Thacker, Bombay, 1951).

INDEX

Abbas, Captain Saied : *quoted*, 121–2

Abell, George (Sir), Private Secretary to the Viceroy : accompanies Lord Ismay to London with draft Plan (May 1947), 183

Aga Khan, The : *quoted*, 42, 45 ; leads Muslim delegation to Round Table Confs., 97

Ahmad, Jamil-ud-Din : *quoted*, 172–3

Ahmed, Mazhar, Lieut. R.P.N. : naval A.D.C. to Jinnah (May 1948), 216–18 ; describes move of Jinnah from Ziarat to Quetta (Aug. 13), 222–3

Ahmed, Nasim : 13

Ahmedabad : Jinnah's speech at (1916), 65

Ahsan, Captain Syed M., R.P.N. : naval A.D.C. to Jinnah, 193, 195

Albert, Prince (The Prince Consort) : on 'The Indians', *quoted*, 37

Alexander, A. V. (Viscount Alexander of Hillsborough) : member of Cabinet Mission to India (1946), 159, 161

Alexander the Great : in the Punjab, 32

Aligarh University (Mohammedan Anglo-Oriental College) : founded 41 ; Jinnah's interest in and bequest to, 43 ; Gandhi's attempted boycott, 87 ; Jinnah's speech to (1938), 100

All-India Muslim League : *see* Muslim League

Amai Bai : Jinnah's boyhood marriage to, 4 ; death, 4

Amiruddin, Mian : 34

Ampthill, 2nd Baron : comments on Council of India Bill (1914), 61

'Amritsar Massacre' (1919) : 80–1

Arnold, Sir Thomas : at Aligarh University, 41

Ashraf, Dr Mohammed : 8, 9

Attlee, C. R. : Prime Minister (1945), 158 ; invites Viceroy and Indian leaders to London (Dec. 1946), 170–1 ; announces June 1948 for transfer of power, 173–4

Auchinleck, Field-Marshal Sir Claude : persuades Jinnah against armed intervention in Kashmir dispute (Oct. 1947), 207 ; tribute to Jinnah, 212

Aurangzeb, Emperor : death of (1707) and decline of Moghul Empire, 36

Bakar, S.N. : conversation with Jinnah, 158–9

Bakhsh, Lt.-Col. Ilahi : Jinnah's doctor during last illness and relationship between, 219–25

Baldev Singh, Sardar (Sikh leader) : flies to London for talks with H.M. Govt. (Dec. 1946), 170 ; returns with Nehru, 171

Baluchistan : Council of Chiefs to vote on Pakistan (1947), 184 ; unanimous acceptance, 187

Bandra Convent School : Fatima Jinnah at, 15–16

Batley, Claude, architect : *quoted*, 135

Bengal : partition of (1905), 24, 25, 44–5 ; outbreak of Indian Mutiny in (1857), 37 ; partition annulled, by royal proclamation (1911), 50 ; partition of (1947), 181, 183, 184

Bengal, East : to vote on Pakistan, 184 ; vote for Pakistan, 187

Benn, W. Wedgwood (Viscount Stansgate) : Sec. of State for India (1929–31), 96

Besant, Dr Annie, Congress leader : attends Muslim League session (1915), 64 ; forms Home Rule League, *q.v.* (1916), 67 ; interned (1917), 67 ; E. S. Montagu's opinion of, 69–70 ; on Montagu-Chelmsford Report (1918), 79 ; withdrawal from Home Rule League, 83

Bihar massacre (1946) : 169–70

Birkenhead, Earl of : succeeds as Sec. of State for India (1924), 92 ; pessimism over self-govt. for India

INDEX

(1924), 93 ; challenge to Indians to produce a constitution (1928), 93

Birnie, Col. E. St J. B., first military secretary to Jinnah as Gov.-Gen. of Pakistan (1947–48) : relationship with Jinnah, 203–5, 207–10 ; quotations from diary describing, plight of refugees, 204, 205, Jinnah's visit to Lahore during Kashmir crisis, 207, Jinnah's health, 208, 209

Bombay Muslim Students Union : Jinnah's address to (1915), 62

Bonnerjee, W. C. (first President of Indian Congress) : *quoted*, 23

Boundary Commission (1947) : *see* Radcliffe Award

Cabinet Mission : arrives in India (1946), 159 ; plans for 'Union of India', 159 *et seq.*

'Calcutta Killing' (1946) : 169

Caliphate (Ottoman) : Muslim sympathy with during 1914–18 war, 63 ; Treaty of Sèvres (1920), 81 ; Caliphate Movement in India, 81–2

Campbell-Bannerman, Sir Henry : Prime Minister, 25

Campbell-Johnson, Alan : Press Attaché to the Viceroy, author of *Mission with Mountbatten, quoted*, 178, 179, 183, 184, 185–6

Canning, Lord : Governor-General (later Viceroy) of India (1855–62), 36 ; *quoted*, 36, 37–8

Casey, R. G. : explains Govt. of India Act (1935), 109–10 ; refers to Congress rejection of Cripps offer (1942), 139 ; on self-government of India, 141 ; his estimate of Jinnah, 166–7

'Caucus Case, The' : 20

Cawnpore : massacre at (1857), 37

Caxton Hall, London : Jinnah's speech to London Indian Association (1913), 56–7

Central Legislative Assembly : introduced under 1919 Govt. of India Act, 88 ; Jinnah elected to (1923), 88, (1926) 90

Chaman Lall, Diwan : describes Jinnah's break with Congress (1920), 85 ; accompanies Jinnah to England (1928), 91 ; account of Mrs Jinnah's illness in Paris (1928), 91–2 ; describes Jinnah's return to India (1934–35), 106 ; attempt to reconcile Jinnah and Gandhi (1940), 136–7

Chamberlain, Austen (Sir) : succeeded by E. S. Montagu as Sec. of State for India (1917), 68

Chamberlain, Neville, Prime Minister : Munich (1938), 117 ; declares war on Germany (1939), 123

Chelmsford, Lord : Viceroy of India (1916–21), 65 ; Jinnah's dislike of, 69 ; letter to King George V on educated Indians (1918), 69 ; *see also* Montagu-Chelmsford Report

Chitty, Sir R. K. Shanmukhan : tribute to Jinnah (1940), 133

Christian Missionary Society High School, Karachi : 4

Churchill, W. S. (Sir) : on Cripps Mission (1942), *quoted*, 139 ; criticizes F. D. Roosevelt's views on 'Indian problem', 139–40

Communal Award (Govt. of India Act, 1935) : Jinnah's comments on, 110

Congress, Indian National, The : first conception and history, 22–6, 40 ; effect of partition of Bengal on, 24–6 ; Jinnah joins (1906), 26, 44 ; uproar at Surat meeting (1907), 46 ; extreme nationalists expelled from (1908), 46 ; Jinnah's speech at 1913 session, 58 ; tribute to Muslim League (1913), 58 ; price for co-operation, during 1914–18 war, 62 ; and Muslim League form 'Lucknow Pact' (1916), 66 ; extreme nationalists readmitted (1916), 67 ; condemns Montagu-Chelmsford Report (1918), 79 ; adopts non-co-operation and boycott to achieve absolute freedom (1920), 84–5 ; Jinnah resigns from (1920), 78, 84–5 ; contest 1937 elections, 111–13 ; strength in NW. Frontier Province (1937), 112 ; treatment of Muslim

INDEX

League criticized by Sir P. Griffiths, 114 ; policy condemned by Jinnah (1937), 115 ; withdraws Ministries and demands immediate independence (1939), 124 ; rejects Cripps offer (1942), 139 ; leaders imprisoned (1942), 143 ; leaders freed (1945), 157 ; oppose Muslim League demand for exclusive Muslim nomination to Interim Govt. (1945), 157 ; and Interim Govt., 157, 160, 162, 163 ; rebuked by Jinnah, 165 ; invited by Viceroy to form Interim Govt. (Aug. 1946), 167 ; Muslim League 'black flag' protest against (Sept. 1946), 168 ; Jinnah's comment on, to Lord Mountbatten, 179 ; failing power of, in NW. Frontier Province, 182 ; ratifies Plan for transfer of power (June 1947), 187

Connaught, H.R.H. Duke of : visits India (1921), 87

Constituent Assembly : Cabinet Mission's plan for (1946), 159 ; elections for (1946), 162 ; Jinnah orders Muslim League members to abstain from, 168–9 ; opens (Dec. 9, 1946), 172

Constituent Assembly of Pakistan : Jinnah's Presidential Address to (Aug. 11, 1947), 197

Cotton, Sir Henry : *quoted*, 26

Council of India Bill : Jinnah leads delegation to England (1914), 59–61 ; read and 'postponed', House of Lords, 59–61 ; Jinnah's comments on, 60–1 ; Lord Ampthill's comments on, 61 ; re-presented as Govt. of India Act of 1915, 64 ; Royal Assent to, 64

Council of State : introduced under Govt. of India Act of 1919, 88

Cow-slaughter : Gandhi's view, during 1918 riots, 73 ; Muslim cow-protection societies (1920), 82

Criminal Law Amendment Bill (1913): Jinnah's speech supporting, 52–3

Cripps Mission (1942) : proposes 'a new Indian Union', 138–9 ; Gandhi's comments on proposals, and rejection by Congress, 139 ; comments by R. G. Casey on rejection, 139 ; Jinnah on, 140

Cripps, Sir Stafford : Jinnah recalls 1940 visit of, 138 ; and Cripps Mission (1942), *q.v.*, 138–40 ; member of Cabinet Mission to India (1946), 159, 161 ; praises Jinnah but denies his authority, 163–4 ; tribute to Jinnah, 212

Croft, Frederick Leigh : 7

Cunningham, Sir George : 199

Dacca : Jinnah's speech to students at (March 1948), 215

Dawn newspaper : created by Jinnah (1938), 142, 143

Dunham, Sister Phyllis : nurse to Jinnah during last illness, 221–5

Durbar, The : King George V at (Dec. 1911), 49, 50

Dwarkadas, Kanji : *quoted*, 79 ; at funeral of Mrs Jinnah (1929), 95 ; Jinnah's comments to, after talks with Gandhi (1944), 151–2

Dyer, Brig.-Gen. R. E. H. : and 'Amritsar Massacre' (1919), 81

Edinburgh, Prince Alfred Duke of : visit to Lahore (1870), 33

Edward VII, King-Emperor : visit 1875–76 recalled, 46 ; Address (1908), 46 ; death (1910), 49

Fatima Bai, 4, 5, 6, 195

Freeth, Mrs G. H. B. : tribute to Jinnah (1929), *quoted*, 96

Gandhi, Mohandas Karamchand : on Indian National Congress, 22 ; in South Africa, 49, 67 ; attends Muslim League session (1915), 64 ; compared with Jinnah, 67, 83, 84, 86, 87, 97–8, 147 ; influence over Hindus, 67, 79, 81 ; E. S. Montagu's opinion of, 70 ; and cow-slaughter, 73 ; protest against Rowlatt Act (1919), 80 ; called *Mahatma*, 81 ; influence over Muslims, 81 ; espouses Caliphate Movement (1920), 81–2 ; leader of Home Rule League, 83 ; induces Congress to

INDEX

demand absolute freedom (1920), 84–5 ; Dr Besant on, 86 ; boycotts visit Prince of Wales (1921), 88 ; imprisoned (1922–4), 88, 89 ; refuses to attend 1st Round Table Conf. (1930), 97 ; imprisoned (1930–31) 97n. ; Lord Irwin on, in letter to King George V. (1931), 98 ; condemnation of Jinnah's Lucknow speech (1937), 115 ; correspondence with Jinnah (1937–8), 115, 116 ; Jinnah's compliment to, 122 ; comment on Cripps offer (1942), 139 ; inaugurates 'Quit India' movement (1942), 143 ; imprisoned (1942), 143 ; released from prison (1944), 146 ; exchange of letters with Jinnah (1944), 146–7 ; medical analysis of, 147 ; talks and correspondence with Jinnah (1944), 148–52 ; referred to, 178 ; signs 'Peace Appeal' (April 1947), 181 ; meets Jinnah after three years (May 1947), 183 ; assassination (Jan. 30, 1948), 210

Ganji, Mohammed Ali : 4

Gardiner, Major W. H. : letters from Jinnah, criticizing Sir S. Cripps (1940), 138, and criticizing Lord Linlithgow (1941), 138 ; exchange of letters with Jinnah on health (1941), 141–2

Garhmukteswar massacre (1946) : 169

George V., King-Emperor : visits India (1911), 49 ; early visit (1905) and conversation with G. K. Gokhale recalled, 49–50 ; proclaims revision of partition of Bengal (1911), 50 ; opens 1st Round Table Conf. (1930), 97

Gladstone, W. E. :return to power (1892), 10

Gokhale, Gopal Krishna : *quoted*, 23, 25 ; conversation with King George V. (1905), 49–50 ; his Elementary Education Bill, 51 ; friendship with Jinnah and their voyage to England (1913), 54–8 ; biographical note, 55 ; death (1915) and tributes from Jinnah and Mrs Naidu, 62, 63

Gokul Das Tej Primary School, Bombay : 4

Government of India Acts : 1915 : Royal Assent to, 64 (*see also* Council of India Bill) 1919 : inauguration of new constitution by Duke of Connaught (1921), 87 ; Act explained, 87–8, 1935 : 98 ; explained by R. G. Casey, 109–10

Gracey, Gen. Sir Douglas : first meeting with Jinnah (1925), 89–90 ; mentioned, 199

Granville, Earl : Lord Canning's letter to, 37–8

Griffiths, Sir Percival (author of *The British Impact on India*) : *quoted*, 45 ; criticizes Congress treatment of Muslim League, 114 ; conversation with Jinnah on 'Pakistan', *quoted*, 127

Habibullah, Ibrahim : mentioned, 119

Hardinge of Penshurst, Lord : Viceroy (1910–16), 49 ; welcomes King George V and Queen Mary (1911), 49

Hawkins, William : emissary of James I to Moghul Court, 33–4

Hayat Khan Tiwana, Sir Khizr : leader Punjab Ministry, opposed to Jinnah and Muslim League (1945), 157

Hindus : anger over partition of Bengal (1905), 24–5 ; ascendancy over Muslims in government, 38 ; movement to replace Urdu by Hindi (1867), 40 ; anti-Muslim riots (1893), 41–2 ; Sir Syed Ahmed Khan's fear of, 42 ; revision of partition of Bengal (1911), 50 ; Gandhi's influence on, (in 1916) 67, (in 1919) 81 ; anti-Muslim riots over cow-slaughter (1918), 73–4 ; offer from Muslim League to guarantee representation to Hindu minorities (1927), 90 ; Jinnah's fear of Hindu *Raj* (1940), 125 ; Jinnah-Gandhi talks (1944), 148–52 ; representation in Interim Govt., 157 ; predominance in Constituent Assembly elections

INDEX

(1946), 162; 1946 massacres, 169–70; Nehru speaks to, on June 3 Plan (1947), 186; ruling class of, in Kashmir, during dispute (Oct. 1947), 206

Home Rule (*Swaraj*): Dadabhai Naoroji's demand for, 26; joint Congress-Muslim League demand for, 50–1; Congress tributes to Muslim League policy (1913), 58; Dr Besant forms Home Rule League, *q.v.* (1916), 67; Congress demands complete independence (1920), 84–5, (1939), 124; Ramsay MacDonald's hopes for (1928), 96–7; advances under Act of 1935, 109–10; offer of Cripps Mission (1942), 138; comments on by R. G. Casey, 141; and Cabinet Mission plan (1946), 159 *et seq.*; Mr Attlee promises transfer of power by June 1948 (1947), 173–4; granted to India and Pakistan (Aug. 15, 1947), 184 *et seq.*

Home Rule League: formed by Dr Besant (1916), 67; Jinnah becomes President Bombay branch (1917), 67; criticized by Lord Willingdon (1918), 76–7; Jinnah resigns from (1920), 78, 83; Dr Besant resigns from, 83; Gandhi changes name of League to *Swaraj Sabha*, 83

Hume, Allan Octavian: formation of Indian National Congress (1885), 22, 23; influence of Syed Ahmed Khan on, 40

Hunter, Sir William: *cited*, 38n, quoted, 53

Imperial Legislative Council: inauguration (1910), 47; Jinnah's membership of, 47–8, 52, 65; Jinnah resigns from (1919), 78, 80; replaced under 1919 Act by Council of State, *q.v.*, and Central Legislative Assembly, *q.v.*, 88

India: British conquest of, 36; Lord Canning, Gov.-Gen. and Viceroy (1855–62), 36, 37–8; misconceptions in British Parliament, 44; Lord Minto, Viceroy (1905–10), 44–5, 48; Government of, as composed in 1908, 47; Lord Hardinge of Penshurst, Viceroy (1910–16), welcomes King George V and Queen Mary (1911), 49; King George V proclaims annulment of partition of Bengal (1911), 50; Council of India Bill (1914), *q.v.*; during 1914–18 war, 61 *et seq.*; Govt. of India Act (1919), 69, 87; Montagu-Chelmsford Report Viceroy (1916–21), 65; E. S. Montagu succeeds Austen Chamberlain as Sec. of State (1917), 68; Govt. of India Act (1919), 69, 87; Montagu-Chelmsford Report (1918), 69, 78–9; Duke of Connaught's visit to inaugurate new constitution (1921), 87; Lord Reading, Viceroy (1921–26), 88; Prince of Wales's visit (1921), 88; visit of Simon Commission, *q.v.* (1928), 90; Lord Irwin (Earl of Halifax), Viceroy (1926–31), 92; Lord Birkenhead, Sec. of State (1924–28), 92; W. Wedgwood Benn (Viscount Stansgate), Sec. of State (1929–31), 96; Round Table Conferences, *q.v.*, inaugurated (1930), 97; Govt. of India Act (1935), 98, and Royal Assent to, 109; Lord Willingdon, Viceroy (1931–36), 98n; Lord Linlithgow, Viceroy (1936–43), 123; war on Germany declared (1939), 123; Jinnah condemns British democratic system as unsuited to India (1940), 125–6; visit of Cripps Mission, *q.v.* (1942), 138–40; Lord Wavell, Viceroy (1943–47), 157; visit of Cabinet Mission (1946), 159 *et seq.*; Lord Pethick-Lawrence, Sec. of State (1945–47), 159; massacres (1946), 169–70; Mr Attlee announces June 1948 as date for transfer of power, 173; Lord Mountbatten, Viceroy (1947), 174; Kashmir dispute (1947–48), *q.v.*, 179; transfer of power date advanced to Aug. 15, 1947, 184; H.M. Govt. agree to

INDEX

Partition, 184; Boundary Commission appointed, 188; accession of Native States at Partition, 205–6

India, after Partition: Lord Mountbatten becomes first Governor-General (Aug. 15, 1947), 193; Independence Day (Aug. 15), 198; Kashmir accedes to, and Indian troops sent (Oct. 26, 1947), 207

Indian Association, London: formation of, and Jinnah's speech to (1913), 56–7

Indian Councils Act, Amendment to (1892): 9–10

Indian Mutiny, The (1857): 37–9, 40; Queen Victoria on, 37; Lord Canning on, 37–8; Sir Syed Ahmed Khan on, 39–40

Indian National Congress, The: *see* Congress

Indian States: circumstances during transfer of power (1947), 184; Lord Mountbatten's advice to rulers, on accession to India or Pakistan, 205–6

Indians in South Africa: Imp. Leg. Council debate on (1910), 48; Gandhi's leadership of, 49

Interim Government: proposals for (1945–46), 157, 159–60; Jinnah's criticism of Lord Wavell's changes to, 162, 163; Viceroy invites Congress to form (Aug. 1946), 167; reconstituted to admit Muslim League members (Oct. 1946), 168

Iqbal, Sir Muhammad: delegate to Round Table Confs., 98; biographical note, 99; demands 'Consolidated Muslim State' (1930), 99; influence on Jinnah, 99; letters to Jinnah (1937), 114–15; death and last letter to Jinnah (1938), 118

Irwin, Lord (Earl of Halifax): Viceroy of India (1926–31), 92; letter on Gandhi to King George V (1931), 98

Islamia College, Peshawar: Jinnah's bequest to, 43

Ismay, General Lord: Chief of Viceroy's Staff, 177, 181; comments on 'communal feeling' (March 1947), 181; talks with Jinnah on partition of Punjab and Bengal, 181; flies to London with draft Plan (May 1947), 183; returns to India with Viceroy, 184; talk with Jinnah on partition of army, 188; mentioned, 193, 199, 206

Jafar, Nanji: 5, 195
Jafri, Fareed: 165n
James, Sir Frederick: tribute to Jinnah (1940), 133
Jardine, Sir John: *quoted*, 26
Jefford,–Rear-[Vice-]Admiral J. W.: creation of Pakistan Navy and relationship with Jinnah, 200–3
Jehangir, Sir Cowasjee: tributes to Jinnah, 59, 133
Jinnah, Dina (Mrs Neville Wadia), only child of M. A. Jinnah: birth (1919), 86; with her father in England (1932), 101, 102; comment on his alleged 'rudeness', 212
Jinnah, Fatima, sister of M. A. Jinnah: 6; enters Bandra Convent School 15, 16; joins brother in London (1931), 101; *cited*, 165; accompanies Jinnah on flight into Karachi (Aug. 7, 1947), 193, 194; Jinnah speaks of debt to, 209; recalls relationship between her brother and doctors, 219; with her brother during last illness and death, 219 *et seq.*
Jinnah Gardens, Lahore: 33, 35
Jinnah Hall, Bombay: 78
Jinnah, Mohammed Ali: parents, 3; birth, 3; ancestry, 4; boyhood and early education, 4–7; first marriage, 4 (recalled, 73); sails for England, 7; at Lincoln's Inn, 8–13; lodgings at 35 Russell Road, Kensington, 8; first interest in Liberalism, 9–12; Lord Morley's influence on, 9; Dadabhai Naoroji's influence on, 11–12; experience as an actor, 13; return to Karachi (1896), 14; sails for Bombay (1897), 14; early years as an advocate, 15–21; temporary Presidency Magistrate (1900), 15, 16;

INDEX

relationship with his sister, Fatima, 15, 16; 'The Caucus Case', 20; first political aim—Indian National Congress, 22; his first session of Congress (1906), 25, 44; secretary to Dadabhai Naoroji, 26; Mrs Naidu's devotion to, 27; compared with Alexander the Great, 32-3; *Jinnah Gardens*, Lahore, named after, 33, 35; Syed Ahmed Khan's influence on, 38, 40-1, 42-3; his will, 43, (Liaquat Ali Khan an executor), 154; elected to Imp. Leg. Council (1910), 47; and Lord Minto, on Indians in South Africa, 48, 49; attends Muslim League session (1912), before becoming a member, 50-1; speech in support of Gokhale's Elementary Education Bill (1912), 51-2; nominated, for second term, Imp. Leg. Council (1913), 52; speech on Criminal Law Amendment Bill (1913), 52-3; introduction of, speech on, and Viceroy's Assent to, Mussalman Wakf Validating Bill (1913), 53-4; Mrs Naidu's tribute to, on Wakf Bill, 54; friendship with Gokhale and their voyage to England (1913), 54-8; speech to London Indian Association (1913), 56-7; joins Muslim League, in London (1913), 57, 58; speech to Congress, Karachi (1913), 58; Sir Cowasjee Jehangir's tributes to, 59, 133; leads Congress delegation to England (1914), 59-61; speech on Council of India Bill, and comments, in *The Times* (1914), 60, 61; speech to Bombay Muslim Students Union (1915), 62; sorrow over death of Gokhale (1915), 62; efforts for greater Congress-Muslim League unity, 63-4; secures Congress support at Muslim League session (1915), 64; re-election to Imp. Leg. Council (1916), 65; speech on 'separate electorates', Ahmedabad (1916), 65; and the 'Lucknow Pact' (1916), 66; described as 'Ambassador of Hindu-Muslim Unity', 66; compared with Gandhi, 67, 83, 84, 86, 87, 97, 147-8; President of Bombay Home Rule League (1917), 67; protest against internment of Dr Besant (1917), 67-8; welcomes appointment of E. S. Montagu as Sec. of State (1917), 68; opinion of Lord Chelmsford, 68, 82; E. S. Montagu's tribute to, 70; courtship and marriage to Ruttenbai Petit (1918), 74-5; relationship with Lord Willingdon, 75-7; signs manifesto demanding 'responsible government' (1918), 76; attacks Lord Willingdon for his opinions (1918), 77; leads anti-Willingdon demonstration, 77-8; *Jinnah Hall*, Bombay, built as tribute to, 78; resigns from Imp. Leg. Council (1919), 78, 80; resigns from Home Rule League (1920), 78, 83; resigns from Congress (1920), 78, 84-5; on Rowlatt Act (1919), 80; on Gandhi's non-co-operation movement (1920), 82-3, 87; Diwan Chaman Lall's tribute to, 85; birth of daughter, Dina (1919), 86; recalls Gokhale (1921), 87; elected to Central Leg. Assembly (1923), 88; on Gandhi's unwillingness to co-operate with Muslims, 89; visits England on army 'Indianization' committee (1925), 89-90; re-elected Central Leg. Assembly (1926), 90; sails for England after separation from wife (1928), 90-1; illness of wife in Paris (1928), 91-2; on Nehru Report (1928), 93, 94; demands rejected at All-Parties Conf. (1928), 94-5; death and funeral of wife (1929), 95; letter to Ramsay MacDonald suggesting conference (1929), 97; attends 1st Round Table Conf. (1930), 97; talks with Iqbal (1931), 99; decision to live in England, 99; life and legal practice in England (1931-34), 99-102; speech to Leeds Luncheon Club (1932), 100; comparison with

Mustafa Kemal, 102-4; persuaded by Liaquat Ali Khan to return to India (1933), 104-6; re-elected Central Leg. Assembly (1934), 109; comments on Communal Award, *q.v.* (1935), 110; congratulated by Governor of Punjab for conciliating Muslims and Sikhs in Lahore (1936), 110-11; President Muslim League Central Election Board (1936), 111-12; 'equal partners' offer ignored by Nehru (1937), 113-14; Iqbal's tribute (1937), 115; declares impossibility of unity with Hindus (Lucknow, 1937), 115; correspondence with Gandhi (1937-38), 115-16; correspondence with Nehru (1938), 116-17; on treatment of Palestine Arabs by British (1938), 117-18; compares Sudeten Germans with Muslims in India (1938), 118; Iqbal's last letter to (1938), 119; attitude to the young and to students, 119-22; supports All-India Muslim Students Federation (1937), 120-1; speech at Allahabad University, 122; calls for 'Day of Deliverance' from Congress regime (1939), 124; contributes articles on unsuitability of democratic government for India, to English journals (1940), 125-6; his 'two nations' theory, described to Sir P. Griffiths (1940), 127; visits wounded Khaksars, Lahore (1940), 128; on women in politics, 128; and 'Pakistan Resolution' (1940), 128-9; first called *Quaid-i-Azam*, the 'Great Leader' (1940), 133; tributes to, on 64th birthday (1940), 133-4; builds new house (1939-40), 134-5; and his architect, Claude Batley, 135; relationship with staff, 135-6; gives Viceroy 'Tentative Proposals' for Muslim support during war (1940), 137; orders resignation Muslim Premiers from Nat. Defence Council (1941), 137-8; letter to Major Gardiner criticizing Lord Linlithgow (1941), 138; letter to Major Gardiner *re* Sir S. Cripps (1940), 138; pledges 'unwavering support' in war effort (1942), 139; disappointment over Cripps Mission (1942), 140; creates *Dawn* newspaper, 142-3; attitude towards 'press', 142-3; Gandhi's impatience with (1942), 143; attempted assassination of (1943), 144-5; interviewed by Beverley Nichols (1943), 145-6; exchange of letters with Gandhi (1944), 146-7; medical analysis of, 147-8; first sign of lung disease (1944), 148; talks and correspondence with Gandhi (1944), 148-52; reviews Muslim demands in interview with London *News Chronicle* (1944), 151; comments on Gandhi talks, to Kanji Dwarkadas (1944), 151-2; Begum Liaquat Ali Khan recalls stories of, and her husband's relationship with, 152-4; Viceroy and Congress reject Muslim League demand for exclusive Muslim nomination to Interim Govt. (1945), 157; and Muslim League success in 1946 elections, 158; speech to Muslim League workers, Calcutta (1946), 158; talk with S. N. Bakar, 158; supports Cabinet Mission 'grouping' plan (1946), 160; his doctor's comments (1946), 160-1; negotiations with Lord Wavell (1946), 162, 163; protest against Congress interpretation of Mission Plan (1946), 163; praised, but his authority denied by Lord Pethick-Lawrence and Sir S. Cripps (1946), 164; criticizes Lord Pethick-Lawrence and Sir S. Cripps, 164; and 'Direct Action' to achieve Pakistan (1946), 165; expects imprisonment, 165-6; R. G. Casey's estimate of, 166-7; criticizes Lord Wavell (1946), 167-8, 169; compromise with Lord Wavell on Interim Govt., 168; orders Muslim League to abstain from Constituent Assembly, 168-9; flies to England for talks with H.M. Govt. (Dec.

INDEX

Mehta, Sir Pherozeshah : 20, 46

Messervy, Gen. Sir Frank : 200

Miéville, Sir Eric, Principal Sec. to the Viceroy (1947) : 177, 184

Minto, 4th Earl of : Viceroy of India (1905–10), receives Muslim deputation, 44–5 ; and Jinnah, on Indians in South Africa, 48

Mohamed Ali, Maulana : induces Jinnah to join Muslim League (1913), 57 ; criticizes Jinnah (1920), 85

Mohammedan Educational Conference : founded, 41

Montagu, Edwin S. : Sec. of State for India (1917), 68 ; Declaration of August 1917, 68–9 ; visits India (1917) and his opinions of Dr Besant, Gandhi, and Jinnah, 69–70 ; *see also* Montagu–Chelmsford Report

Montagu–Chelmsford Report : referred to, 69 ; published (1918), 78–9

Morley, John (Lord Morley of Blackburn) : influence on Jinnah, 9 ; Sec. of State for India (1906), 25 ; tribute to Gokhale (1906), 55

Mount Pleasant Road, Bombay : Jinnah's bungalow, 73, 91, 106 ; Jinnah's new house (1939–40), 134–5

Mountbatten of Burma, Admiral the Earl : reference to boyhood, 49 ; Viceroy (1947), appointment announced, 174 ; arrives in Delhi (March 1947), 177 ; negotiates with Jinnah, Nehru, and other Indian leaders, and with H.M. Govt., for transfer of power, 177–87 ; asks Nehru for 'estimate' of Jinnah, 178 ; Ian Stephens' comment on Lord Mountbatten's alleged 'pro-Hindu' prejudices (Oct. 1947), *quoted*, 179 ; appreciation of Jinnah, 180 ; induces Jinnah and Gandhi to sign 'Peace Appeal' (April 14, 1947), 181 ; sends Lord Ismay to London with draft Plan, 183 ; flies to London and returns with final Plan, 184 ; announces August 15, 1947, as date for transfer of power, and concedes Pakistan ,184 ; broadcasts terms of Plan (June 3), 186 ; Jinnah's appreciation of, 187 ; Gov.-Gen. of new India, 193 ; at inauguration of Jinnah as Gov.-Gen. of Pakistan, 198, 201 ; advice to rulers of Indian States on accession to India or Pakistan, 205–6 ; concern over indecision of Maharaja of Kashmir, 206

Mudie, Sir Francis : 199 ; tribute to Jinnah, 208 ; last meeting with Jinnah (May 1948), 215–16

Muslim League, All-India : formation, 41, 44–5 ; adoption of *Swaraj* policy of Congress, 50–1 ; Jinnah joins in London (1913), 56, 57, 58 ; Congress tribute to (1913), 58 ; Jinnah's efforts for greater unity with Congress, 63–4 ; 1915 session attended by Congress leaders, 64 ; and Congress form 'Lucknow Pact' (1916), 66 ; Jinnah's speech at League meeting (1920) on Gandhi's non-cooperation campaign, 82–3 ; demand for representation of minorities (1927), 90 ; Iqbal demands 'Consolidated Muslim State' (1930), 99 ; contests 1937 elections, 111–13 ; Congress treatment of, criticized by Sir P. Griffiths, 114 ; Nehru belittles (1938), 117 ; growing power of (1939), 118 ; 'Pakistan Resolution' passed, Lahore (1940), 127, 128–9 ; Jinnah orders resignation Muslim League Provincial Premiers from Nat. Defence Council (1941), 137–8 ; Jinnah's speech, on Cripps Mission (1942), 140 ; Viceroy and Congress oppose demand for exclusive Muslim nomination to Interim Govt., 157 ; opposition of Punjab Prime Minister to, 157 ; success in 1946 general elections, 158 ; and the Interim Govt., 160, 162, 163 ; accepts Cabinet Mission Plan (1946), 160 ; success in elections for Constituent Assembly (1946), 162 ; cancels acceptance of Cabinet Mission Plan and sanctions 'Direct Action'

INDEX

(July 1946), 164–5; 'black flag' protest against Interim Govt. (Sept. 1946), 168; appoints members to reconstituted Interim Govt. (Oct. 1946), 168; Jinnah orders members to abstain from Constit. Assembly (Nov. 1946), 168–9; British branch welcomes Jinnah (Dec. 1946), 172–3; increasing strength in Punjab (March 1947), 180; civil disobedience in NW. Fontier Province (March 1947), 180; anti-Congress revolt in NW. Frontier Province (April 1947), 182; ratifies Plan for transfer of power (June 1947), 187

Muslim Students Federation, All-India: formation under Jinnah's encouragement (1937), 120–1

Muslims: and the partition of Bengal (1905), 24n, 44, 45, 50; 'Pakistan Resolution', referred to, 32; decline of, 36–40; Sir Syed Ahmed Khan on, 39, 42; revival of learning at Aligarh, 41; anti-Muslim riots, Bombay (1893), 41–2; Aga Khan on, *quoted*, 42, 45; minority in Indian National Congress, 44; Sir Percival Griffiths on, 45; the Wakf Validating Bill (1913), 53–4; Jinnah's plea for separate electorates (1915), 65, (1924), 89; riots against, caused by 'cow-slaughter' (1918), 73–4; Gandhi's influence on, 81; reaction to Sèvres Treaty (1920), 81, 82; Aga Khan leads delegation to Round Table Confs., 97; Iqbal demands 'Consolidated Muslim State' (1930), 99; separate electorates guaranteed under Communal Award (1935), 110; dispute with Sikhs over mosque, Lahore (1936), 110–11; celebrate 'Day of Deliverance' (1939), 124; Jinnah fears for, under Hindu *Raj*, 125; Lord Linlithgow's pledge to (1940), 137; Jinnah pledges 'unwavering support' of, in war effort, to Sir S. Cripps (1942), 139; Jinnah-Gandhi talks (1944), 148–52; Viceroy and Congress reject Muslim League demand for exclusive Muslim nomination to Interim Govt. (1945), 157; political parties opposed to Jinnah, 157; and Cabinet Mission Plan (1946), 159–60; and Interim Govt., 160 *et seq.*; Lord Wavell's broadcast appeal to, for co-operation (1946), 167; massacres (1946), 169–70; Sikh plot against Punjab Muslims (April 1947), 182; Muslim areas to vote on Pakistan, 184; Jinnah broadcasts to, on June 3 Plan, 186–7; vote for Pakistan, 187; welcome Jinnah at Karachi (Aug. 7, 1947), 194–5; Jinnah's "You are free" speech to (Aug. 11, 1947), 197; Sikh atrocities against, 204, 205; in Kashmir, 206, 207

Mussalman Wakf Validating Bill (1913): introduced by Jinnah, his speech on, 53–4; Viceroy's Assent to, 53

Naidu, Mrs Sarojini (author of *Mohomed Ali Jinnah: An Ambassador of Unity*): biographical note, 6n; quoted, 6, 8, 15, 21–2, 26, 27, 50, 54, 55–6, 57–8, 63, 64, 213–14; her affection for Jinnah, 27; tribute to Jinnah's skill as legislator (1913), 54; comment on Jinnah joining Muslim League, 57–8; on effect of death of Gokhale, 63; attends Muslim League session (1915), and comment on Jinnah, 64; estimate of Jinnah's character, recalled, 213–14

Naoroji, Dadabhai: M.P. for Central Finsbury (1892), 10–12; *quoted*, 11–12, 23, 26; Jinnah, secretary to (1906), 26

Nehru, Pandit Jawaharlal: education, 49; increasing authority in Congress, 113; ignores Jinnah's 'equal partners' offer (1937), 113–14; correspondence with Jinnah (1938), 116–17; belittles Muslim League (1938), 117; pledge to support total war against Japan (1942), 139, 140; imprisoned (1942–45), 143; on

INDEX

Muslim demand for partition of India, 158; threatens 'grouping' plan (1946), 162–3; Vice-Pres. Interim Govt. (Aug. 1946), 167; flies to London for talks with H.M. Govt. (Dec. 1946), 170; *Time* magazine comment on, 170–1; defiant speech at Benares (Dec. 1946), 171; relationship and negotiations with Lord Mountbatten (1947–48), 177 *et seq.*; his 'estimate' of Jinnah, 178; June 3 broadcast speech, 186; love for Kashmir, 206

Nehru, Pandit Motilal (father of Jawaharlal): and Nehru Report, *q.v.* (1928), 93

Nehru Report: published 1928, 93–5; Jinnah's comments on, 93, 94

Newnham Road, Karachi: Jinnah's birth in, 3, 5

News Chronicle, London: Jinnah reviews Muslim demands, in interview (1944), 151

Nichols, Beverley (author of *Verdict on India*): interview with Jinnah (1943), *quoted*, 145–6

Nightingale, Florence: letter to Dadabhai Naoroji, *quoted*, 11

Noman, Mohammed (author of *Muslim India*): *quoted*, 84; forms All-India Muslim Students Federation (1937), 120–1; relationship with Jinnah, 120–1

North-West Frontier Province: strength of Congress in (1937), 112; Muslim League civil disobedience campaign in (March 1947), 180; anti-Congress revolt (April 1947), 182; to vote on Pakistan, 184; vote for Pakistan, 187; Jinnah's visit to (April 1948), 215

Nusserwanjee, Jamshed: tribute to Jinnah and description of his disillusionment in 1928, 94, 95; last meeting with Jinnah (Feb. 1948), 210

Ollivant, Sir Charles: 15, 17
Oudh: British annexation of (1856), 36

Pakistan: the name explained (by Choudhury Rahmat Ali), 125, Jinnah expounds Pakistan demand, to Sir P. Griffiths (1940), 127; 'Pakistan Resolution' passed (1940), 128–9; and Cripps Mission—Jinnah's comments on (1942), 140; referred to during Jinnah–Beverley Nichols interview (1943), 146; and Cabinet Mission Plan (1946), 160; enthusiasm for, at London meeting of Muslims (Dec. 1946), 172–3; Jinnah's negotiations with Lord Mountbatten for, and achievement of, (1947), 177–90; Jinnah chosen as first Gov.-Gen. of, 193; Pres. Address to Constituent Assembly of (Aug. 11), 197; inauguration of Jinnah as Gov.-Gen. of (Aug. 14), 198; Cabinet sworn in (Aug. 15), 198; Independence Day, 198; Jinnah's wish to retain British officers and officials in, 199; creation of navy, 200–2; plight of refugees' 204, 205; sympathy of Kashmiri Muslims for, 206; decision not to take military action in Kashmir (Oct. 1947), 207; regular troops sent in to help 'Azad' Kashmir Govt. (April 1948), 208n; Jinnah opens State Bank of (July 1, 1948), 217–18; concern of Govt. over Jinnah's final illness, 221

'Pakistan Resolution' (1940): referred to, 32; passed at Lahore, 128–9

Palliser, Admiral Sir Arthur: episode preceding official visit to Pakistan (1947), 202–3

Patel, Surgeon-Commander Jal R.: medical examination of Jinnah (1944), 148; (1946), 160–1

Pethick-Lawrence, Lord: Sec. of State for India (1945–47), 159; leads Cabinet Mission to India (1946), 159; praises Jinnah, but denies his authority, 164; criticized by Jinnah, 164

Petit, Sir Dinshaw (father of Ruttenbai Petit): injunction against Jinnah, 74–5

INDEX

Petit, Ruttenbai : *see* Jinnah, Ruttenbai
Punjab : Sikh conquest of, 33, 34, 35 ; British annexation of (1849), 35, 36 ; 'Amritsar Massacre' (1919), 81 ; Prime Minister of, opposed to Jinnah and Muslim League (1945), 157 ; increasing Muslim League strength (March 1947), 180 ; riots in (April 1947), 182 ; Sikh plot to form own state in, 182 ; partition of, 181, 183, 184
Punjab, West : to vote on Pakistan, 184 ; vote for Pakistan, 187

Quaid-i-Azam, the 'Great Leader' : name first given to Jinnah in 1940, 133
Quetta : Jinnah moved to, from Ziarat, during last illness (August 13, 1948), 222–3 ; Jinnah flown from, to Karachi, on day of death (Sept. 11, 1948), 224

Rabbani, Wing-Commander Ata : air A.D.C. to Jinnah, 193–4, 198
Radcliffe Award : frontiers defined by, after Partition (1947), 188 ; Jinnah's comments on, 188
Radcliffe, Sir Cyril (Lord) : Chairman Boundary Commission (1947) ; *see* Radcliffe Award
Rajah, Rao Bahadar M.C. : tribute to Jinnah on behalf of 'Untouchables' (1940), 133–4
Raleigh, Sir Walter : at Aligarh University, 41
Ramsay, T. W. : describes Jinnah leaving England (1934–5), 106
Reading, Lord : Viceroy of India (1921–26), 88
Reddy, Dr C. R. : tribute to Jinnah (1940), 133
Roe, Sir Thomas : visit to Punjab (1615), 34
Roosevelt, F. D. : on perils of India during war (1942), 139 ; views on 'Indian problem' criticized by Sir W. Churchill, 139–40

Round Table Conferences : 1st : opened by King George V (1930), 97 ; attended by Jinnah, 97. 2nd : delegates rebuked by Ramsay MacDonald (1931), 98. 3rd : Jinnah dropped from, 99
Rowlands, Sir Archibald : 199
Rowlatt Act (1919) : Jinnah condemns, 80
Royal Scots : Jinnah dines with, Karachi (Dec. 1947), 209
Russell Road, Kensington, No. 35 : Jinnah's first lodgings in London, 8
Russell, Wilfred (author of *Indian Summer*) : quoted, 180, 182, 200

Sabir Mazangavi, Rafiq : attempts assassination of Jinnah (1943), and trial, 144–5
Saiyid, M. H. (author of *Mohammed Ali Jinnah. A Political Study*) : quoted, 14–15, 78, 125
Salisbury, 3rd Marquess of : insult to Dadabhai Naoroji (1892), 10, 11
Sandhurst : Jinnah's visit to (1925), 89–90
Sapru, Sir Tej Bahadur : criticizes Jinnah (1928), 94
Setalvad, Sir Chimanlal : on Jinnah's break with Congress (1920), 85
Sèvres, Treaty of (1920) : 81, 82
Sikhs : conquest of Punjab, 33, 34, 35 ; dispute over mosque in Lahore (1936), 110–11 ; riots in Punjab (April 1947), 182 ; plot to form own state in Punjab (April 1947), 182 ; Jinnah forbids armed Muslim League action against, 182 ; atrocities (Aug.–Sept. 1947), 204, 205
Simla Conferences : 1st (1945), 157 ; 2nd (1946), 159–60
Simon Commission : protests against, 90 ; arrives Bombay (1928), 90
Simon, Sir John (Viscount) : leader of Simon Commission, *q.v.*, 90 ; advocates Round Table Conference (1929), 97
Sind : Napier's conquest of (1843), 36 ; to vote on Pakistan (1947), 184 ; vote for Pakistan, 187

242

INDEX

Sind Madrasah High School, Karachi: 4, 7; Jinnah's bequest to, 43

Somjee, M. A.: anecdote concerning Jinnah and, 18

State Bank of Pakistan: opened by Jinnah (July 1, 1948), 217–18

Stephens, Ian (author of *Horned Moon*): quoted, 179, 193; conversation with Jinnah (Feb. 1948), 211

Swaraj, or 'self-government': *see* Home Rule

Swaraj Sabha: *see* Home Rule League

Syed Ahmed Khan, Sir: early life and plans for reform, 38–42; on causes of the Indian Mutiny, 39–40; foundation Aligarh University (1877), 41; foundation Mohammedan Educational Conference, 41; on fate of Muslims, quoted, 42; mentioned, 51; and Muslim *Wakfs*, 53

Sylhet: to vote on Pakistan (1947), 184; vote for Pakistan, 187

Symonds, Richard (author of *The Making of Pakistan*): quoted, 38, 180

Tara Singh, Master: incites Punjab Sikhs against Muslims (April 1947), 182

Time and Tide: Jinnah contributes article denouncing democratic government as unsuitable to India (March 9, 1940), 125, quoted, 126–7

Tuker, Lieut.-Gen. Sir Francis (author of *While Memory Serves*): on 1946 massacres, quoted, 169–70; mentioned, 189

Turkey: Muslim sympathy for, during 1914–18 war, 63; Treaty of Sèvres, and Caliphate Movement in India (1920), 81–2; Sultan deposed (1922) and Caliphate abolished (1924), 82; *see also* Caliphate

Untouchables': join in 'Day of Deliverance' celebration (1939), 124; Rao Bahadur M. C. Rajah's tribute to Jinnah on behalf of (1940), 133–4

Victoria, Queen: Empress of India (1876), 4; on the Indian Mutiny, quoted, 37

Wadia, Mrs Neville: *see* Jinnah, Dina

Wakf: *see* Mussalman Wakf Validating Bill; *also* Jinnah, M. A.

Wales, Prince Edward of: visit to India and boycott by Gandhi (1921), 88

Wavell, Countess: tribute to Jinnah, 213

Wavell, Field-Marshal Viscount (Earl): Viceroy of India (1943–47), 157; proposes 'Indianization' of Viceroy's Exec. Council (1945), 157; opposes Muslim League's demand for exclusive Muslim nomination to Interim Govt. (1945), 157; and Interim Govt., 157 *et seq.*; Jinnah's criticism of, 162, 163, 167–8, 169; invites Congress to form Interim Govt. (Aug. 1946), 167; broadcast appeal for Muslim co-operation, 167; reconstitutes Interim Govt. to admit Muslim League (Oct. 1946), 168; flies to London for talks with H.M. Govt. (Dec. 1946), 170; *Time* magazine comments on, 170; criticism of Jinnah, 212

Wedderburn, Sir William: 59–60, 61

Willingdon, Lady (Dowager Marchioness of): alleged incident at Government House, Bombay (1918), 75

Willingdon, Lord (Marquess of): Governor of Bombay (1913–19), relationship with Jinnah, 75–7; criticism of Home Rule League, 76–7; demonstration against (1918), 77–8; Viceroy of India (1931–36), 98n

Wood, Lady Graham: Jinnah buys house from (1931), 101; her tribute to him, 101

World War: (1914–18): pledges and help from India, 61–2; demands by

Congress, 62. (1939–45) : India's declaration of war, 123

Wrench, Sir Evelyn (author of *Immortal Years*) : *quoted*, 6, 8 ; reports conversation with Jinnah (1942), 142

Zam-Zamma, or 'Kim's Gun', Lahore : 33

Ziarat : Jinnah moves to (June 1948), 216 ; last illness at, 219–22 ; Liaquat Ali Khan visits, 221 ; Jinnah moved from, to Quetta, 222